THE HUMAN SIDE *of* ENTERPRISE

ANNOTATED EDITION

Douglas McGregor

UPDATED AND WITH A NEW COMMENTARY
BY Joel Cutcher-Gershenfeld

McGraw-Hill

New York | Chicago | San Francisco | Lisbon | London
Madrid | Mexico City | Milan | New Delhi | San Juan
Seoul | Singapore | Sydney | Toronto

The McGraw·Hill Companies

1 2 3 4 5 6 7 8 9 0 DOC/DOC 0 9 8 7 6 5

ISBN 0-07-146222-8

This book is printed on recycled, acid-free paper containing a minimum of 50% recycled, de-inked fiber.

To My Wife

This book is dedicated to DOUGLAS McGREGOR and the many generations of scholars whose work has been and will continue to be shaped by a deep appreciation for *The Human Side of Enterprise.*

CONTENTS

EDITOR'S NOTE AND ACKNOWLEDGMENTS

Attending to the human side of enterprise is an enduring challenge. When Douglas McGregor authored this classic text in 1960, his conception of Theory Y helped to launch what was then termed the "human relations movement." Theory Y served as a counterpoint to authoritarian, control-oriented Theory X assumptions about people. Today, knowledge-driven work systems and low-cost business strategies clash over these same basic assumptions—are people the engine that creates value or a cost to cut whenever possible? In producing this annotated edition our aim is to foster continued and ever deeper dialogue on these core questions.

Launching us into this volume is a new foreword by Ed Schein, who was recruited by Douglas McGregor to join the MIT faculty in 1956. Ed's comments are immediately practical, providing three vivid examples illustrating the interdependence between Theory Y and strong, commanding leadership, a compelling corporate culture, and the essential roles of trust and respect in various audit roles.

Also at the outset of the volume we have reprinted the original foreword by Douglas McGregor and the foreword written by Warren Bennis for the twenty-fifth anniversary edition of the book. Warren was a student of McGregor's at MIT and has written extensively in celebration of McGregor's work. At the conclusion of the volume, there is a selection of historical documents, articles, and other relevant materials.

A new editor's introduction provides extended commentary on the past, current, and continued importance of the book. Two kinds of annotations appear throughout the volume. First, each chapter is introduced by a paragraph or two that represents a brief summary of key themes from the chapter, grounded in direct quotes from the text. The aim here has been to be true to McGregor's voice and to highlight certain "gems" from the chapter. Then, within each chapter, selected notes are provided alongside the text. Some notes are provided to link McGregor's writing to prior or subsequent scholarship. Other notes serve to highlight key ideas that are of particular importance today. In still other cases, the notes invite dialogue between the reader and McGregor's text. Interspersed are stories and comments from scholars and practitioners. Original footnotes are numbered as in the original text; new footnotes are indicated with an asterisk. Throughout, there is an admitted MIT bias, and a bit of an Antioch bias, reflecting the circles of scholarship and practice that have emanated from the universities where McGregor spent most of his career.

I would like to thank the participants in the Organizational Studies Group (OSG) and Institute for Work and Employment Relations (IWER) lunches at MIT, where we had a brief discussion in advance of this publication, as well as acknowledge the materials and comments contributed by Deborah Ancona, Lotte Bailyn, Stephen Barley, Betty Barrett, Warren Bennis, Matthew Bidwell, Dennis R. Briscoe, Diane Burton, Dennis Dabney, Steve Deneroff, Michael Diamond, David Ellerman, John-Paul Ferguson, Scott Highhouse, Bill Jaeger, Naresh Khatri, Gideon Kunda, Roger Komer, Steven Lipworth, John Lubans, Ron May, Larry Nirenberg, Sally Payne, Margaret Philips, Larry Prusak, Benjamin Schneider, John Shin, Abe Siegal, Stephen Sleigh, and Anil Verma. I would like to particularly thank George Strauss, who shared many reflections from his graduate studies with Douglas McGregor. I would also like to thank David Jacobs, who has written on the moral and value-based dimensions of McGregor's work and who urges that we pay more attention to the more "reformist" and "radical" aspects of Theory Y. Thomas Kochan and Robert McKersie have made extensive, heartfelt comments and suggestions on this manuscript—both of them urging deeper debate on core assumptions relevant for today's challenges. I am also deeply appreciative of the infectious joy and enthusiasm brought to this project by Barbara Gellman-Danley, president, Antioch University McGregor. I would like to thank Maggie Tsui, who conducted the analysis of citations, and IWER librarian Anita Perkins, who helped identify archival materials. Appreciation is also due to Douglas McGregor's two grandsons, Greg and Phil Colvard, who combed family records and found the photographs that we have been able to include on the cover of this volume. Finally, special appreciation is due Ed Schein for writing the new foreword for this edition, which is sure to further clarify and extend Douglas McGregor's legacy.

In producing this volume, I would like to express particular appreciation to Jeanne Glasser, who had the original vision for what this book would be. It has been a pleasure and an honor to work in service of that vision. The production team is also most appreciated for having produced such a striking cover, design, and layout.

On a personal basis, the values articulated by Douglas McGregor are among the values that underlie my marriage, that I work to instill as a parent, that were instilled in me as a child, and that are part of my heritage. So this acknowledgment would not be complete without expressing my deepest appreciation for the support and engagement of these values with my wife, Susan; my children, Gabriel and Aaron; my brothers, Neil and Alan; and my parents, Walter and Gladys. In fact, there ought not to be a distinction between the values and assumptions about people that we advance through business enterprise and the values and assumptions about people that guide the balance of our lives. At the end of *The Human Side of Enterprise*, McGregor invites us to realize "the potential for collaboration inherent in the human resources of industry" so as to provide a model for governments and nations. Ultimately, he saw the journey into *The Human Side of Enterprise* as a journey toward making the world a better place. I hope this new annotated edition helps us along the way.

EDGAR SCHEIN

MAKING THEORY Y CONCRETE

Some Case Examples and Important Lessons

People have read about Theory X and Theory Y for 45 years now, but I think they still do not truly understand what these theories mean in practice. I propose, therefore, in this short essay to illustrate them rather than talk about them.

CASE 1: THE STEREOTYPE OF THE MILITARY AS THEORY X

In the 1970s the MIT Sloan School was involved in a management program for newly promoted admirals at the Naval War College. These were captains of ships who were moving into more senior administrative positions in the Pentagon. When Dick Beckhard and I first designed this course, we anticipated that one of the most important areas of concern would be how managers who were used to absolute authority would master becoming members of a new hierarchy in which they were now at the bottom of the heap rather than on top. If being an autocrat meant holding Theory X, we would have a tough job training them for their new role.

We had available a questionnaire that asked people a series of questions designed to elicit their X or Y assumptions, and we had a good bit of information about managers from other industries. When we gave this questionnaire to class after class of the new admirals, we were surprised to learn that they were consistently higher in Theory Y assumptions than the industrial groups we had tested.

As we got to know these admirals as individuals and heard their stories of what leadership in the Navy meant, it became obvious that command did not automatically mean control. These admirals were acutely aware of how important it was for them to trust their subordinates because they were dependent on those subordinates. They knew that control systems that implied mistrust would backfire. And they told us stories of how commanders who were Theory X–oriented either would become nervous wrecks (as did Captain Queeg in the novel *The Caine Mutiny*) or would not be promoted to higher levels. It became clear that the higher you went, the more important it was to be a Theory Y person, even if you were required by the task to act autocratically (i.e., decisively).

LESSON 1. We must question our stereotype that having total authority and having to act autocratically at times means that you are a Theory X person. Being autocratic has more to do with the task at hand than with assumptions about people. Theory Y leaders act autocratically when the task demands it. Many organizations, especially the military, are labeled Theory X because they have fairly tight controls. Without examining the task and the actual executives, however, you cannot assume that they are Theory X.

LESSON 2. In our management models, we must separate command and control instead of always linking them. Command is consistent with Theory Y. It is in the concept of *control* that we must distinguish controls that presume trust (Theory Y) from controls that assume that the employee will always take advantage unless closely monitored with time clocks, random inspections, and the like (the essence of Theory X). Trusting people does not mean abdicating control.

CASE 2: KEN OLSEN: AN EXAMPLE OF A THEORY Y ENTREPRENEUR

I had the opportunity to work with Ken Olsen, the founder of Digital Equipment Corporation, for over 25 years (Schein, 2003).* Even

* Edgar H. Schein, Paul J. Kampas, Peter Delisi, and Michael Sonduck, (eds.), *DEC Is Dead, Long Live DEC: The Lasting Legacy of Digital Equipment Corporation*, San Francisco: Berrett-Koehler (2003).

though the company ultimately failed as an economic entity, its alumni continue to avow that life at DEC was incredibly inspiring, and they attributed their good experiences and DEC's 30 years of success to the freedom and sense of responsibility that was engendered by Ken Olsen's management style.

In my book on DEC's history, I provide examples of what a true Theory Y management style looks like and what assumptions it is based on. Ken Olsen believed that you start with the best and brightest individuals, that you create a decision-making process based on debate and having to sell your ideas to other bright individuals, that you ask people to propose what they will do and, if approved, that they have and will exercise responsibility for getting it done, that people will learn to monitor themselves and report back if things are not going according to plan (hence there is no need to monitor them all the time), and that people will at all times behave completely ethically with respect to customers and one another. Lying or withholding information was the ultimate sin.

With success and growth, problems arose between various groups that had become empires unto themselves, highlighting some of the limitations of continuing to manage by giving total freedom. But Ken Olsen's faith in people never wavered, and his success in building an innovative organization for over 30 years is unmatched. What brought DEC down in the end was intergroup warfare among engineering groups that were trying to second-guess where the increasingly commodified computer market was heading. What was needed if the economic entity was to survive was strong command, but not Theory X–type controls.

CASE 3: HOW TO BE A HELPFUL AUDITOR

One of McGregor's most powerful examples of Theory Y thinking was his analysis of how auditing and control systems should work. He pointed out that in most organizations, the auditor would go down to some production unit, find some problems, and report them to his superior, who would send the information up the auditing chain. The information would then cross over to the head of operations, who would send the information down the operational chain, where it would eventually land in the office of the supervisor of the production group whose work was at issue. The supervisor would then call in the employee or group and ask why it was doing what it was doing, often catching the group off guard and making its members feel that they were being watched by Big Brother. McGregor also noted that a long period of time will have elapsed between when the problem was identified and when the group is confronted with this information.

McGregor proposed something that, at the time, seemed quite radical but is today much more common: that when the auditor discovers a problem, he or she should initially make the operating group aware of it, even before he or she reported it to his or her own boss in auditing. In most cases that led to the problem's being addressed immediately instead of weeks or months later. It made employees feel that auditing was there to help them, not to "catch" people doing things wrong. The report would still go up the auditing ladder so that information could be collected about possible broader problem issues, but at the local level things would be fixed in a timely fashion and without creating an image of auditing as a group to be feared. McGregor cogently pointed out that if auditing came to be feared, this would motivate employees to hide aspects of how they worked, leading to the proliferation of problems rather than their solution.

Openness, teamwork, and responsibility are frequently touted values in today's industrial climate. The problem is that these values cannot be exercised in an environment created by Theory X managers. If we really want more responsible, open, team-oriented behavior, by far the best way to get it is to start with a manager who deeply holds Theory Y assumptions and weed all Theory X managers out of the system as quickly as possible.

Edgar Schein
Sloan Fellow Professor of
Management, Emeritus
Sloan School of Management, MIT

FOREWORD TO THE TWENTY-FIFTH ANNIVERSARY PRINTING

WARREN BENNIS

Every so often, someone encapsulates a timely idea in such striking wording that the idea quickly penetrates the general consciousness. Such is the case with this book, Douglas McGregor's seminal work, his first and only book. I feel so privileged to be invited to write this Foreword.

Doug McGregor was an epochal figure in his own time, and remains one, for that matter. He created a "new taste" across the entire field of management and the newer fields of "organizational behavior" and "organization development." One can agree or disagree with his writings, but they are always there as something to shoot for or at, depending on one's viewpoint. All of us who live and work in large organized settings—practitioners and scholars alike—sing his exultant chants, or lament their popularity, or question their validity. Just as every economist, knowingly or not, pays his dues to Keynes, we are all, one way or another, disciples of McGregor.

When I say that *The Human Side of Enterprise* created a "new taste," I'm dead serious, since this book, more than any other book on management, changed an entire concept of organizational man and replaced it with a new paradigm that stressed human potentials, emphasized human growth, and elevated the human role in industrial society. Perhaps more importantly, a large segment of Doug's (and my own) professional field operated in an environment which he created and of which this book laid the foundation. Much of the work that goes on now could not have happened if this book hadn't been written.

Nothing McGregor wrote before or after this book failed to reflect, in one way or another, his later-to-be-developed trademark, now immortalized by that simple initial, "Y."

His famous "Theory Y" speech was delivered at the Fifth Anniversary Convocation of MIT's Alfred P. Sloan School of Management in April 1957. "The Human Side of Enterprise" was the title of that speech, and it was under that title that McGregor published this book in 1960, just twenty-five years ago.

What did McGregor say to captivate the managerial public he was addressing? Basically, he was asking all of us, interested in empowering and motivating the workforce, to examine our assumptions (implicit as well as explicit) about the most effective way to manage people. He then proposed a new theory of the human being (partly influenced by the psychological theorists of "self-actualization," especially Abraham Maslow), a new theory of power, and a new set of values that would guide the spirit of the industrial workplace.

All of the themes that informed his earlier work and those that culminated in *The Human Side of Enterprise* can be seen and are reflected in virtually every book written on management today. They can be summed up, I believe, with the following propositions:

- Active participation by all involved
- A transcending concern with individual dignity, worth, and growth
- Reexamination and resolution of the conflict between individual needs and organizational goals, through effective interpersonal relationships between superiors and subordinates
- A concept of influence that relies not on coercion, compromise, evasion or avoidance, pseudosupport, or bargaining, but on openness, confrontation, and "working through" differences
- A belief that human growth is self-generated and furthered by an environment of trust, feedback, and authentic human relationships

This last proposition about "feedback" reminds me of a personal (and telling) anecdote about Doug. It seemed to me that he was always open to experience, to feedback; he did not seem to require the ordinary cuticles of protection most of us carefully develop. This appetite for feedback apparently began early in his career because, shortly after starting teaching at Harvard in 1935, he asked one of his senior professors for some help and guidance on his teaching style. After several paragraphs of praise, the professor, Gordon Allport, wrote:

> The only possible points I can think of that you might still learn are (1) not to jingle coins and keys, (2) keeping hands out of pockets would automatically prevent this, (3) generally speaking, feet belong on the floor rather than the lecture desk (though I am aware of the charm of informality especially in a personality like yours …), (4) the trouble you will have next year is to get a theoretical framework into which to put things. I haven't succeeded very well in 12 years with this most difficult task.

Doug never succeeded in keeping his feet off the desk, and when he was president of Antioch College, students' sensibilities were offended by this, but he did conquer the coin-jingling habit unless he become impatient with late-staying guests. He did, though, finally construct "a theoretical framework into which to put things," which resulted in this book.

Getting back to the main themes in this book, I would add this: In the end, the employee must take the responsibility for his or her own growth. McGregor would not tolerate "pseudogrowth" forced on the individual by the overzealous manager—no matter how well intentioned—who manipulates, or by a sadist who uses fear as a crutch to hide personal fears. Growth is organic, natural. The best a leader can do is understand the conditions creating a climate of growth and do everything possible to irrigate. The leader intervenes only rarely—and at great risk.

The Human Side of Enterprise facilitated—if not directly influenced—a number of related developments in the practice of management. The application of "encounter groups" (or "T-groups," sensitivity training, and so forth) to actual, on-line, real-life organizations began in earnest after this book was published. It helped provide the badly needed theory that could translate a "small group" model of change—basically an interpersonal one—from an artificial laboratory situation, distant in time and space from the sweaty and plebeian day-to-day life of the real world, to intact, functioning organizations. The work of Peters and Waterman, Ouchi, Kanter, Likert, Argyris, Schein, Blake and Mouton, Beckhard, Shepard, and too many others to mention here owes in large part its acceptance and development to this book.

In addition, the newer fields of organizational behavior and organizational development emerged from the tradition McGregor established and they have since matured into an important area of theory, research, and practice. One example of the practical consequences of this development is the establishment of new departments and corporate vice presidents of organizational development, or OD. These departments and executives take as their chief responsibility the examination and promotion of work environments that facilitate Theory Y responses.

That this book attracted devoted disciples and devoted critics should come as no surprise. It was bound to. Any radically new idea always bootlegs in prescriptive and moral imperatives that stand at an angle to conventional practices. Of course, there were some who criticized this book because they detected in it (quite correctly) a style of behavior antithetical to their own value system.

Basically, the nerve this book touched has to do with the underlying premise of the book, the question it addresses, namely the assumptions we hold about human behavior. McGregor's detractors, now quieted somewhat by the results of their failed leadership results, wondered how a Theory Y manager could run a railroad. They questioned whether a leader could *listen* so much without appearing passive, weak, or too "permissive." They wondered how a philosophy of management that would "give away" the prerogatives of decision making to subordinates could work. That sounds suspiciously like communism, wrote one critic in the early 60s.

Those aren't concocted criticisms; they represent only a mild sampling of typical responses. The one about communism is (or used to be) frequently expressed and is undoubtedly the least relevant to McGregor's argument. McGregor steadfastly held to the accountability and responsibility of the formal organization's leadership. "Power equalization," a term applied to Theory Y by some critics, just doesn't hold water. McGregor never hinted or implied any surrender of power.

Indeed, he argued that a trusting, open, and honest leader-follower relationship *adds to*, rather than subtracts from, the leader's ability to influence the workforce. (Which also means that it adds to the subordinate's ability to influence his or her superior.)

Doug McGregor was a genius, not necessarily for the originality of his ideas, which were often "in the air" or developed by similarly creative spirits. He was a genius because he had clarity of mind, a rare empathy for managers, and a flair for the right metaphor that grounded and established a new idea.

Ideas are always invented before their founders hit on them. Surely there must have been an "identity crisis" long before Erickson coined the phrase. Theory X and Theory Y certainly existed before McGregor. But he named them, labeled them. The old joke about the umpire in the bottom of the last inning of the determining game of the World Series comes to mind. The score is tied, the bases are loaded, two out, and the batter has a 3-2 count. The ball is pitched, and the umpire hesitates. The batter turns around angrily and yells: "Well, what the hell is it?" And the umpire responds: "It ain't nothin' till I call it!"

"Calling it" in science or in practice requires not only those other remarkable attributes of McGregor but that important and decisive element: courage. He had the courage to call it—in abundance.

McGregor was also a genius in the direct influence he has had on so many of us now profiting from his ideas and courage. In a recent article about the top ten leaders in the field of OD, eight of the ten, when asked what the most important influence on their career was, singled out Doug McGregor (and, indirectly, this book). More importantly, when we read that General Motors, perhaps the most influential organization in the world, is attempting to move toward a Theory Y corporate culture, we can fully understand the impact of this book. It used to be that the old fashioned GM philosophy of management could be summed up by this phrase: "DON'T THINK, DUMMY—DO WHAT YOU'RE TOLD!" Now, in GM's Buick City plant as well as a number of others, there is a new and very different credo which goes: "THINK! I'M NOT GOING TO TELL YOU WHAT TO DO."

It's called participate management. Its ancestor is Theory Y. In 1950, McGregor wrote:

> Out of all this has come the first clear recognition of an inescapable fact: we cannot successfully *force* people to work for management's objectives. The ancient conception that people do the work of the world only if they are forced to do so by threats or intimidation, or by the camouflaged authoritarian methods of paternalism, has been suffering from a lingering fatal illness for a quarter of a century. I venture the guess that it will be dead in another decade.*

He was characteristically optimistic about the death of authoritarianism, but he was unerring, as usual, in putting his finger on the right issue at the right time. He might have helped, had he lived, to bring it about a lot sooner. There are a lot of us who believe that McGraw-Hill's decision to reissue this masterpiece will bring about the inevitable a little sooner than even Doug predicted.

Warren G. Bennis
The Joseph DeBell Distinguished Professor of
Management and Organization
University of Southern California
School of Business Administration

* From a personal communication.

PREFACE

DOUGLAS McGREGOR

Some years ago during a meeting of the Advisory Committee of MIT's School of Industrial Management, Alfred Sloan raised some questions related to the issue of whether successful managers are born or made. I was aware—as he was—that his questions were not easily answered. The discussion, however, served to sharpen certain interests I had had for some time in a systematic examination of the many common but inconsistent assumptions about what makes a manager.

In 1954 the Alfred P. Sloan Foundation made a grant to Alex Bavelas and me to explore some of these ideas more fully. Bavelas' interests lay in some laboratory experiments, while mine centered on research in industry, but they had a common focus on a more adequate theory of management.

After Bavelas went to the Bell Laboratories in 1956, the laboratory work waned. I am not an experimentalist. Another colleague, Theodore M. Alfred, and I continued a comparative study of the operation of management development programs in a number of large companies. The subjects were a group of former Sloan Fellows, but our studies ranged widely within their companies as we sought to learn more about the way in which theories and practices within different organizations influence the making of managers.

These studies are not yet complete, but this book has grown out of them and is to a large extent the fruit of Mr. Sloan's questions and the opportunity to pursue them afforded by the Alfred P. Sloan Foundation.*

---

*In order to better develop successful managers, Alfred P. Sloan provided funding to develop "a more adequate theory of management." This connection between theory and practice is at the heart of *The Human Side of Enterprise.*

It seems clear to me that the making of managers, in so far as they are made, is only to a rather small degree the result of management's formal efforts in management development. It is to a much greater degree the result of management's conception of the nature of its task and of all the policies and practices which are constructed to implement this conception. The way a business is managed determines to a very large extent what people are perceived to have "potential" and how they develop. We go off on the wrong track when we seek to study management development in terms of the formal machinery of programs carrying this label.

Without in the least minimizing the importance of the work that has been done to improve the selection of people with managerial potential, I have come to the conviction that some of our most important problems lie elsewhere. Even if we possessed methods enabling us to do a perfect job of selecting young men with the capacity to become top executives, the practical gain for industry would be negligible under today's conditions. The reason is that we have not learned enough about the utilization of talent, about the creation of an organizational climate conducive to human growth. The blunt fact is that we are a long way from realizing the potential represented by the human resources we now recruit into industry. We have much to accomplish with respect to utilization before further improvements in selection will become important.

Two decades after the publication of this book, Dr. W. Edwards Deming echoed McGregor with his injunction: "Don't blame the people, fix the system."

This volume is an attempt to substantiate the thesis that the human side of enterprise is "all of a piece"—that the theoretical assumptions management holds about controlling its human resources determine the whole character of the enterprise. They determine also the quality of its successive generations of management.

Of course the process is circular, and herein lies the possibility and the hope of future progress. The key question of top management is: "What are your assumptions (implicit as well as explicit) about the most effective way to manage people?" From the answer to this question flow the answers to the questions Mr. Sloan raised in our discussion about the making of managers, as well as answers to many other questions which perplex and confound management as it seeks to achieve more successfully the economic objectives of enterprise. It will be clear to the reader that I believe many of our present assumptions about the most effective way to manage people are far from adequate.

University of Toronto Professor Anil Verma (and a Sloan alum) writes that:

The preface/intro to the book was not only memorable, but it shaped my thinking for decades to come. McGregor saw the way work is structured as key. To him, personnel functions of recruitment, performance appraisal, bonuses, etc., were all peripheral unless they were designed to support the structure of work organization. This view stands in contrast with the current focus in the HR field.

It is completely impossible for me to acknowledge individually the help I have received in evolving the ideas presented here. Many professional colleagues, past and present, and many close friends in management have encouraged, criticized, and inspired me for twenty years. I cannot hold them responsible for what is in this volume, but they taught me most of what I now believe I know about management, about social science, and about the relevance of the latter to the former.

I have tried to protect the anonymity of the companies from which illustrative materials have been drawn. May I, however, acknowledge with deep gratitude the time given to Mr. Alfred and me by some thirty former Sloan Fellows and more than a hundred managers in their companies to answer our questions, the frankness with which they were answered, and the interest these men took in our studies.

To Patricia Macpherson, my secretary, I owe much. Were it not for her cheerful patience with innumerable rewritings and editings, this book would never have been completed.

Finally, to the Alfred P. Sloan Foundation, and to Mr. Sloan personally, my sincere thanks, not only for the funds which made this book possible, but for the freedom to pursue my not always intelligible interests where they led.

Douglas McGregor

INTRODUCTION TO THE ANNOTATED EDITION

Joel Cutcher-Gershenfeld

Like a beacon across the generations, Douglas McGregor's insights into what he termed "the human side of enterprise" continue today to reveal deep truths about people and organizations.

McGregor begins this 1960 management classic with a seemingly simple question: "What are your assumptions (implicit as well as explicit) about the most effective way to manage people?" At the time, this question drove a fundamental transformation in the work of scholars and practitioners alike. It is just as pertinent today.

When *The Human Side of Enterprise* was published, it codified principles in the then-emerging "human relations" movement in management. By identifying two contrasting assumptions about human nature—what McGregor called "Theory X" and "Theory Y"—he highlighted the role of core assumptions and values in a management system. He stated that: "If there is a single assumption which pervades conventional organizational theory it is that authority is the central, indispensable means of managerial control" (page 24). He thus launched a debate in theory and practice between management systems rooted in authority versus those rooted in influence.

At the time, McGregor was challenging the prevailing view that management control was required because employees needed to be "coerced, controlled, directed, [and] threatened with punishment to get them to put forth adequate effort toward the achievement of organizational objectives" (p. 45). By turning the spotlight on these basic assumptions, McGregor was able to identify popular practices—what he called "gimmicks" and today we would call management fads—that were without empirical or theoretical foundations. The limits of management by objectives, performance appraisal systems, and simple incentive schemes were clearly revealed. These practices either rested on flawed assumptions or were implemented in ways that rested on flawed assumptions. What was the alternative?

McGregor offered Theory Y, which paired the assumption that employees are worthy of trust and respect with the view that, with proper support, employees would be intrinsically motivated to do the best job they could. McGregor rejected any simple notion of replacing a control-oriented approach with permissive management. Instead, he was engaged in a much more comprehensive process of advancing management practice on the basis of well-constructed theory. He urged the development of a theory of management based on the assumptions of interdependent actors in less hierarchical organizations, who must succeed more on the basis of influence than authority.[1] This was a radical notion then, and it is still at the cutting edge.

AN ENDURING LEGACY

Today, careful attention to core assumptions and values remains an enduring legacy of this book. *The Human Side of Enterprise*

[1] McGregor did not originally begin with the terminology "Theory X" and "Theory Y." George Strauss, who studied at MIT under Douglas McGregor in the mid-1940s, reports that, prior to coining these terms, he was then focused on the contrast between what he termed "augmentative" and "reductive" approaches to management.

is a foundational text in the fields of organizational behavior, organizational development, industrial relations, human resource management, industrial/organizational psychology, organizational sociology, and others. It has spawned extensions, such as William Ouchi's *Theory Z*, which sought to incorporate assumptions grounded in the clan-oriented structure of Japanese society and lessons from the quality-focused management models that had been perfected in many Japanese corporations.[2] Indeed, McGregor partly anticipated key points in *Theory Z* in his discussion of staff-line relations, where he states, "It is probable that one day we shall begin to draw organization charts as a series of linked groups rather than as a hierarchical structure of individual 'reporting' relationships" (p. 237). The spread of team-based work systems and the rise of what some term the knowledge economy has put an even greater premium on examining these underlying assumptions about what motivates people in organizations and society.

Unfortunately, too much of what is written today—in scholarly publications and in the popular business press—gives insufficient attention to these core assumptions. This gap can, perhaps, be best understood by using the framework that McGregor's MIT colleague Ed Schein developed for the study of organizational cultures.[3] He identifies three levels of culture: the surface-level visible artifacts of an organizational culture, the midlevel stated polices and procedures, and the deep, underlying values and assumptions. Because so much of the management and organizational literature is limited to the

---

[2] William Ouchi, *Theory Z: How American Business Can Meet the Japanese Challenge,* New York: Addison-Wesley, 1981.

[3] Edgar Schein, *Organizational Culture and Leadership,* San Francisco: Jossey-Bass, 1988.

artifact level or the policies and procedures level, it is vulnerable to being seen as superficial, faddish, and, ultimately, inadequate.[4] In a recent book review and reflective essay, David Jacobs observes:

> ***McGregor's Theories X and Y are still prominently featured in textbooks on management and organizational theory. However, contemporary management scholars have largely rejected McGregor's arguments, preferring contingency theories emerging from empirical studies. Even leading disciples of McGregor seem to follow the fashion and downplay the critical moral core of his thinking. Partly as a result, management scholars fail to perceive the need for profound reforms in organizations.[5]***

In commenting on the moral side of Douglas McGregor, Berkeley professor George Strauss, who was a student of McGregor at MIT, states that:

> ***In a sense he was a fourth generation preacher (his great-grandfather was a Scottish Presbyterian minister; his grandfather founded a mission for the homeless, which Doug's father continued; Doug as a boy would play the piano in evening services). True, Doug preached to corporate CEOs rather than the down-and-out and religion does not appear explicitly in his writing, but this background may be one key***

---

[4] It is also true that few authors turn a phrase so effectively as did Douglas McGregor—with keen insight, blunt clarity, and the right hint of humor.

[5] David Jacobs, "Book Review Essay: Douglas McGregor—The Human Side of Enterprise in Peril," *Academy of Management Review*, vol. 29, no. 2, 2004, pp. 293–311. David is professor of management at Morgan State University.

to understanding his personal values and his tendency to preach.[6]

Over the years, a relatively small number of high-profile industry leaders in many sectors of the economy have innovated in ways consistent with Theory Y values and assumptions. Ken Olsen, founding CEO of Digital Equipment Corporation (DEC), operationalized Theory Y assumptions about people by creating an innovative, nonhierarchical, participative organization that helped to shape the culture of the entire computer industry during the 1970s and 1980s. In the retail trades, Nordstrom Corporation is renowned for empowering front-line employees to solve customer problems and drive innovation. Thousands of corporations have adopted Scanlon plans or other forms of gain-sharing or goal-sharing arrangements with the participative approach advocated by McGregor, including companies such as Wescast Industries, Herman Miller, Donnelley, Motorola, and Beth Israel Hospital–Boston—all of which have also been cited on various lists of "The 100 Best Companies to Work For in America." In connecting the Scanlon plan with core assumptions, Max Dupree, retired CEO and chairman of Herman Miller, comments:

The Scanlon Plan is a process that enables a growing number of people in an organization to serve customers, to serve employees, to serve owners, to serve the public. It's built on the assumption that the great majority of people are well

---

[6] George Strauss, "Book Review," *Relations Industrialles*, vol. 57, no. 1, Hiver/Winter 2002. Although Mcgregor had a strong religious upbringing, he was not deeply oriented around religion. His grandchildren Greg and Phil Colvard indicated that it was their understanding that he was a Secular Humanist who primarily believed in the inherent goodness and nobility of all humankind.

motivated, come to work as adults, need the opportunity to meet their personal potential at the same time the organization meets its potential.[7]

The Nucor Corporation, which has become one of the major producers of steel in the United States, attributes its success to four employment relations principles[8] that signal Theory Y assumptions. These are

1. Management is obligated to manage Nucor in such a way that employees will have the opportunity to earn according to their productivity.
2. Employees should be able to feel confident that if they do their jobs properly, they will have a job tomorrow.
3. Employees have the right to be treated fairly and must believe that they will be.
4. Employees must have an avenue of appeal when they believe they are being treated unfairly.

McGregor would have been surprised, however, to find that Nucor is an aggressively non-union employer. At the time he was writing, unions were responsible for the gains in wages, benefits, and fair treatment on the job that corresponded with the growth of the middle class. McGregor saw these gains as a necessary foundation for further human development in organizations. This is an assumption that is no longer shared by many

---

[7] DuPree is also author of *Leadership Is an Art* and *Leadership Jazz.* This quote is from http://www.scanlonleader.org/Scanlon/ScanlonWebSite/aboutus/quotesm.html.

[8] For more detail on how this company presents these principles as core underlying business assumptions, see www.nucor.com.

managers in the human resources field—a matter further addressed in the next section of this introduction.

Overall, McGregor's work makes it clear that a focus on basic assumptions can be transformative. Consider the reflections of Ron May, senior vice president of operations for DTE Energy, which is the leading provider of gas, electric, and other energy services in Michigan:

> *My father was a WW II airborne veteran. He started with General MacArthur in Australia, released the Bataan Death March prisoners, and, after years of fighting, arrived in Japan at the beginning of the occupation. I grew up with Theory X–style command and control culture. If you were to be a leader, he taught, this was the tool of strength and survival.*
>
> *Later, in college, I learned from McGregor's book that there was another style. This began the journey of a lifetime. I have looked to the human side of management in activities from front-line supervision to union relations to the executive office, as well as in technical activities such as engineering and accounting. I sum up my approach to leadership as "do the right thing, based upon values of respect and integrity." I also add, "If you can help, do it."*
>
> *The idea is that people want the freedom to excel. They will provide so much more of themselves in solving problems, doing their daily work, and building great relationships. This is the difference in Theory X and Theory Y assumptions.*
>
> *Strong command is needed in emergencies. This was certainly the case when I led the August 2003 Blackout Recov-*

ery for my company. But even then the Theory Y human side of how to treat people was employed. Just because we were in a crisis mode, it did not mean that we suddenly shifted to distrusting people's motivation and commitment to do an excellent job. In fact, the sense of shared purpose was at its highest during this crisis.

Unquestionably, *The Human Side of Enterprise* is a classic. Not only has this book affected the thinking of countless organizational leaders like Ron May, but it is a touchstone for scholars. Consider the frequency with which it is cited in leading publications, as indicated in Figure 1. The *Social Science Citation Index* began tracking citations in 1966, so we don't have a record of the immediate response to the book, but we do see a clear progression toward a peak in popularity in the mid-1970s. (The *Social Science Citation Index* tracks references from approximately 1,700 social science journals and books, spanning many fields and disciplines.) This is, of course, the peak of what has come to be termed the "Human Relations Movement," which views McGregor as one of its founders. Perhaps more interesting, however, is the pattern from 1980 forward. This is the portrait of a classic—a book that continues to be cited on a steady basis for many decades after its peak. As Peter Drucker commented in a 2000 volume in which Heil, Bennis, and Stephens celebrated McGregor's work: "With every passing year, McGregor's message becomes ever more relevant, more timely, and more important."[9]

---

[9] Gary Heil, Warren Bennis, and Deborah Stephens, *Douglas McGregor, Revisited: Managing the Human Side of the Enterprise*, New York: John Wiley & Sons, 2000.

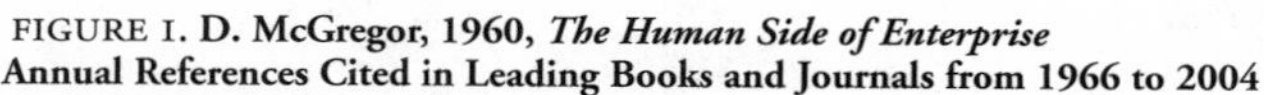

FIGURE I. **D. McGregor, 1960, *The Human Side of Enterprise***
Annual References Cited in Leading Books and Journals from 1966 to 2004

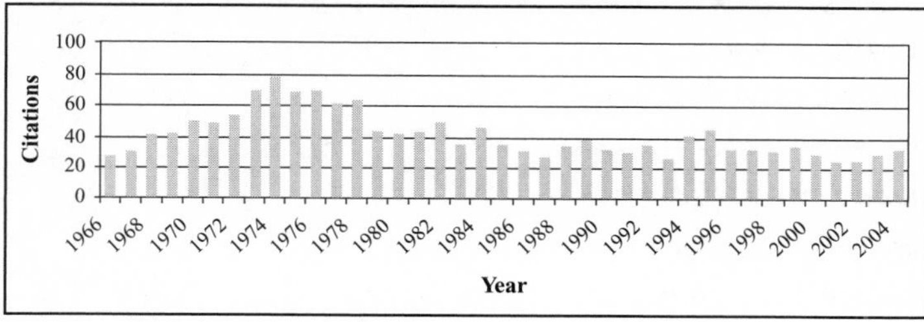

In addition to the frequency of citations, consider the diversity. Some of the journals with articles citing McGregor just in 2004 and 2005 include

Academy of Management Executive
Academy of Management Review
Annual Review of Psychology
Biochemistry and Molecular Biology
Education
Education and Urban Society
Educational Policy
Gender, Work and Organization
Human Resource Management
International Journal of Cooperative Information Systems
International Studies Quarterly
Journal of Applied Social Psychology
Journal of Business Ethics
Journal of Healthcare Management
Journal of Higher Education
Journal of International Business Studies
Journal of Organizational Change Management
Journal of Vocational Behavior
Organizational Science

Personnel Review
Policing
Prison Journal
Public Health Nursing
School Psychology International
Small Group Research
Social Work in Health Care
Systems Research and Behavioral Science

A CONTINUING DEBATE

Certainly a fair question would be why management practice is not now dominated by Theory Y, which has been widely taught in business schools, industrial relations schools, psychology departments, professional development seminars, and other settings for over four decades. This very question was raised by MIT Professor Lotte Bailyn at a recent lunch meeting of the MIT Organizational Studies Group (OSG). This group and the Institute for Work and Employment Relations (IWER), which also held a similar lunch discussion, both have their roots in the MIT Industrial Relations Section, which McGregor helped to found in 1937. The answers that surfaced at these two lunch sessions were many. MIT Professor Thomas Kochan noted that many other aspects of management education have roots in economics, which has historically emphasized competitive assumptions about people and organizations.[10] So mixed messages are conveyed in our management training with respect to the prevailing assumptions about human nature. It was also noted that

[10] Institutional economics has historically been a counterpoint to more market-based approaches to economic forces, and, more recently, important advances in economics have come from scholars who have relaxed simple competitive assumptions.

the competing aspects of human behavior highlighted by McGregor have endured for thousands of years—the emphasis on influence and respect, on the one hand, and the reliance on authority and control on the other. So, it is no surprise that the issues remain in debate. As well, John-Paul Ferguson, currently a doctoral student at MIT, calls attention to McGregor's assumption that advances in the first half of the twentieth century in protection of workers' rights, the broad reach of collective bargaining, and improvements in working conditions would continue to expand in the future. In fact, the last three decades in the United States have seen a contentious gridlock on collective labor policy issues and an almost incoherent patchwork quilt of new individual employment rights, a declining percentage of the workforce covered under collective bargaining, and the erosion of health-care and pension benefits. These and other contextual conditions, McGregor would point out, shift people's focus back to what Abraham Maslow termed basic safety and security concerns, rather than personal development and self-actualization.[11]

There is, today, a continuing debate in practice between Theory X and Theory Y assumptions. The General Electric Corporation is renowned, for example, for embodying the core assumption that internal competition will drive excellence. This involves selling off entire companies that can't stay on top of their markets, and it involves employee relations practices that pit individuals against one another. Although the company has slightly relaxed its "10-80-10" employee performance review policy (in which the top 10 percent of the workforce is highly rewarded and the bottom 10 percent of the workforce is on notice that they are at risk of being fired), this fierce competitive culture and the success enjoyed by this corporation have

[11] Abraham Maslow, *Motivation and Personality*, New York: Harper & Brothers, 1954.

earned high marks in the business press, directly or indirectly reinforcing a Theory X approach.

The prevalence of Theory X assumptions among leading corporations was highlighted in an e-mail exchange that followed the announcement of this annotated edition. John Shin, a corporate strategist at Samsung Electronics and a former member of the research staff at the Harvard Business School's Strategy and Competition Unit, attributes Samsung's business success, in part, to what he terms the influence of "a Theory X–style command and control culture that permeates the organization." He reports that "on the semiconductor and LCD fab floor, men and women, who are well past the minimum pay and benefits hurdle bar as in McGregor's book, toil 70 hours a week without much in the way of forward-looking self-development. These people [presumably managers] with an average pay of USD 100,000 have never heard of Theory Y, and they probably won't in the future." He also describes "insular, control-dominated communication between the European outpost and the HQ." Yet, he points out, "Popular business press ranging from *BusinessWeek* to the *Wall Street Journal* and the *Financial Times* in recent times hailed Samsung's meteoric rise as nothing but a miracle. Samsung's profit numbers since 2002 consistently beat the sum total profits of the top 10 Japanese electronics companies."[12]

Wal-Mart, too, is a highly visible business success in which a Theory X view of employees permeates the culture. Employee theft is a concern in the retail sector, but the approach to this

---

[12] He also adds, "Samsung's mobile phones unit is winning market share at Nokia's expense, especially in high ASP segments. Samsung's memory chip unit is leading the DRAM market with premium DDR2 chips. Samsung's NAND flash memory is the industry standard, and Intel is losing lustre with its position in NOR flash."

issue reveals deeper underlying assumptions. For example, one real estate professional described a negotiations session at the corporate headquarters where, at the time, the corporate boardrooms had video cameras installed and employees were instructed to always keep their hands above the tables in order to ensure that no underhanded deals were being made. In 2004 the *New York Times* reported that some Wal-Mart stores locked their employees in at night to avoid theft of merchandise, prompting one reader to ask whether the company had yet to join the twentieth, let alone the twenty-first century.[13] Wal-Mart has been under significant public pressure from community groups, unions, and the media in recent years. The more overt practices may be tempered, but the underlying Theory X assumptions are likely to persist.

More prevalent and perhaps more insidious are the practices that are proclaimed as being motivated by a valuing of human resources but that have subtle forms of control embedded in them. McGregor had a keen ability to see, for example, how the delegation of employee monitoring to a human resources, finance, or industrial engineering function was not an example of enlightened delegation, but a more insidious form of control. The issue here is whether the more overt and the less visible forms of Theory X control are more or less effective than the emphasis on self-control, commitment, and integration that flows from Theory Y.

This debate is not new—it dates back to the introduction of McGregor's work.[14] Although he advocated the benefits of Theory Y for both the individual and the organization, McGre-

[13] Steven Greenhouse, "Workers Assail Night Lock-Ins by Wal-Mart," *New York Times,* Jan. 18, 2004.

[14] Indeed, in the appendix to this volume, the debate is featured in a special 1962 *BusinessWeek* article.

gor was not just offering a normative polemic. He sought to explain the practices and relationships that he observed. In this sense, he would understand that operating on the basis of Theory Y assumptions may be harder today than it was in 1960.

CURRENT AND FUTURE CHALLENGES

At the time when McGregor was writing, the pressing issues included performance appraisal, line-staff relations, the Scanlon approach to gain sharing, management development, and other matters—all of which merited one or more chapters in *The Human Side of Enterprise*. If the book were to be written today, what might merit a chapter? What assumptions would need careful attention? In part, there are new challenges for which the focus on Theory X and Theory Y assumptions is still relevant. As well, there are challenges in which additional assumptions about work, technology, organizations, markets, and other matters might be added to the debate.[15] Consider the following challenges:

- The rise of the global economy, the information revolution, and the growth of knowledge-driven work, which call for us to reconsider assumptions about technology, markets, and the nature of work
- The collapse of the traditional social contract around work

[15] In considering the renewed relevance of McGregor's work, we may just be participating in one of many successive iterations between a humanistic, normative focus and a more mechanistic, rational focus. This thesis is advanced in Stephen R. Barley and Gideon Kunda, "Design and Devotion: Surges of Rational and Normative Ideologies of Control in Managerial Discourse," *Administrative Science Quarterly*, vol. 32, 1992, pp. 363–399. In this respect, linking McGregor's work with the analysis by Barley and Kunda leads us to ask whether it is the larger social and economic context that brings ideas to the fore, or whether certain ideas are sufficiently compelling as to propel changes in the social and economic context.

and expansion of the "independent consultant" model of employment, which calls for us to reconsider assumptions about the legal and institutional frameworks associated with employment

- The connections between the stock market and practices such as reengineering and "rightsizing," as well as the moves in many sectors toward deregulation and privatization, all of which have reinforced and accelerated the impact of Theory X assumptions
- The succession of quality, lean, and Six Sigma initiatives;[16] joint ventures and strategic alliances; and related systems change initiatives, all of which can be fruitfully regrounded in Theory Y assumptions
- Many other innovations, such as "principled" or "interest-based" approaches to negotiation, robust systems for dispute resolution in the workplace, new frontiers around work-life balance, and others, all of which call for expanded assumptions about how we interact in today's organizations with today's workforce
- The increasingly deep cultural divides around religious fundamentalism, personal identity, and other complex challenges in society, all of which can become interwoven with assumptions about people and organizations

These and other challenges would draw McGregor's attention; they can still benefit from the wisdom in *The Human Side of Enterprise*, and these challenges spur us on to explore additional underlying values and assumptions. Let us consider how Douglas McGregor might engage these points.

[16] Six Sigma initiatives represent a structured set of tools and methods aimed at achieving exceptional levels of enterprise quality (statistical control established at six standard deviations from the mean). These initiatives feature successive levels of demonstrated capability in cost savings, which earn change leaders "green belts," "black belts," and "master black belts."

First, McGregor would quickly cut through so much of today's rhetoric that "employees are our most valuable resource" and the plethora of participative practices implemented by using unilateral command and control methods. He would point out how Theory X assumptions virtually guarantee that any immediate gains from top-down reengineering will have to be balanced against longer-term challenges in rebuilding trust and relationships. He would be outraged at how, during the 1990s, stock valuations rose with each successive layoff announcement. His focus would not be just a surface response, but a call to examine the core assumptions about human behavior that guide these institutions. He would push to engage the debate at this deeper level.

Similarly, McGregor would look at the many U.S. industries that have been deregulated—trucking, airlines, telecommunications, energy, banking, and others—and point out that the organizational implications were barely mentioned in the policy debates in advance of these decisions. He would look at the situation facing the airline industry, for example, and understand why the leading pollster of employees in this industry describes the workforce as angry, militant, and lacking any trust or confidence in the business or management models of the employers.[17] The core assumptions about the virtues of competition for consumers (which dominated the policy debates) were never connected to the unstated, but clearly implicit, assumptions about the effects of unfettered price competition on employee and managerial behavior, motivation, and welfare. In fact, the ultimate "story" in each deregulated industry has been powerfully shaped, and in some cases completely dominated, by the human and organizational implications. In addition to assumptions about

---

[17] Attitude survey results reported by Phil Comstock, president, Wilson Center for Public Research, to the Airline Industry Council, Labor and Employment Relations National Policy Forum Meetings, June 16, 2005.

people, these issues bring to the surface underlying assumptions about the very purpose of corporations (shareholder value maximization versus what is termed today a double bottom line).[18]

McGregor's lens also helps us to avoid painting all of the information-intensive work, the outsourcing, and the globalization with a single brush. This lens urges that we ask whether the issues around both the legacy jobs and the new jobs are being addressed from an integrative point of view. Is the attention on the interests and capabilities of both the employees and the employer? McGregor would disparage some of the new customer service call centers that re-create, with modern technology, industrial sweatshops. At the same time, he would celebrate call centers such as those established by UK Fujitsu, where employees are empowered to first understand what work the customer is trying to accomplish with the Fujitsu products, and then what systemic solutions are needed to address the immediate inquiry and prevent such problems in the future.[19] A single customer call may prompt two or three hours of assistance and follow-up on the part of the call-center employee. The result? Gains that are orders of magnitude better than the performance of traditional call centers—just as McGregor would predict. The assumptions here are not just about human potential, but also about

---

[18] The concept of a double bottom line refers to organizations that systematically pursue (and track) both social and financial outcomes (this is sometimes expanded as a triple bottom line around "profits, people, and planet"). For an important study on this matter, see Catherine Clark, William Rosenzweig, David Long, and Sara Olsen, "Double Bottom Line Project Report: Assessing Social Impact in Double Bottom Line Ventures—Methods Catalogue," Rockefeller Foundation, 2005.

[19] See the case study in Chapter 12 of Joel Cutcher-Gershenfeld and J. Kevin Ford, *Valuable Disconnects in Organizational Learning Systems*, New York: Oxford University Press, 2005; see also Stephen Parry, Sue Barlow, and Mike Faulkner, *Sense and Respond: The Journey to Customer Purpose*, London: Palgrave/Macmillan, 2005.

organizations being customer-driven, team-based, and adaptable. There are also assumptions about technology enabling rather than supplanting or stifling people.[20]

What about the decline of unions—an aspect of the institutional landscape that McGregor was counting on to expand as a mechanism to foster the integration of employee and employer interests? On the one hand, McGregor would certainly celebrate the efforts that are taking place to bring to the surface underlying interests and foster increased problem-solving during collective bargaining. After all, even with the decline, there are still approximately 50,000 public- and private-sector collective bargaining agreements negotiated every year in the United States, and a growing number of cases feature some experimentation with these methods. Similarly, he would deeply appreciate the advances in alternative approaches to dispute resolution—replacing the adversarial assumptions of the legal system with a problem-solving and relationship-building orientation. These and related experiments are signaled by the following comment from Stephen Sleigh, director of strategic resources for the international Association of Machinists:

> *McGregor's seminal work spurred managers and union leaders alike to rethink the command and control work environment. Now, a full generation and a half later, my own union has dedicated substantial resources to fostering high-performance work systems rooted in McGregor's view that workers can think, plan, and be creative. In this information age, this view should be dominant, rather than unusual, as it remains today.*

---

[20] There is, of course, a debate about technology assumptions that precedes McGregor's work (including, of course, Karl Marx, Sydney and Beatrice Webb, Adam Smith, and others) and that continues following McGregor's contributions (with the work of Harry Braverman and others).

On the other hand, McGregor would likely look at the way collective bargaining has become almost exclusively oriented around wages, hours, and working conditions and share Sleigh's concern with the diffusion of new work systems. He would point out that the institution of collective bargaining has been primarily limited in its focus to only what Maslow would call lower-order human needs. McGregor would ask, rightly, why haven't collective negotiations further developed around helping individuals at work to realize their full potential throughout a career? Why hasn't the process pushed the frontiers of work-life balance? He would look at the limited number of experiments with agreements aimed at generating mutual gains and point out that collective bargaining could not expand without pioneering new ways to deliver deeper value to employers and employees—not just a succession of new agreements. The key underlying assumption here is whether the institutions associated with the collective interests of the workforce are "add-ons" rather than integral to the business operations and the lives of the workforce.

And the lessons from *The Human Side of Enterprise* go further, much further. Consider McGregor's simple observation that management climate and employment relations do not derive from formal policies or statements, but emerge through countless daily interactions. These interactions, McGregor noted, serve to build or undermine a reciprocal relationship in which employees and employers either are committed to mutual success or are working at cross purposes. There is a direct parallel with the teachings of Buddhist philosophers, who also observe that all of our daily actions create "imprints" that shape the way our lives unfold. If these imprints are rooted in fear, jealousy, and mistrust, they shape a life characterized by these same assumptions.[21]

[21] For a modern presentation connecting Buddhist principles with business practices, see Geshe Michael Roach, *The Diamond Cutter: The Buddha on Managing Your Business and Your life*, New York: Doubleday, 2000.

You reap what you sow. Or, as the philosopher William James famously observed, "The greatest discovery of our generation is that human beings can alter their lives by altering their attitudes of mind. As you think, so shall you be." McGregor's argument was similar. He was not advocating a naive stance of unquestioning trust. Rather, he was urging that assuming the best about people creates an environment in which, most of the time, people will indeed rise to meet those expectations. The pattern becomes self-reinforcing, and a positive cycle is enabled.[22] Today, the emerging movement around what is termed "appreciative inquiry" is rooted in the view that a pattern of positively framed, constructive questions (avoiding negative, distrustful questions) builds mutual understanding and effective relationships.[23] Similarly, some of the leading work in complexity theory utilizes agent-based models in which a few simple underlying principles guide microinteractions and can account for the characteristics of vast, complex systems.[24] In these regards, the focus of

---

[22] Note the contrast between this focus on patterns of interaction and the focus on outcomes (the contours of agreements) in another contemporary classic, John Dunlop's *Industrial Relations systems* (New York: Henry Holt, 1958).

[23] See, for example, S. Srivastva and David Coorperrider (eds.), *Appreciative Management and Leadership: The Power of Positive Thought and Action in Organizations*, San Francisco: Jossey-Bass, 1990; F. Barrett, G. F. Thomas, and S. P. Hocevar. "The Central Role of Discourse in Large-Scale Change: A Social Construction Perspective," *Journal of Applied Behavioral Science*, vol. 31, 1995, pp. 352–372; David Cooperrider and M. Avital (eds.), *Advances in Appreciative Inquiry: Constructive Discourse and Human Organization*. New York: Elsevier Publishing, 2004.

[24] M. Mitchell Waldrop, *Complexity: The Emerging Science at the Edge of Order and Chaos*, New York: Simon and Schuster, 1992; Ravindra K. Ajuja, Thomas L. Magnanti, and James B. Orlin, *Network Flows: Theory, Algorithms, and Applications*, New York: Prentice-Hall, 1993; John

Theory Y on patterned interactions and core underlying assumptions is at once ancient and at the cutting edge.

In addressing the deep ideological and moral divides in the United States and around the world, with the associated links to religious fundamentalism, McGregor would undoubtedly share a profound concern, but he would also be likely to be drawn to the patterns of interaction that build bridges across these divides. The South African Truth and Reconciliation Process, groups such as "Seeds of Peace" that bring Palestinian and Israeli teenagers together, and other such reconciliation efforts are dedicated to the principles of integration and to advancing the constructive assumptions about human nature that McGregor highlighted.[25] McGregor, with his own deeply moral and

---

Hollad, *Hidden Order: How Adaptation Builds Complexity*, Boston: Addison-Wesley, 1996; Joshua M. Epstein and Robert L. Axtell, *Growing Artificial Societies: Social Science from the Bottom Up*, Washington: Brookings Institution, 1996.

[25] In considering the larger issues of values in society, a word or two is in order about the title of the book. I admit, as others will as well, that I have been sometimes guilty of inadvertently or purposely restating the title as "The Human side of *the* Enterprise." In the early stages of this project, I inadvertently sent a note to thousands of colleagues with "the" added to the title. The 2000 book *Douglas McGregor Revisited* purposely included the subtitle *Managing the Human Side of the Enterprise.* Indeed, with today's focus on enterprise transformation, this attention to the social aspects of the enterprise makes the slightly reworded title very timely. But McGregor's focus was not just on the business organization as such; he was focused on the core values and assumptions that underlie enterprise itself in our economy. In that sense, he does call into question economic assumptions about competition, foreign policy assumptions around control, and other arrangements that fail to foster reciprocal capability and integration of interests. This theme is reinforced by a more recent book to come out of MIT's industrial relations community, *The Mutual Gains Enterprise*, by Paul Osterman and Thomas Kochan (Boston: Harvard Business School Press, 1994).

humanistic orientation, would certainly struggle with (but not avoid) the opportunities and tensions around personal identity and affinity groups in organizations, which interweave issues of race, religion, gender, ethnicity, sexual identity, and attitudes on abortion, stem cell research, religious fundamentalism, and other matters.

At the fiftieth anniversary of MIT's Sloan School of Management, one of the featured presentations built on McGregor's framework and outlined additional assumptions relevant for the twenty-first century, as reflected in the following chart.

Contrasting Assumptions in Twentieth- and Twenty-First-Century Organizations[26]

Assumptions About:	Assumptions Characterizing Twentieth-Century Organizations	Assumptions That May Characterize Twenty-First-Century Organizations
People	Theory X: People are a cost that must be monitored and controlled	Theory Y: People are an asset that should be valued and developed
Work	Segmented, industrially based, and individual tasks	Collaborative, knowledge-based projects

[26] Source: Thomas Kochan, Wanda Orlikowski, and Joel Cutcher-Gershenfeld, "Beyond McGregor's Theory Y: Human Capital and Knowledge-Based Work in the 21st Century Organization," in Thomas Kochan and Richard Schmalensee (eds.), *Management: Inventing and Delivering Its Future*, Cambridge, Mass.: MIT Press, 2003.

Assumptions About:	Assumptions Characterizing Twentieth-Century Organizations	Assumptions That May Characterize Twenty-First-Century Organizations
Technology	Design technology to control work and minimize human error	Integrate technology with social systems to enable knowledge-based work
Leadership	Senior managers and technical experts	Distributed leadership at all levels
Goals	Unitary focus on returns to shareholders	Multidimensional focus on value for multiple stakeholders

In this analysis, Theory X and Theory Y are the foundation for a much further exploration of basic assumptions about people and organizations. As this introduction suggests, even the assumptions in this chart are just the beginning of the sort of exploration that McGregor urged.

LIMITATIONS OF THE TEXT

There are, of course, aspects of the book that do not stand the test of time. Early on, Warren Bennis observed that the book is too focused on the internal supervisor/subordinate relationships and does not sufficiently take into account the external organizational context. He also noted the dilemma and challenge of a Theory Y supervisor needing Theory Y supervision as well.[27]

---

[27] Warren Bennis, "Chairman Mac," *Harvard Business Review*, vol. 50, no. 4, September–October 1972, p. 140.

The use of vignettes to illustrate key points in the book is welcome, but in masking the organizational context for virtually all of them, we lose the ability to independently verify the points and probe further—an aspect of scientific verification that has now become an expected practice (where feasible) in organizational research. Similarly, the occasional citations of relevant research studies are welcome, as are the bibliographic entries at the end of each chapter, but today's standards of scholarship would demand that many more points be supported with appropriate citations and references. Of course, the use of the masculine pronoun throughout the book dates it.[28] As was noted earlier, McGregor's assumption that there would be continued stability and expansion with respect to employee rights, working conditions, and collective bargaining is now jarring in its optimism. In railing against standardization, which he does in numerous places, McGregor failed to anticipate a unique twist pioneered by Drs. Deming and Juran and then embodied in the Toyota Production System and other effective lean or Six Sigma systems. Instead of the oppressive "one size fits all" models that McGregor rightfully disparaged, he failed to anticipate the way that standardization in the hands of the front-line workforce (through self-inspection of quality, self-managed preventive maintenance procedures, structured organizational learning processes, and other such standardized processes) would prove an essential foundation for continuous improvement.

Perhaps most complicated of all is the way McGregor positioned Theory X and Theory Y as resting on contrasting, wholly incompatible assumptions. Five years after the publication of *The Human Side of Enterprise*, another classic text, *A Behavioral*

[28] McGregor's sparing use of commas is a quibble that I note only after having retyped so many wonderful quotes where I had to stop myself from adding commas in order to preserve the original text.

Theory of Labor Negotiations, was also published by McGraw-Hill. The coauthors, Richard Walton and Robert McKersie,[29] expanded the concept of integration, but also noted that what they termed "integrative bargaining" was in a dynamic tension with "distributive bargaining."[30] Although the integrative and distributive dimensions were clearly opposite one another in ways similar to Theory X and Theory Y, the authors noted that they were invariably both present in a negotiation (along with two additional dimensions, attitudinal structuring and intraorganizational bargaining). McGregor's work is crystal clear and compelling because he makes such a sharp differentiation between Theory X and Theory Y. An almost sacrilegious point can be made, however, about the importance of better understanding how organizations can persist for so long with these inconsistent assumptions coexisting in policies and practices. At a metaphysical level, can Theory Y or other similarly constructive assumptions exist in the absence of Theory X as a counterpoint? At a practical level, even enlightened practitioners may be operating on a basis closer to the ancient Sufi aphorism that you should "trust in Allah, but tie up your camel." Does this mean that Theory X and Theory Y are in some ways interdependent—that a small degree of Theory X caution about the worst in people is a necessary counterbalance to Theory Y? Or is it just the case that we need a robust conception of Theory Y?[31]

This is an enduring tension that was never fully resolved by Douglas McGregor. What about situations in which strong leaders must act in ways that override expressed individual or col-

---

[29] Now emeritus professors from Harvard and MIT, respectively.

[30] See Richard Walton and Robert McKersie, *A Behavioral Theory of Labor Negotiations*, New York: McGraw-Hill, 1965.

[31] George Strauss, Book Review, *Relations Industrialles*, vol. 57, no. 1, Hiver/Winter 2002.

lective interests? What of situations in which leaders must unilaterally remove individuals who will not abandon Theory X approaches? These situations in which power becomes interwoven with a commitment to Theory Y are cause for deep introspection. As Berkeley Professor George Strauss notes:

> *Psychoanalysis was very much in the air in the 1930s and Doug had a personal analysis. Psychoanalytic concepts, such as transference, popped up frequently in his teaching. It may also have something to do with the difficulties he faced coming to grips with the concept and exercise of authority. As he sometimes put it, boss-subordinate relations replicate those between parents and children. Subordinate dependence is a problem that can be alleviated but never entirely eliminated.*

Strauss further observes, "Doug saw his presidency of Antioch, already a highly democratic college, as an opportunity to put Theory Y into practice." Strauss quotes McGregor[32] as stating:

> *I believed ... that a leader could operate successfully as a kind of adviser to his organization. I though I could avoid being a "boss." ... I couldn't have been more wrong.... I finally began to realize that a leader cannot avoid the exercise of authority any more than he can avoid responsibility for what happens to his organization. In fact, it is the major responsibility of the top executive to take on his own shoulders the responsibility for resolving the uncertainties that are always involved in important decisions.... The boss must boss.*

---

[32] The quote is from Douglas McGregor, "On Leadership," *Antioch Notes*, vol. 31, no. 9, May 1, 1954, reprinted in Warren Bennis and Edgar Schein (eds.), *Leadership and Motivation: Essays of Douglas McGregor*, with the collaboration of Caroline McGregor, Cambridge, Mass.: MIT Press, 1966.

Ed Schein's foreword extends this point, making clear that strong command is a highly consistent and necessary aspect of Theory Y.[33] But what about the other side of the equation—the employees? In commenting on the diffusion of Theory Y assumptions, Thomas Kochan Observes:

> *We might infer that only when employees have sufficient power to discipline and limit the ability of Theory X management, will managers widely adopt Theory Y assumptions and practices. When managerial power meets no effective resistance, executives turn their attention to financial stakeholders and others that do wield power over them. Diffusion of Theory Y may well depend on a more balanced set of power relationships among different organizational stakeholders than is found in many workplaces today.*

So, even if the tension cannot be fully resolved, there is at least some guidance in wrestling with the dilemmas. As McGregor put it, "Good human relations develop out of strength, not of weakness."[34]

CONCLUSION

Douglas McGregor's legacy at Antioch has taken on a unique, tangible form. Antioch is a federation of separate, related institutions, and, in 1992, the campus offering undergraduate and graduate programs in management, conflict resolution, educa-

---

[33] In a recent presentation, Lynn Williams, former president of the United Steelworkers of America, was asked about the union's lessons from having representatives serve on the boards of struggling steel companies. His response was, "We learned that good management is really important." (Presentation on June 2, 2005 to DTE Energy and Utility Workers Local 223.)

[34] From "On Leadership."

tional administration, and other topics was renamed to honor Douglas McGregor.[35] Barbara Gellman-Danley, president, Antioch University McGregor, comments that

> *Douglas McGregor's work helps define the heart of our institution. I often find myself telling my staff, "What would McGregor do in this situation?" One time we gave extra time off during the winter holiday season and some questioned our supposed generosity. I recall saying, "We are named after Douglas McGregor; we walk the talk." I often explain the meaning of "McGregor" in our name, and it makes me proud to see how many people still revere his teachings, over a half century later.*[36]

A century ago, we made the transition across what Michael Piore and Charles Sabel termed the first industrial divide as we moved from a craft to an industrial model of work.[37] Published in 1960, McGregor's work was at the forefront in identifying the limits of the industrial model that resulted. As McGregor put it, "The

---

[35] Initially named the McGregor School of Antioch University, it was renamed Antioch University McGregor in 2000 to reflect the fact that all programs, graduate and undergraduate, were covered on this campus. It is part of Antioch University, which includes the original Antioch College campus (also located in Yellow Springs, Ohio) and additional operations on campuses in New Hampshire, California, and Washington.

[36] Dr. Gellman-Danley also teaches classes in organizational behavior and related the following personal experience: "I was teaching a group of graduate management students about our namesake, Douglas McGregor, and referred to his May 1, 1944, commencement remarks when he was president of Antioch College. I noticed, purely by coincidence, it was exactly 50 years to the day of the speech. In Antioch terms, we call that 'karma!'" For more information on the Antioch University McGregor school, see http://www.mcgregor.edu.

[37] Michael Piore and Charles Sable, *The Second Industrial Divide*, New York: Basic Books, 1984.

modern, large, industrial enterprise is ... a social invention of great historical importance. Unfortunately, it is already obsolete. In its present form it is simply not an adequate means for meeting the future economic requirements of society" (p. 327). Today, there is indeed growing evidence to suggest that we are in the early or middle stages of a second industrial divide, which has been variously characterized as involving an information revolution, increased interconnection across global markets, the rise of flexible specialization in production and service operations, and a transformation toward knowledge-driven work in all sectors of the economy.

McGregor understood, anticipated, and helped point the way toward what may well emerge as a future model of work, organizations, and society that is rooted in core assumptions driving participative, interdependent, authentic, inventive, and productive relationships. However, the alternative, an economic "race to the bottom" based on increasingly individualistic, control-oriented, and competitive assumptions, is also a very real possibility. As we venture forth, McGregor's insights about *The Human Side of Enterprise* continue to be a beacon, guiding the way and pointing us, again and again, to engage the debate at the level of core values and assumptions. We must continue to ask, as he did: "What are your assumptions (implicit as well as explicit) about the most effective way to manage people?

PART ONE

THE THEORETICAL ASSUMPTIONS OF MANAGEMENT

MANAGEMENT AND SCIENTIFIC KNOWLEDGE

In Chapter 1, McGregor challenges us to conduct a simple exercise the next time we are in a managerial meeting or other situation where policies are under discussion. "Tune your ear," he suggests, "to listen for assumptions about human behavior, whether they relate to an individual, a particular group, or people in general." He further notes, "The engineer does not blame water for flowing downhill rather than up, nor gases for expanding rather than contracting when heated. However, when people respond to managerial decisions in undesired ways, the normal response is to blame them. It is *their* stupidity, or *their* uncooperativeness, or *their* laziness which is seized on as the explanation of what happened, not management's failure to select appropriate means for control." At the core, McGregor states, "There is, in fact, no prediction without theory; all managerial decisions and actions rest on assumptions about behavior." Thus, it is in this chapter that we are invited to begin the journey at the level of fundamental or core assumptions about human behavior.

Implicitly, McGregor is also posing a question that remains only partly answered today. He is suggesting, by analogy, that the social sciences should and will develop a predictive capability comparable to that of the physical sciences (a theme he develops further in later chapters in the book). In fact, the fields of management science, organizational science, and decision

science[1] have progressed substantially since 1960, including important work about biases in human judgment, optimization of complex networks, and many other matters. But predictive, scientific advances about the fundamental nature of human beings at work remain elusive.

---

[1] For example, journals published by the Institute for Operations Research and the Management Sciences include *Decision Analysis, Information Systems Research, INFORMS Journal on Computing, Interfaces, Management Science, Manufacturing & Service Operations Management, Marketing Science, Mathematics of Operations Research, Operations Research, Organization Science, Transportation Science,* and *INFORMS Transactions on Education.*

CHAPTER 1

MANAGEMENT AND SCIENTIFIC KNOWLEDGE

Every professional is concerned with the use of knowledge in the achievement of objectives: the engineer as he designs equipment, the medical practitioner as he diagnoses and prescribes for the ills of his patients, the lawyer or the architect as he serves his clients. The professional draws upon the knowledge of science and of his colleagues, and upon knowledge gained through personal experience. The degree to which he relies upon the first two of these rather than the third is one of the ways in which the professional may be distinguished from the layman.

From the outset, McGregor connects "knowledge" with the achievement of economic and other objectives, focusing at the time on the professional workforce. Today, these principles apply more broadly as many forms of work become more knowledge-driven. (See Joel Cutcher-Gershenfeld et al., *Knowledge-Driven Work: Unexpected Lessons from Japanese and United States Work Practices*, New York: Oxford University Press, 1998.)

It is beginning to be possible for the industrial manager to be a professional in this respect. He can draw upon a reasonable and growing body of knowledge in the social sciences as an aid to achieving his managerial objectives. He need not rely exclusively on personal experience and observation.

Progress in any profession is associated with the ability to predict and control, and this is true also of industrial management. One of the major tasks of management is to organize human effort in the service of the economic objectives of the enterprise. Every managerial decision has behavioral consequences. Successful management depends—not alone, but significantly—upon the ability to predict and control human behavior.

Our ability along these lines today is spotty. It is remarkably good in some respects. Consider such everyday acts as making an appointment, signing a purchase agreement, placing a long-distance call, asking a subordinate to prepare a report, making a hotel reservation, mailing a letter. In literally thousands of ways we predict with a high degree of accuracy what others will do, and we control their behavior in the sense that our actions lead to the desired consequences.

At the same time, it is true that other attempts at prediction and control are quite inadequate. Many of the important social problems of our time reflect this inadequacy: juvenile delinquency, crime, the high traffic fatality rate, management-labor conflict, the cold war.

The results so far achieved in the management of business and industry reflect considerable ability to predict and control human behavior. The fact that a company is economically successful means, among other things, that management has been able to attract people into the organization and to organize and direct their efforts toward the production and sale of goods or services at a profit. Nevertheless, few managers are satisfied with their ability to predict and control the behavior of the members of their organizations. The interest expressed in new developments in this field is an indication of management's recognition of the opportunity for improvement. The frequent success of the outright charlatan in peddling managerial patent medicines also reflects the consciousness of inadequacy. Many managers would agree that the effectiveness of their organizations would be at least doubled if they could discover how to tap the unrealized potential present in their human resources.

I share with some of my colleagues the conviction that the social sciences could contribute more effectively than they have to managerial progress with respect to the human side of enterprise. There are, of course, many reasons why improvement has been slow. Some have to do with the social sciences themselves: they are still in their adolescence in comparison with the physical sciences; their findings are piecemeal and scattered; they lack precision; many critical issues are still in controversy. These are relative matters, however. One need only contrast the situation today with that thirty years ago to recognize that much has been accomplished. The social sciences are a rich resource today for management even though they have not reached full maturity.

I am not particularly impressed with arguments that social scientists do not publish their findings in language intelligible to the layman. Neither do physicists! Also, while it is lamentable that some social scientists jump incautiously from relatively precarious theory to practical applications, and others refuse to concern themselves at all with applications, there is nothing unique about social science in these respects. Today most managers are forced to rely on "middlemen" in the form of social scientist consultants or staff, or on literature intermediate between scientific journals and the Sunday supplements to interpret theory and research or to help them judge the scientific adequacy of claims or proposals. The time is not far off when the competent manager—like any other professional practitioner—will find it a necessity to be well enough versed in the scientific disciplines relevant to this work to be able to read the literature and judge the adequacy of scientific findings and claims.*

This is not to say that we social scientists can ignore our responsibilities. It is to say that the position of the manager vis-à-vis the social sciences will one day be no different than that of the engineer vis-à-vis the physical sciences or the doctor vis-à-vis chemistry or biology. The professional need not be a scientist, but he must be sophisticated enough to make competent use of scientific knowledge.

---

* It is striking to see the degree of optimism concerning the likely advances and impacts of the social sciences that McGregor expressed.

EVERY MANAGERIAL ACT RESTS ON THEORY

There are some other reasons why management has been relatively slow to utilize social science knowledge. Two of these are especially important. The first is that every manager quite naturally considers himself his own social scientist. His personal experience with people from childhood on has been so rich that he feels little real need to turn elsewhere for knowledge of human behavior. The social scientist's knowledge often appears to him to be theoretical and unrelated to the realities with which he must deal, whereas his own experience-based knowledge is practical and useful.

This frequent, invidious comparison of the practical and the theoretical with respect to the management of human resources has been a severe handicap to progress in this field. It has led to premature and misguided attempts to translate scientific findings into action; it has permitted the quack and the charlatan to peddle worthless gimmicks and programs.

Every managerial act rests on assumptions, generalizations, and hypotheses—that is to say, on theory. Our assumptions are frequently implicit, sometimes quite unconscious, often conflicting; nevertheless, they determine our predictions that if we do *a, b* will occur. Theory and practice are inseparable.*

Next time you attend a management staff meeting at which a policy problem is under discussion or some action is being considered, try a variant on the pastime of doodling. Jot down the assumptions (beliefs, opinions, convictions, generalizations) about human behavior made during the discussion by the participants. Some of these will be explicitly stated ("A manager must himself be technically competent in a given field in order to manage professionals within it."). Most will be implicit, but fairly easily inferred ("We should require the office force to punch time clocks as they do in the factory."). It

---

* The inseparability of theory and practice builds on work advanced by Kurt Lewin, who preceded Douglas McGregor at MIT. (See Kurt Lewin, *Field Theory in the Social Sciences*, New York: Harper & Brothers, 1951.)

will not make too much difference whether the problem under discussion is a human problem, a financial or a technical one. Tune your ear to listen for assumptions about human behavior, whether they relate to an individual, a particular group, or people in general. The length and variety of your list will surprise you.

Learning to "tune your ear to listen for assumptions about human behavior" is a skill later advanced by Peter Senge in helping people to listen for and understand alternative "mental models" in organizations. In *The Fifth Discipline*, Senge quotes Hanover CEO Bill O'Brien as follows:

In the traditional authoritarian organization, the dogma was managing, organizing and controlling. In the learning organization, the new "dogma" will be vision, values and mental models. The healthy corporations will be the ones which can systematize ways to bring people together to develop the best possible mental models for the situation at hand.

It is possible to have more or less adequate theoretical assumptions; it is not possible to reach a managerial decision or take a managerial action uninfluenced by assumptions, whether adequate or not. The insistence on being practical really means, "Let's accept *my* theoretical assumptions without argument or test." The common practice of proceeding without explicit examination of theoretical assumptions leads, at times, to remarkable inconsistencies in managerial behavior.

A manager, for example, states that he delegates to his subordinates. When asked, he expresses assumptions such as, "People need to learn to take responsibility," or, "Those closer to the situation can make the best decisions." However, he has arranged to obtain a constant flow of detailed information about the behavior of his subordinates, and he uses this information to police their behavior and to "second-guess" their decisions. He says, "I am held responsible, so I need to know what is going on." He sees no inconsistency in his behavior, nor does he recognize some other assumptions which are implicit: "People can't be trusted," or, "They can't really make as good decisions as I can."

With one hand, and in accord with certain assumptions, he delegates; with the other, and in line with other assumptions, he takes actions which have the effect of nullifying his delegation. Not only does he fail to recognize the inconsistencies involved, but if faced with them he is likely to deny them.*

Another common way of denying the importance of theory to managerial behavior is to insist that management is an art. This also precludes critical examination of the theoretical assumptions underlying managerial actions by placing reliance on intuitions and feelings, which are by definition not subject to question. The issue is not whether management is a science. It is not. Its purposes are different. Science is concerned with the advancement of knowledge; management, like any profession, is concerned with the achievement of practical objectives. The issue is whether management can utilize scientific knowledge in the achievement of those objectives. To insist that management is an art is frequently no more than a denial of the relevance of systematic, tested knowledge to practice. So long as the manager fails to question the validity of his personal assumptions, he is unlikely to avail himself of what is available in science. And much is there. The knowledge in the social sciences is not sparse, but frequently it contradicts personal experience and threatens some cherished illusions. The easy way out is rejection, since one can always find imperfections and inadequacies in scientific knowledge.

CONTROL IS SELECTIVE ADAPTATION

An equally important reason for management's failure to make effective use of current social science knowledge has to do with a mis-

---

* This gap between rhetoric and reality has achieved wide currency today via the comic strip *Dilbert*.

conception concerning the nature of control in the field of human behavior. In engineering, control consists in adjustment to natural law. It does not mean making nature do our bidding. We do not, for example, dig channels in the expectation that water will flow uphill; we do not use kerosene to put out a fire. In designing an internal combustion engine we recognize and adjust to the fact that gases expand when heated; we do not attempt to make them behave otherwise. With respect to physical phenomena, control involves the selection of means which are *appropriate* to the nature of the phenomena with which we are concerned.*

In the human field the situation is the same, but we often dig channels to make water flow uphill. Many of our attempts to control behavior, far from representing selective adaptations, are in direct violation of human nature. They consist in trying to make people behave as we wish without concern for natural law. Yet we can no more expect to achieve desired results through inappropriate action in this field than in engineering.

Individual incentive plans provide a good example of an attempt to control behavior which fails to take sufficient account of "natural law"—in this case, human behavior in the industrial setting.

The practical logic of incentives is that people want money, and that they will work harder to get more of it. In accord with this logic, we measure jobs, establish standards for "a fair day's work," and determine a scale of incentive pay which provides a bonus for productivity above the standard.

Incentive plans do not, however, take account of several other well-demonstrated characteristics of behavior in the organizational

---

* Control theory and principles of feedback in technical systems were at the heart of important advances in the field of engineering at the time this book was written. (See David Mindell, *Between Human and Machine: Feedback, Control, and Computing before Cybernetics*, Baltimore: Johns Hopkins University Press, 2002.) Today, the principles of control theory in technical systems and in social systems are being linked in MIT's newly established Engineering Systems Division (ESD).

setting: (1) that most people also want the approval of their fellow workers and that, if necessary, they will forgo increased pay to obtain this approval; (2) that no managerial assurances can persuade workers that incentive rates will remain inviolate regardless of how much they produce; (3) that the ingenuity of the average worker is sufficient to outwit *any* system of controls devised by management.

A "good" individual incentive plan may bring about a moderate increase in productivity (perhaps 15 per cent), but it also may bring a considerable variety of protective behaviors—deliberate restriction of output, hidden jigs and fixtures, hidden production, fudged records, grievances over rates and standards, etc. In addition, it generally creates attitudes which are the opposite of those desired—antagonism toward those who administer the plan, cynicism with respect to management's integrity and fairness, indifference to the importance of collaboration with other parts of the organization (except for collusive efforts to *defeat* the incentive system).

All of these results are costly, and so are the managerial countermeasures which must be established to combat them (staff effort, elaborate control procedures, closer supervision, concessions with respect to rates, down-time provisions, setup arrangements, etc.). If the *total* costs of administering the incentive program—both direct and indirect—were calculated, it would often turn out that they add up to more than the total gains from increased productivity. Certainly the typical incentive plan is of limited effectiveness as a method of control if the purpose is to motivate human beings to direct their efforts toward organizational objectives.

Another fallacy is often revealed in managerial attempts to control human behavior. When we fail to achieve the results we desire, we tend to seek the cause everywhere but where it usually lies: in our choice of inappropriate methods of control. The engineer does not blame water for flowing downhill rather than up, nor gases for expanding rather than contracting when heated. However, when people respond to managerial decisions in undesired ways, the normal response is to blame them. It is *their* stupidity, or *their* cooperativeness, or *their* laziness which is seized on as the explanation of what happened, not management's failure to select appropriate means for control.*

The director of operations research in a large company is concerned because fewer than half of the solutions to operating problems developed by his research team have been adopted by the line organization. He is currently trying to persuade higher management to issue orders to the line regarding the implementation of certain of his findings. "If they can't recognize what's good for the organization, they will have to be told what to do," is his conclusion. Not only is his assumption of the line's stupidity incorrect, but so also is his further assumption that commands from higher management will solve the problem. Yet, for him, the whole problem is "out there." It does not occur to him to question his own methods of control.

Effective prediction and control are as central to the task of management as they are to the task of engineering or of medicine. If we would improve our ability to organize and direct human effort toward economic ends, we must not only recognize that this is so, we must also recognize and correct some common fallacies with respect to these matters.

Human behavior is predictable, but, as in physical science, accurate prediction hinges on the correctness of underlying theoretical assumptions. There is, in fact, no prediction without theory; all managerial decisions and actions rest on assumptions about behavior. If we adopt the posture of the ostrich with respect to our assumptions under the mistaken idea that we are thus "being practical," or that "management is an art," our progress with respect to the human side of enterprise will indeed be slow. Only as we examine and test our theoretical assumptions can we hope to make them more adequate, to remove inconsistencies, and thus to improve our ability to predict.

---

* For a subsequent treatment of these points, see Kerr's "On the Folly of Rewarding A, While Hoping for B," *Academy of Management Journal*, vol. 18, 1975.

We can improve our ability to control only if we recognize that control consists in selective adaptation to human nature rather than in attempting to make human nature conform to our wishes. If our attempts to control are unsuccessful, the cause generally lies in our choice of inappropriate means. We will be unlikely to improve our managerial competence by blaming people for failing to behave according to our predictions.

CONTROL AND PROFESSIONAL ETHICS

Discussions of the idea of controlling human behavior raise justifiable apprehensions about possible manipulation and exploitation. These concerns are not new, but they will be intensified as the manager becomes more professional in his use of social science knowledge to achieve the objectives of the economic enterprise. We must pause, therefore, to consider another characteristic of the professional: his conscious concern with ethical values.

Scientific knowledge is indifferent with respect to its uses. In this sense (and only in this sense) science is independent of values. Scientific knowledge can be used for good or evil purposes; it can be used to help mankind or to destroy him, as we have seen so dramatically in recent times with respect to certain applications of nuclear physics. It is obvious, therefore, that the more professional the manager becomes in his use of scientific knowledge, the more professional he must become in his sensitivity to ethical values. He must be concerned both with broad social values and with those involved in his attempts to control the members of his own organization.

Management's freedom to manage has been progressively curtailed in our society during the past century. Legislation with respect to child labor, the employment of women, workmen's compensation, collective bargaining, and many other matters reflects society's concern with the ethics of management. One approach to these problems is to see all restrictions on management as unreasonable and to fight blindly against them. This was fairly typical of industrial management a generation or two ago. The other approach is to become more sensitive to human values and to exert self-control through a positive, conscious, ethical code. It is this latter approach which characterizes the concept of the "social responsibility" of management about which we hear so much today.

John-Paul Ferguson, currently a doctoral student at MIT, comments:

McGregor assumes that the Theory X approach has become inoperative, in part, because of the widespread growth of collective bargaining between 1935 and 1960, which both secured great material gains for employees and reduced managerial discretion. Thus, I would argue, McGregor saw Theory Y not as a substitute for unions and collective bargaining, but as a complement to it. Most of McGregor's heirs in HR have not taken this point. They seem not to understand that the incentive for large organizations to employ Theory Y practices—and the HR professionals who espouse them—has declined in parallel with, if at a lag to, unionization.

Even though some managers are increasingly aware of these problems and are making sincere attempts to keep their behavior in line with high ethical principles, we have a way to go before the ethics of management are comparable to those, for example, of medicine. There are many instances in which essentially unethical practices are either ignored or defended with rationalizations.

It is usual today for big corporations to encourage, and sometimes to require, their executives to have annual physical examinations. Not many years ago it was common practice to make the data from these examinations available to top management to use in making decisions affecting the individual's career. Today, most large companies have a firm policy that these personal data about the individual are shared by the doctor only with the patient himself. It is up to the individual executive whether he will make this information known to his superiors. Most managements today are scrupulous in observing this policy.

Contrast this practice with that used in psychological testing and in the clinical diagnosis of the personalities of executives for purposes of placement. The reference here is not to initial selection but to administrative practices affecting the career of the individual after he has become an accepted member of the organization.

The data obtained from such tests and clinical interviews are private information which the individual gives about himself unwittingly. He has, in effect, no choice, since he does not know what significance will be placed upon his responses by the test or the interviewer. To use such data for administrative purposes seems quite clearly to be as much an invasion of individual rights as to use medical data in this way. Yet, many companies have opposite policies with respect to these two kinds of information.

It is natural to expect management to be committed to the economic objectives of the industrial organization. However, the history of social legislation has indicated that society will grant management freedom in its pursuit of these objectives only to the extent that human values are preserved and protected. Professions like medicine, education, and law in general maintain high ethical standards with respect to the influences they exert on human beings. In directing the human resources of the industrial organization, management is in a similar position. Here, as elsewhere in our society, the price of freedom is responsibility.

REFERENCES

Drucker, Peter F., "Thinking Ahead: The Potentials of Management Science," *Harvard Business Review*, vol. 37, no. 1 (January–February), 1959.

Gouldner, Alvin W., "Theoretical Requirements of the Applied Social Sciences," *American Sociological Review*, vol. 22, 1957, pp. 91–102.

Selekman, Benjamin M., "Sin Bravely: The Danger of Perfectionism," *Harvard Business Review*, vol. 37, no. 1 (January–February), 1959.

Wilensky, Harold L., "Human Relations in the Workplace: An Appraisal of Some Recent Research," *Research in Industrial Human Relations*. New York: Harper & Brothers, 1957, pp. 25–50.

SELECTED REFERENCES TO THE ANNOTATED EDITION

Cutcher-Gershenfeld, Joel, et al. *Knowledge-Driven Work: Unexpected Lessons from Japanese and United States Work Practices*, New York: Oxford University Press, 1998.

Kerr, S., "On the Folly of Rewarding A, While Hoping for B," *Academy of Management Journal*, vol. 18, 1975, pp. 769–783.

Mindell, David, *Between Human and Machine: Feedback, Control, and Computing before Cybernetics*, Baltimore: Johns Hopkins University Press, 2002.

Senge, Peter, *The Fifth Discipline: The Art and Practice of the Learning Organization*, New York: Doubleday, 1990, p. 180.

DISCUSSION QUESTIONS FOR CHAPTER 1

1. Once people's basic safety and security needs are met, do you assume that the majority of people will need incentives, monitoring, and control if they are expected to accomplish organizational objectives? Or do you assume that the majority of people will need clear goals, opportunities to excel, and support if they are expected to accomplish organizational objectives? Whichever you have selected, what is your evidence or basis for making this assumption?

2. McGregor states that "every managerial act rests on assumptions, generalizations, and hypotheses—that is to say, on theory." Identify a particularly visible or salient management act—what are the relevant underlying assumptions, generalizations, and hypotheses?

3. Are the physical sciences (and, in particular, physics) an appropriate model for social science research on people and organizations, as McGregor suggests?

METHODS OF INFLUENCE AND CONTROL

In Chapter 2, McGregor is critical of traditional managerial and supervisory training for being rooted in "armchair speculation rather than ... empirical research." He states that, "If there is a single assumption which pervades conventional organizational theory it is that authority is the central, indispensable means of managerial control.... Most of the other principles of organization, such as unity of command, staff and line, span of control, are directly derived from this one [assumption]." Instead of a sole reliance on control, McGregor points us toward various forms of influence, which can and should be employed "when there is some degree of dependence of the one party on the other." He concludes, "The power to influence others is not a function of the amount of authority one can exert. It is, rather, a function of the appropriate selection of the means of influence which the particular circumstances require.... [R]elinquishing authority is seen as losing the power to control. This is a completely misleading conception."

In the fields of communications and negotiations, we do see important advances in our understanding of the nature of influence and integrative ways of resolving disputes.[1] The literatures

[1] Richard Walton and Robert McKersie, *A Behavioral Theory of Labor Negotiations*, New York: McGraw-Hill, 1965; Roger Fisher and William Ury, *Getting to Yes: Negotiating Agreement without Giving In*, New York: Houghton Mifflin, 1981; William Ury, Jeanne Brett, and Stephen Goldberg, *Getting Disputes Resolved: Designing Systems to Cut the Costs of Conflict*, San Francisco: Jossey-Bass, 1988; Barbara Grey, *Collaborating*, San Francisco: Jossey-Bass, 1989.

on leadership and power have delved deeply into the many ways in which leaders act through influence, rather than control—often explicitly citing McGregor as a seminal thinker in this regard.[2] But the practice in industry and other walks of life of relying on hierarchically derived control systems has proved remarkably persistent, while the skills and orientation for managing via influence continue to be underdeveloped in many organizational settings. Individuals do operate in this way, but it is more often in spite of the systems in which they work, not because things have been set up to foster this form of leadership. Consider too the power of the workforce to exercise influence with managers in organizations that emphasize Theory X assumptions. In all, McGregor is prescient in pointing out that "interdependence is a central characteristic of the modern, complex society" and that influence, much more than authority, is central to success in such a context.

---

[2] Samuel B. Bacharach, *Power and Politics in Organizations: The Social Psychology of Conflict, Coalitions, and Bargaining*, San Francisco: Jossey-Bass, 1980; John Kotter, *Power and Influence: Beyond Formal Authority*, New York: The Free Press, 1985; P. Hershey and K. H. Blanchard, *Management of Organizational Behavior: Utilizing Human Resources*, 5th ed., Englewood Cliffs, N.J.: Prentice-Hall, 1988; Warren Bennis, *On Becoming a Leader*, Boston: Addison-Wesley, 1989; Allan Cohen and David Bradford, *Influence without Authority: The Use of Alliances, Reciprocity and Exchange to Accomplish Work*, New York: John Wiley & Sons, 1989.

CHAPTER 2

METHODS OF INFLUENCE AND CONTROL

Formal theories of organization have been taught in management courses for many years, and there is an extensive literature on the subject. The textbook principles of organization—hierarchical structure, authority, unity of command, task specialization, division of staff and line, span of control, equality of responsibility and authority, etc.—comprise a logically persuasive set of assumptions which have had a profound influence upon managerial behavior over several generations.* Despite the fact that they rest primarily on armchair speculation rather than on empirical research, the literature gives the impression that these classical principles are beyond challenge. (The manual for a supervisory training program in one large company suggests that the instructor point out by analogy and example that the principles of organization are "like the laws of physics."†

Formal textbook principles have blended into personal assumptions in many ways. In some instances the formal theory has been consistent with these assumptions; sometimes there have been sharp inconsistencies. Since it is rare for deep-rooted emotional convictions to be abandoned in favor of conflicting academic theory, at least in the field of the social sciences, some managers simply reject the formal principles (and the "long-haired" professors who propound them) and retain their own assumptions. In other instances there are varying degrees of accommodation between academic theory and

---

* Ironically, a classic text along these lines is *Concept of the Corporation*, by Alfred P. Sloan. McGregor is responding to the work of Faol and many popular textbooks at the time.

† The use of the "laws of physics" as a basis for legitimacy is a recurrent theme throughout the text—here as a critique of existing scholarship, and later as an aspirational goal for social science.

personal conviction. Out of this process of rejection and accommodation have come many innovations, some of which have been successful. It is not difficult, in fact, to find examples which contradict almost every one of the textbook principles of organization. The arguments with respect to these exceptions are naturally vehement, but regardless of their merit, it is becoming clear that the traditional principles fall considerably short of being like the laws of physics. Among many reasons, three are especially significant:

1. The conventional principles were derived primarily from the study of models (the military and the Catholic Church) which differ in important respects from modern industrial organizations. It is a plausible idea that there should be universal principles of organization, and that they could be derived from the study of such old and successful institutions. However, if there are universal principles common to all forms of organization, it is now apparent that they are not the ones derived by classical theorists from the Church and the military. As an example, unity of command (the principle that each member of an organization must only have one boss) may be essential on the battlefield, but it is not a universal principle. Whatever the organization chart may show, the typical middle-level manager in the modern industrial organization finds that his behavior is controlled not by one but by several "superiors." In some companies, project groups are formed to carry out complex tasks, and the members of these groups report both to the project supervisor and to their functional superiors. Moreover, there is one organization where subordinates always have had two bosses: the family!

In challenging the assumption that "each member of an organization must only have one boss," McGregor is anticipating the principles of matrix management. He is challenging principles that come from Max Weber and others who celebrated the merits of hierarchy as an innovative organizational form (in com-

parison to preceding systems dominated by favoritism or pure dictatorial rule). (See Max Weber, *The Theory of Social and Economic Organization*, London: Oxford University Press, 1947.)

2. Classical organization theory suffers from "ethnocentrism":* It ignores the significance of the political, social, and economic milieu in shaping organizations and influencing managerial practice. We live today in a world which only faintly resembles that of a half century ago. The standard of living, the level of education, and the political complexion of the United States today profoundly affect both the possibilities and limitations of organizational behavior. In addition, technological changes are bringing about changes in all types of organization. In the military, for example, it is becoming increasingly difficult to manage a weapons team in the field as a typical infantry unit was managed a couple of decades ago. Such a team requires a high degree of autonomy.† Instead of following explicit orders from superiors, it must be able to adjust its behavior to fit local circumstances within the context of relatively broad objectives. (It is interesting to note the attempts that are made—by "programming" for example—to retain central control over the operations of such units. Established theories of control are not abandoned easily, even in the face of clear evidence of their inappropriateness.
3. Underlying the principles of classical organization theory are a number of assumptions about human behavior which are at best only partially true.‡ In this respect organizational theory is in

* McGregor's concern with "ethnocentrism" is still timely, as is his urging us to consider the political, social, and economic context of organizations.

† This focus on "autonomy" is concurrent with the sociotechnical systems literature and anticipates the literatures on teams and groups that followed this work.

‡ Although not stated by name, the reference is likely to the principles of scientific management. (See Frederick W. Taylor, *Principles of Scientific Management*, New York: Harper & Brothers, 1911.)

> much the same state today as was economic theory at the turn of the century. Knowledge accumulated during recent decades challenges and contradicts assumptions which are still axiomatic in conventional organization theory. It will be necessary to examine some of these assumptions in detail.

Unfortunately, those classical principles of organization—derived from inappropriate models, unrelated to the political, social, economic, and technological milieu, and based on erroneous assumptions about behavior—continue to influence our thinking about the management of the human resources of industry. Management's attempts to solve the problems arising from the inadequacy of these assumptions have often involved the search for new formulas, new techniques, new procedures. These generally yield disappointing results because they are adjustments to symptoms rather than causes. The real need is for new theory, changed assumptions, more understanding of the nature of human behavior in organizational settings.

METHODS OF INFLUENCE

If there is a single assumption which pervades conventional organizational theory it is that authority is the central, indispensable means of managerial control. This is the basic principle of organization in the textbook theory of management. The very structure of the organization is a hierarchy of authoritative relationships. The terms *up* and *down* within the structure refer to a scale of authority. Most of the other principles of organization, such as unity of command, staff and line, span of control, are directly derived from this one.*

The first thing to be noted about authority is that it is but one of several forms of social influence or control. Direct physical coercion

---

* The contrast between organizations and leadership based on control versus influence is a central contribution by McGregor that is all the more relevant today in the context of strategic alliances, public-private partnerships, and other efforts requiring alignment of independent, but interdependent organizations.

is the most powerful and the most primitive of these. It was almost universal a few centuries ago, and we still resort to it sometimes, although its use is limited by social prohibitions in our culture today. Physical coercion is a legitimate means of social control over certain forms of criminal behavior; it occurs occasionally in severe labor disputes; and it is common in parental control of small children. We are devoting a substantial portion of our national budget today to prevent its most frightening use: in war.

Persuasion, in its many forms, represents another means of social control. In the sales field, where authority and physical coercion are clearly inappropriate, we place major reliance on this type of influence. Within management, consultation and discussion provide at least a partial substitution of persuasion for authority. In certain kinds of relationships, but not in others, there is the expectation that authority or even physical coercion will be resorted to if persuasion is ineffective. This situation is common in labor relations and in the international field. Within industrial organizations, managers frequently speak euphemistically of "selling" an idea or a course of action to someone when both parties are fully aware that if persuasion is not successful resort will be had to authority as the means of control. In a genuine sales relationship one cannot fall back on authority if persuasion fails. This makes quite a difference!

Finally, there is the form of influence involved in professional "help." While the nature of this influence is relatively poorly understood, it is different from ordinary methods of persuasion. Most professionals—lawyers, doctors, architects, engineers—simply rely on "the authority of knowledge." Their relationships with clients represent an extreme form of authoritarianism in which "help" is conceived in completely unilateral terms. They are often indifferent to the fact that the client can ignore their advice, or even terminate the relationship, at will.

True professional help, as typified by the exceptionally sophisticated and sensitive individual in any professional field, does not consist in playing God with the client, but in placing the professional's knowledge and skill at the client's disposal. It is a particularly important form of social influence which is not at all well understood. We will have occasion to examine its nature in some detail in Chapters 5 and 12.

All these methods of social control are relative; none is absolute. The appropriateness of a given form of control is a function of several other variables. Effective control consists in "selective adaptations" to these variables. The engineer does not dig channels to make water flow uphill; the salesman does not give commands to a customer; the superintendent does not give orders to the president; a nation at war does not offer professional help to the enemy; the parent does not give advice to his year-old child.

The success of any form of social influence or control depends ultimately upon altering the ability of others to achieve their goals or satisfy their needs. The modification may be an enhancement of this ability (for example, through the offer of a product, the provision of professional advice, or the promise of a reward) or a curtailment of it (for example, through a disciplinary action, a jail sentence, the termination of employment, or the threat of a punishment). Such modifications in the ability of the individual to achieve goals or satisfy needs may be relatively minor (as is the case with product advertising in mass media) or major (as is the case with the superior in an organizational relationship who may affect the long-term career expectations of his subordinates in important ways). However, in either case, the influence can occur only when there is some degree of dependence of the one party on the other. The dependence may be quite small or very great, it may be unilateral or mutual, but if there is no dependence there is no opportunity to control. Unless I perceive that you can somehow affect my ability to satisfy my needs, you cannot influence my behavior.

Thus the nature and degree of dependence is a critical factor in determining what methods of control will be effective.* Selective adaptation to these aspects of organizational relationships is a matter of great importance. Let us consider in a little more detail what this means.

THE LIMITATIONS OF AUTHORITY

In general, both the literature on organization and management practice accept authority as an absolute rather than a relative concept. Little recognition is given to control as a process of selective adaptation to such varying conditions as the nature and degree of dependence in organizational relationships. The consequences are of considerable significance. Some of our most troublesome problems in managing the human resources of industry in the United States today are directly traceable to the assumption that authority is an absolute and to inappropriate attempts to control behavior which flow from this assumption.

The effectiveness of authority as a means of control depends first of all upon the ability to enforce it through the use of punishment. In the two organizations which have been the models for classical organization theory, the situation with respect to enforcement is clear. In the military, authority is enforceable through the court-martial, with the death penalty as the extreme form of punishment. In the Church, excommunication represents the psychological equivalent of the death penalty.

A half century or more ago, industrial management had, in the threat of unemployment, a form of punishment which made the use of authority relatively effective. Discharge as the ultimate punishment was even further reinforced by yellow-dog contracts and employer

---

* This link between influence and dependence is highlighted as crucial in "determining what methods of control will be effective." McGregor is signaling a contingency approach, although it is not clear how many cases would qualify as featuring such complete dependence so as to justify the imposition of authority.

blacklists. The situation today is vastly different. The social legislation of the 1930s, unemployment compensation, the limitations on arbitrary discharge brought about by a generation of widespread collective bargaining, and the far greater mobility of our citizens all serve to make discharge a considerably less severe form of punishment than it once was. As a means of enforcing authority it is certainly not comparable to excommunication from the Church or to the military court-martial.

McGregor saw a steady progress toward increasing protection of the individual and collective rights of employees that would further constrain authoritarian management. In fact, the trend in the United States has been the reverse, with the erosion of collective bargaining, the elevated importance of what is termed "employment at will," and the globalization of work operations.

What this indicates is that the employment relationship involves substantially less dependence than it did a half century ago. Alternative relationships, alternative ways of satisfying needs and achieving goals are sufficiently available that a particular employment relationship can be terminated with a relatively smaller loss. Moreover, the dependence is further reduced by the various negotiated limitations on management's freedom to exercise the authority to discharge.

This phenomenon of decreased dependence in social relationships is not confined entirely to industry. Consider, for example, what has happened in the last fifty years in the United States to the position of the wife in the marital relationship, or of the older adolescent child in the family. We have tended to recognize more readily in these relationships the effect of lessened dependence upon the appropriateness of authority as a means of social control. The significance of the parallel change in the employment relationship—within management or between the worker and management—has been less well understood.

The second limitation upon the effectiveness of authority as a means of control is the availability of countermeasures. These can range, depending upon conditions, from a minimal but relatively ineffective compliance to open rebellion. The elaborate legalism of certain collective bargaining relationships provides one illustration of the use of countermeasures to render authority less effective. Likewise, restriction of output, featherbedding, and other more subtle forms of sabotage of organizational objectives are symptoms which suggest that management leans on a weak crutch if it relies too much on authority today. Moreover, these countermeasures are not limited to workers or to unionized plants. Although given different labels, restriction of output and featherbedding can often be observed within management! They are not unknown even at the vice-presidential level.

Less obvious, but equally effective in defeating managerial purposes, are such things as indifference to organizational objectives, low standards of performance, ingenious forms of protective behavior, and refusal to accept responsibility. The fact is that these phenomena are so familiar that most managers tend in daily practice to rely less and less on the exercise of personal authority except in the crisis situation when other methods fail. This becomes more evident the higher one goes in the organization. The use of commands and orders within the higher levels of management is relatively rare. This was not true fifty or even twenty-five years ago.

The outstanding fact about relationships in the modern industrial organization is that they involve a high degree of *inter*dependence. Not only are subordinates dependent upon those above them in the organization for satisfying their needs and achieving their goals, but managers at every level are dependent upon all those below them for achieving both their own and organizational goals.

An agent of the Textile Workers Union of America likes to tell the story of the occasion when a new manager appeared in the mill where he was working. The manager came into the weave room the day he arrived. He walked directly over to the agent and said, "Are you Belloc?" The agent acknowledged that he was. The manager said, "I am the new manager here. When I manage a mill, I run it. Do you understand?" The agent nodded, and then waved his hand. The workers, intently watching this encounter, shut down every loom in the room immediately. The agent turned to the manager and said, "All right, go ahead and run it."

In "The Human Side of Enterprise: Don't Turn Managers into Executioners!" in the May 1997 issue of *Apparel Industry*, management consultant Thomas Brown connected McGregor's work with that of utopian philosopher and textile manufacturer Robert Owen:

Robert Owen, a successful textile manufacturer in Scotland, published a tract in 1813 advising his fellow manufacturers to care for their people "at least" as well as their industrial equipment: "If, then, due care as to the state of your inanimate machines can produce such beneficial results, what may not be expected if you devote equal attention to your vital machines [workers], which are far more wonderfully constructed?"

This is a dramatic illustration of the fact that every manager at every level is dependent upon those below him in the organization. The dependence may be more pronounced—it is certainly more explicit—when those below are organized in a militant union. It is nevertheless a fact whether or not workers are formally organized, and within the management framework as well. The trouble with focusing explicitly on the concept of authority is that it blinds us to this dependence downwards. Some people are strongly motivated toward the managerial role because they perceive it as an escape from dependence. Their reliance on authority, their attempted escape, tends in fact to be self-defeating.

Interdependence in organizations involves more than dependence upward and downward; it also involves lateral dependence. Interdependence is characteristic of staff-line relationships. It is equally characteristic of relationships between many line departments (particularly where the output of one department is the input of another), and it is characteristic of the relationship among any group of subordinates who report to a common boss. The competition which is so common within such a group for power and position and recognition is a reflection of the interdependence inherent in the situation.

Conventional organization theory gives full recognition to dependence upward, but it fails to recognize the significance of interdependence. This is a result again of the theorist's choice of models. The Church as an organization rests on dependence which is essentially one-way. The ultimate source of all authority and all power is God, and all members of the organization are, therefore, dependent upward. In the military—under the conditions of war which are the conditions for which the military organization is built—individuals are required to sacrifice their personal goals and needs to the necessities of the national crisis, and to accept dependence upward. As we have noted above, both these organizations have a means of reinforcing this dependence.

Industry, on the other hand, is the economic organ of society, of all of us. Its ultimate purpose is to serve the common good. There is no superhuman source of authority; there is no sound basis for expecting the individual to sacrifice his personal goals or needs for the organization (except possibly under crisis conditions), and there is no successful way to enforce this expectation if it does exist. In a free enterprise society such as ours there is no final sanction that can be applied to enforce managerial authority. In fact, because the dependence is mutual, sanctions can be applied in both directions. Management can attempt to enforce its authority through disciplinary action, but the individual can resign; he can join a powerful union; he can resort to a variety of tactics which influence the ability of those above him to satisfy *their* needs and to fulfill their responsibilities to the organization. They are dependent upon him, just as he is dependent upon them.

It is fundamental, therefore, to any theory of organization that the nature of the dependency relationships be understood and allowed for. In the social, economic, and political milieu of the United States today the management of industry is becoming unable to rely on authority as the sole, or even the primary, method of accomplishing organizational objectives through people. Its dependence downward is too great to permit this unilateral means of control.

The curve in Figure 1 is a rough schematic representation of the way in which the appropriateness of authority probably varies as a function of dependence.* When the dependence in the relationship is relatively complete (as in a slave economy or between a parent and a small child), authority can be used almost exclusively without fear

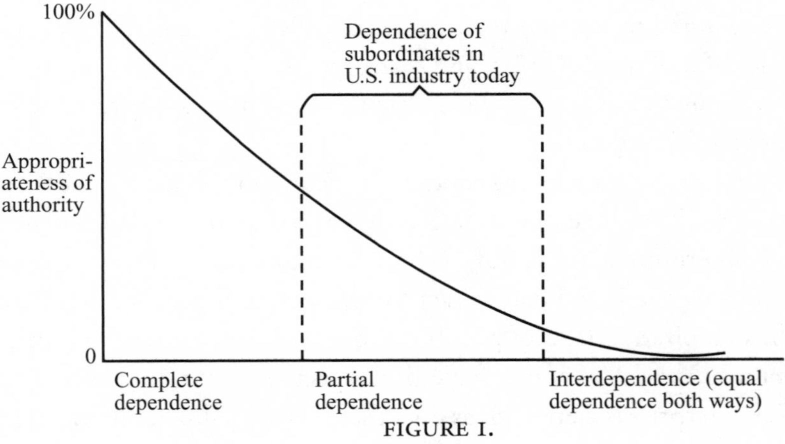

FIGURE I.

* The concepts of situational leadership developed by Hershey and Blanchard, which include "directing," "supporting," "coaching," and "delegating," build on this core distinction between authority and dependence. (See Hershey and Blanchard, *Management of Organizational Behavior: Utilizing Human Resources*, 5th ed., Englewood Cliffs, N.J.: Prentice-Hall, 1988.)

of negative consequences. At the other extreme, when dependence is approximately equal, authority is useless as a means of control (consider the relationship between friends, for example).

In United States industry today, employees are in a relationship of partial dependence. Authority, as a means of influence, is certainly not useless, but for many purposes it is less appropriate than persuasion or professional help. Exclusive reliance upon authority encourages countermeasures, minimal performance, even open rebellion. The dependence—as in the case of the adolescent* in the family—is simply not great enough to guarantee compliance.

THE PSYCHOLOGY OF DEPENDENCE

One of the reasons why these limitations on the effectiveness of authority are not so well recognized as one would expect is that dependence involves deep-seated emotional reactions. To be dependent is in some ways satisfying. It is nice to be taken care of, to be secure. In other ways it is frustrating. To be dependent is to be limited in freedom, to be subject to influences which are frequently perceived as arbitrary and unjust.

Likewise, independence is satisfying. It is nice to be able to stand on one's own feet, make one's own decisions, lead one's own life. On the other hand, independence can be threatening. One can be too far out on a limb; the risks can be frightening.

These emotional concomitants of dependence and independence stem from a series of universal human experiences. Each of us is born into a relationship of relatively complete dependence. As infants and small children we would not survive unless we were taken care of completely. The process of growing up involves a gradual shift out of this state of dependence as we become able to take more and more responsibility for ourselves.

---

* This analogy to adolescents is at once clarifying and complicated—it illustrates well the difficulties of imposing control, but it has the implication that employees are in a comparable role. See the related note on page 56.

The end product, however, is not independence. No individual in society is completely independent. *Inter*dependence is a central characteristic of the modern, complex society. In every aspect of life we depend upon each other in achieving our goals. We do not grow our own food, make our own clothes, provide our own transportation or shelter, educate ourselves. We have learned that as a society we can have more of everything we want by specializing individually. However, the price of specialization is dependence on others.

Growing up and learning to live in this complex of interdependent relationships is not without its emotional conflicts. Our contrary emotional needs and anxieties are profoundly influential. No matter how we resolve them as we grow up, we remain sensitive when we are placed in a situation which resembles, even remotely, the dependence of infancy. To be a subordinate in an organization is to be placed in a dependent relationship which has enough of the elements of the earlier one to be sensitive and, under certain conditions, explosive.

The desirable end of the growth process is an ability to strike a balance—to tolerate certain forms of dependence without being unduly frustrated, and at the same time to stand alone in some respects without undue anxiety. Some of us never learn to tolerate even a moderate amount of dependence with comfort. We remain rebellious; any hint of the exercise of personal authority over us is threatening. Others of us tend to be unhappy if we are too much on our own. We like to lean on those above and to be sure of some degree of protection and security. The variations in these patterns are, of course, infinite. Whatever they are, few of us achieve that degree of emotional maturity which makes us able to accept dependence with complete objectivity. Dependent relationships are sensitive ones.

ROLE RELATIONSHIPS

The common-sense assumption is that the managerial relationship is essentially a single, uniform one. We tend to think that the boss is a boss is a boss is a boss. This is not the case at all. The circumstances change from hour to hour and from day to day as the manager undertakes different activities, and the methods of influence which are appropriate shift accordingly.

In describing all forms of social relationships, we tend to attach labels which define their more obvious characteristics and which assign to the parties single and unchanging roles. Thus we speak of the parent, the husband, the friend, the manager. In each of these, however, the individual occupies a variety of different roles over time. The parent, for example, may at times be a playmate, at other times a teacher, at other times an arbitrator, at other times a protector. The parent's behavior and the forms of influence he utilizes shift appreciably as the conditions demand different roles.

The same thing is true of the manager. At times he may be in the role of the leader of a group of subordinates; at other times he may be a member of a group of his peers. Sometimes he is in the role of teacher; at other times he may be a decision maker, a disciplinarian, a helper, a consultant, or simply an observer. When he is helping a subordinate to analyze a problem and decide how to deal with it, the methods he uses to influence the subordinate will be quite different than when he is dealing with a disciplinary problem. The very nature of the relation shifts as the circumstances change. Moreover, the manager adopts different roles as he deals with the manager of another department, or with his immediate superior, or with a superior several levels higher in the organization.*

The managerial role is not a single, invariant one, but a complex of different roles. Ordinarily we adjust to the changing circumstances without conscious thought, but an observer will detect major changes in behavior and attitude, and in the resulting behavior of the other party to the relationship. Conventional theories of organization do

---

* Henry Mintzberg, an MIT doctoral student in the early 1970s, expanded on this notion in his classic study of what managers actually do (in comparison to the stereotypes in so many managerial textbooks). (See Henry Mintzberg, "The Manager's Job: Folklore and Fact," *Harvard Business Review*, vol.53, no. 4, 1978.)

not recognize the significance of role flexibility in the managerial relationship.

The degree of flexibility in managerial roles which would be most appropriate in influencing behavior is limited not only by the manager's own theoretical assumptions and attitudes but by the expectations of his subordinates. They, too, tend to make the common-sense assumption that a boss is a boss is a boss. The formal position which the superior occupies in the organizational hierarchy and the emphasis upon authority as *the* managerial method of influence make it difficult for subordinates to perceive and respond to a boss as a colleague or as a consultant. Only if the manager is genuinely sensitive to the differing role requirements, and is in addition explicit about the role he is adopting, can subordinates learn to respond appropriately. The latter are sometimes considerably confused when a boss who has consistently occupied a single authoritarian role in all his dealings with them suddenly becomes "participative" without making explicit his own conscious attempt to shift his role.

Despite these difficulties, it is clear that the circumstances of the superior-subordinate relationship do shift in ways which demand considerable role flexibility. If we accept the theoretical hypothesis that appropriate control is a function of the conditions, we cannot ignore its implications.

Of course, there are times when the role of boss is the only appropriate one. It is sometimes necessary to issue a direct order, to take a formal disciplinary action, to terminate a subordinate's employment. There are other instances, however, where we tend unnecessarily to think of the boss role as inevitable. A superior acting explicitly as an "arbitrator" in resolving an issue between subordinates, or in deciding upon one course of action among several proposed alternatives is in a role which can carry quite different overtones for subordinates than if the superior is inflexible in his role of boss.

The necessity for role flexibility sometimes places the manager in an impossible situation. This happens when he is forced to occupy incompatible roles in a relationship with another individual or a group. Performance appraisal programs, for example, often require the superior to occupy simultaneously the role of judge and the role of counselor to a subordinate. Members of staff departments are frequently required to be specialists offering professional service and advice, and *in addition*, policemen administering managerial controls.

Obviously, circumstances which force incompatible roles on the individual create tension and confusion in the relationship. The consequent costs for the organization may be substantial. We will have occasion to examine these problems of role incompatibility further in Chapter 6, and again in Chapter 12 when we consider staff-line relationships.

FROM PHYSICAL COERCION TO SELECTIVE ADAPTATION

For all of these reasons, it would appear that authority is an inappropriate method of control on which to place exclusive reliance in United States industry today if management's purpose is to influence behavior toward the achievement of organizational objectives. It is obvious that it cannot be dispensed with altogether. Under certain circumstances it may be essential, but for promoting collaboration it is at best a weak crutch.

Over the long sweep of history there have been two major transitions with respect to the central means of controlling human behavior in organizational settings. The first was the transition from sheer physical force to reliance on formal authority.* It took centuries. Even today we tend to slip back into reliance on force when other attempts to influence fail. The transition is clearly further along in the United States and Western Europe than it is in some parts of the world. At

---

* In the negotiations and dispute resolution literature, the distinction is made between resolution of conflict on the basis of power, rights, and interests, which parallels McGregor's focus on the transitions from physical force to authority to influence. (See William Ury et al., *Getting Disputes Resolved*, San Francisco: Jossey-Bass, 1988.)

the level of international relations, it is evident that we have only a precarious foothold on the transitional ladder from primitive force to "higher" forms of influence.

The second transition has been under way for at least a century, and it has its roots deep in the past. But it is far from complete today. In domestic politics authoritarianism is suspect; in child rearing we have made some wild swings, but exclusive reliance on authority is generally recognized today to create more problems than it solves; in religious organizations authority carries less force than it once did; husbands in our culture can no longer rely on authority to control the behavior of their wives.

A major difficulty is that we are not at all clear what we are trending *toward.* It is becoming evident after some trial-and-error learning that abdication is not an appropriate antithesis to authoritarianism, nor is there an answer in the simple compromise position halfway between the extremes. Only if we can free ourselves from the notion that we are limited to a single dimension—that of more or less authority—will we escape from our present dilemma. There are many alternatives to authority, not one. Each is appropriate for certain purposes and under certain conditions.

Authority is perfectly appropriate as a means of influencing behavior under certain circumstances. There is nothing inherently wrong or bad about giving an order or making a unilateral decision. There are many circumstances, however, when the exercise of authority fails to achieve the desired results. Under such circumstances, the solution does not lie in exerting more authority or less authority; *it lies in using other means of influence.*

If authority is the only tool in the manager's kit, he cannot hope to achieve his purposes very well, but it does not follow that he ought to throw away this tool. There are times when he will need it, when other tools will not be appropriate for his purposes.

The power to influence others is not a function of the amount of authority one can exert. It is, rather, a function of the appropriate selection of the means of influence which the particular circumstances require. Conventional organization theory teaches us that power and authority are coextensive. Consequently, relinquishing authority is seen as losing the power to control. This is a completely misleading conception.

We have today at least the basic knowledge to enable us to discriminate among several forms of influence and to recognize some of the conditions within which each is appropriate. That knowledge—limited though it is—has important implications for industral management.

REFERENCES

Argyris, Chris, *Personality and Organization.* New York: Harper & Brothers, 1957.

Bakke, E. Wight, *Bonds of Organization.* New York: Harper & Brothers, 1950. Yale Labor and Management Series.

Barnard, Chester I., *The Functions of the Executive.* Cambridge, Mass.: Harvard University Press, 1938.

Boulding, Kenneth E., *The Organizational Revolution.* New York: Harper & Brothers, 1953.

Drucker, Peter F., *The New Society.* New York: Harper & Brothers, 1950.

Drucker, Peter F., *The Practice of Management.* New York: Harper & Brothers, 1954.

Haire, Mason (ed.), *Modern Organization Theory.* New York: John Wiley & Sons, Inc., 1959.

Harbison, Frederick, and Charles A. Myers, *Management in the Industrial World.* New York: McGraw-Hill Book Company, Inc., 1959.

Jacobson, E., W. W. Charters, Jr., and S. Lieberman, "The Use of the Role Concept in the Study of Complex Organizations," *Journal of Social Issues,* vol. 7, no. 3, 1951.

Metcalf, Henry C., and L. Urwick (eds.), *Dynamic Administration: The Collected Papers of Mary Parker Follett.* New York: Harper & Brothers, 1942.

Simon, Herbert A., *Administrative Behavior*, 2d ed. New York: The Macmillan Company, 1959.

Simon, Herbert A., "Authority," *Research in Industrial Human Relations.* New York: Harper & Brothers, 1957.

SELECTED REFERENCES TO THE ANNOTATED EDITION

Brown, Tom, "The Human Side of Enterprise: Don't Turn Managers into Executioners!" *Apparel Industry*, vol. 58, May 1997.

Hershey, P., and K. H. Blanchard, *Management of Organizational Behavior: Utilizing Human Resources*, 5th ed., Englewood Cliffs, N.J.: Prentice-Hall, 1988.

Mintzberg, Henry, "The Manager's Job: Folklore and Fact," *Harvard Business Review*, vol. 53, no. 4, 1978, pp. 49–61.

Taylor, Fredrick W., *Principles of Scientific Management*, New York: Harper & Brothers, 1911.

Ury, William, *Getting Disputes Resolved*, San Francisco: Jossey-Bass, 1988.

Weber, Max, *The Theory of Social and Economic Organization*, London: Oxford University Press, 1947.

DISCUSSION QUESTIONS FOR CHAPTER 2

1. What are examples that you can cite of leadership based on authority and control? What are examples of leadership based on influence? What do you notice when you compare them?
2. McGregor identifies many forms of influence that might be used by managers, including persuasion, consultation, and professional "help." Would you expect that employees would use those same forms of influence in their dealings with management, or are there other forms of influence that would be relevant?
3. Examine Figure 1 on page 32. What data would need to be collected to make this an actual representation of the relationship between the "appropriateness of authority" and the degree of interdependence?

THEORY X: THE TRADITIONAL VIEW OF DIRECTION AND CONTROL

In Chapter 3, McGregor again reminds us, "Behind every managerial decision or action are assumptions about human nature and human behavior." Theory X, he notes, rests on three core assumptions, which are:

1. The average human being has an inherent dislike of work and will avoid it if he can....
2. Because of this human characteristic of dislike of work, most people must be coerced, controlled, directed, threatened with punishment to get them to put forth adequate effort toward the achievement of organizational objectives....
3. The average human being prefers to be directed, wishes to avoid responsibility, has relatively little ambition, wants security above all.

McGregor observes that these assumptions are "rarely expressed so bluntly" and that "a good deal of lip service is given to the ideal of the worth of the average human being." In fact, he notes, it is this set of Theory X assumptions that "materially influences managerial strategy in a wide sector of American Industry." While acknowledging that "these assumptions would not have persisted if there were not a considerable body of evidence to support them," he also notes that "there are many readily observable phenomena in industry and elsewhere which are not consistent with this view of human nature." In particular,

he points to "the growth of knowledge in the social sciences during the past quarter century [that] has made it possible to reformulate some assumptions about human nature and human behavior in the organizational setting." Alluding to Maslow's hierarchy of needs, for example, he observes that "a satisfied need is not a motivator of behavior!" McGregor also notes that attention to underlying assumptions is as important with respect to the process or method of implementation as it is to the substance: "What sometimes appear to be new strategies—decentralization, management by objectives, consultative supervision, 'democratic' leadership—are usually old wine in new bottles because the procedures developed to implement them are derived from the same inadequate assumptions about human nature."

While McGregor's observations are compelling, it was not clear then and is still not clear today what is the relative distribution of managers and workers holding Theory X assumptions. We see plenty of cases where managers—in the public, private, and not-for-profit sectors—take actions that seem rooted in a Theory X view of the world. Systematic research on this topic would be most welcome.

CHAPTER 3

THEORY X: THE TRADITIONAL VIEW OF DIRECTION AND CONTROL

Behind every managerial decision or action are assumptions about human nature and human behavior. A few of these are remarkably pervasive. They are implicit in most of the literature of organization and in much current managerial policy and practice:

1. *The average human being has an inherent dislike of work and will avoid it if he can.*

This assumption has deep roots. The punishment of Adam and Eve for eating the fruit of the Tree of Knowledge was to be banished from Eden into a world where they had to work for a living. The stress that management places on productivity, on the concept of "a fair day's work," on the evils of featherbedding and restriction of output, on rewards for performance—while it has a logic in terms of the objectives of enterprise—reflects an underlying belief that management must counteract an inherent human tendency to avoid work. The evidence for the correctness of this assumption* would seem to most managers to be incontrovertible.

2. *Because of this human characteristic of dislike of work, most people must be coerced, controlled, directed, threatened with punishment*

*Today, this assumption would not seem incontrovertible, partly as a result of the influence of McGregor. Still, we see the emphasis on control and incentives that is rooted in this assumption. Indeed, principal-agent and other incentive-oriented models of organizations dominate in the growing and increasingly influential field of organizational economics.

to get them to put forth adequate effort toward the achievement of organizational objectives.

The dislike of work is so strong that even the promise of rewards is not generally enough to overcome it. People will accept the rewards and demand continually higher ones, but these alone will not produce the necessary effort. Only the threat of punishment will do the trick.

The current wave of criticism of "human relations," the derogatory comments about "permissiveness" and "democracy" in industry, the trends in some companies toward recentralization after the postwar wave of decentralization—all these are assertions of the underlying assumption that people will only work under external coercion and control. The recession of 1957–1958 ended a decade of experimentation with the "soft" managerial approach, and this assumption (which never really was abandoned) is being openly espoused once more.

3. *The average human being prefers to be directed, wishes to avoid responsibility, has relatively little ambition, wants security above all.*

This assumption of the "mediocrity of the masses" is rarely expressed so bluntly. In fact, a good deal of lip service is given to the ideal of the worth of the average human being. Our political and social values demand such public expressions. Nevertheless, a great many managers will give private support to this assumption, and it is easy to see it reflected in policy and practice. Paternalism has become a nasty word, but it is by no means a defunct managerial philosophy.

I have suggested elsewhere the name Theory X for this set of assumptions. In later chapters of this book I will attempt to show that Theory X is not a straw man for purposes of demolition, but is in fact a theory which materially influences managerial strategy in a wide sector of American industry today. Moreover, the principles of organization which comprise the bulk of the literature of management *could only have been derived from assumptions such as those of Theory X.* Other beliefs about human nature would have led inevitably to quite different organizational principles.

An auto supply human resource manager interviewed in 1990 for *Strategic Negotiations* proudly declared that "we take a Theory X approach." This was an organization that had just emerged from a bitter, violent strike and was ostensibly trying to repair relations with the workforce. (See Richard Walton et al., *Strategic Negotiations: A Theory of Change in Labor-Management Relations*, Boston: Harvard Business School Press, 1994.)

Theory X provides an explanation of some human behavior in industry. These assumptions would not have persisted if there were not a considerable body of evidence to support them. Nevertheless, there are many readily observable phenomena in industry and elsewhere which are not consistent with this view of human nature.

Such a state of affairs is not uncommon. The history of science provides many examples of theoretical explanations which persist over long periods despite the fact that they are only partially adequate. Newton's laws of motion are a case in point. It was not until the development of the theory of relativity during the present century that important inconsistencies and inadequacies in Newtonian theory could be understood and corrected.*

The growth of knowledge in the social sciences during the past quarter century has made it possible to reformulate some assumptions about human nature and human behavior in the organizational setting which resolve certain of the inconsistencies inherent in Theory X. While this reformulation is, of course, tentative, it provides an improved basis for prediction and control of human behavior in industry.

SOME ASSUMPTIONS ABOUT MOTIVATION

At the core of any theory of the management of human resources are assumptions about human motivation. This has been a confusing

---

* The focus on prediction in the spirit of physics is an important subtext to this book.

subject because there have been so many conflicting points of view even among social scientists. In recent years, however, there has been a convergence of research findings and a growing acceptance of a few rather basic ideas about motivation. These ideas appear to have considerable power. They help to explain the inadequacies of Theory X as well as the limited sense in which it is correct. In addition, they provide the basis for an entirely different theory of management.

The following generalizations about motivation are somewhat oversimplified. If all of the qualifications which would be required by a truly adequate treatment were introduced, the gross essentials which are particularly significant for management would be obscured. These generalizations do not misrepresent the facts, but they do ignore some complexities of human behavior which are relatively unimportant for our purposes.

Man is a wanting animal—as soon as one of his needs is satisfied, another appears in its place. This process is unending. It continues from birth to death. Man continuously puts forth effort—works, if you please—to satisfy his needs.

Human needs are organized in a series of levels—a hierarchy of importance.* At the lowest level, but preeminent in importance when they are thwarted, are the physiological needs. Man lives by bread alone, when there is no bread. Unless the circumstances are unusual, his needs for love, for status, for recognition are inoperative when his stomach has been empty for a while. But when he eats regularly and adequately, hunger ceases to be an important need. The sated man has hunger only in the sense that a full bottle has emptiness. The same is true of the other physiological needs of man—for rest, exercise, shelter, protection from the elements.

A satisfied need is not a motivator of behavior! This is a fact of profound significance. It is a fact which is unrecognized in Theory X and is, therefore, ignored in the conventional approach to the man-

* Maslow's hierarchy of human needs was a core influence on McGregor. (See Abraham Maslow, "A Theory of Human Motivation," *Psychological Review*, vol. 50, pp. 370–396, 1943.)

agement of people. I shall return to it later. For the moment, an example will make the point. Consider your own need for air. Except as you are deprived of it, it has no appreciable motivating effect upon your behavior.

When the physiological needs are reasonably satisfied, needs at the next higher level begin to dominate man's behavior—to motivate him. These are the safety needs, for protection against danger, threat, deprivation. Some people mistakenly refer to these as needs for security. However, unless man is in a dependent relationship where he fears arbitrary deprivation, he does not demand security. The need is for the "fairest possible break." When he is confident of this, he is more than willing to take risks. But when he feels threatened or dependent, his greatest need is for protection, for security.

The fact needs little emphasis that since every industrial employee is in at least a partially dependent relationship, safety needs may assume considerable importance. Arbitrary management actions, behavior which arouses uncertainty with respect to continued employment or which reflects favoritism or discrimination, unpredictable administration of policy—these can be powerful motivators of the safety needs in the employment relationship at every level from worker to vice president. In addition, the safety needs of managers are often aroused by their dependence downward or laterally. This is a major reason for emphasis on management prerogatives and clear assignments of authority.

When man's physiological needs are satisfied and he is no longer fearful about his physical welfare, his social needs become important motivators of his behavior. These are such needs as those for belonging, for association, for acceptance by one's fellows, for giving and receiving friendship and love.*

---

* Although Maslow's hierarchy of needs was not validated through formal, falsifiable research, the findings were widely accepted, in part, because of the concurrent and related work taking place in the fields of psychotherapy and psychology. This was a domain of great interest to McGregor, who chose to undergo psychotherapy at this time.

Management knows today of the existence of these needs, but it is often assumed quite wrongly that they represent a threat to the organization. Many studies have demonstrated that the tightly knit, cohesive work group may, under proper conditions, be far more effective than an equal number of separate individuals in achieving organizational goals. Yet management, fearing group hostility to its own objectives, often goes to considerable lengths to control and direct human efforts in ways that are inimical to the natural "groupiness" of human beings. When man's social needs—and perhaps his safety needs, too—are thus thwarted, he behaves in ways which tend to defeat organizational objectives. He becomes resistant, antagonistic, uncooperative. But this behavior is a consequence, not a cause.

Above the social needs—in the sense that they do not usually become motivators until lower needs are reasonably satisfied—are the needs of greatest significance to management and to man himself. They are the egoistic needs, and they are of two kinds:

1. Those that relate to one's self-esteem: needs for self-respect and self-confidence, for autonomy, for achievement, for competence, for knowledge

2. Those that relate to one's reputation: needs for status, for recognition, for appreciation, for the deserved respect of one's fellows

Unlike the lower needs, these are rarely satisfied; man seeks indefinitely for more satisfaction of these needs once they have become important to him. However, they do not usually appear in any significant way until physiological, safety, and social needs are reasonably satisfied. Exceptions to this generalization are to be observed, particularly under circumstances where, in addition to severe deprivation of physiological needs, human dignity is trampled upon. Political revolutions often grow out of thwarted social and ego, as well as physiological, needs.

The typical industrial organization offers only limited opportunities for the satisfaction of egoistic needs to people at lower levels in the hierarchy. The conventional methods of organizing work, particularly in mass production industries, give little heed to these aspects of human motivation. If the practices of "scientific management" were deliberately calculated to thwart these needs—which, of course, they are not—they could hardly accomplish this purpose better than they do.

This is a clear reference to Frederick Taylor's *Scientific Management*, where statements such as the following were made:

This loafing or soldiering proceeds from two causes. First, from the natural instinct and tendency of men to take it easy, which may be called natural soldiering. Second, from more intricate second thought and reasoning caused by their relations with other men, which may be called systematic soldiering.

It should also be noted that Taylor placed the responsibility for this behavior not on the worker, but on management for failing to organize work properly and not providing the right incentives. In that sense, there is also some degree of alignment between Taylor and McGregor.

Finally—a capstone, as it were, on the hierarchy—there are the needs for self-fulfillment. These are the needs for realizing one's own potentialities, for continued self-development, for being creative in the broadest sense of that term.

The conditions of modern industrial life give only limited opportunity for these relatively dormant human needs to find expression. The deprivation most people experience with respect to other lower-level needs diverts their energies into the struggle to satisfy *those* needs, and the needs for self-fulfillment remain below the level of consciousness.

Now, briefly, a few general comments about motivation:

We recognize readily enough that a man suffering from a severe dietary deficiency is sick. The deprivation of physiological needs has behavioral consequences. The same is true, although less well recognized, of the deprivation of higher-level needs. The man whose needs for safety, association, independence, or status are thwarted is sick, just as surely as is he who has rickets. And his sickness will have behavioral consequences. We will be mistaken if we attribute his resultant passivity, or his hostility, or his refusal to accept responsibility to his inherent "human nature." These forms of behavior are *symptoms* of illness—of deprivation of his social and egoistic needs.

The man whose lower-level needs are satisfied is not motivated to satisfy *those* needs. For practical purposes they exist no longer. (Remember my point about your need for air.) Management often asks, "Why aren't people more productive? We pay good wages, provide good working conditions, have excellent fringe benefits and steady employment. Yet people do not seem to be willing to put forth more than minimum effort." It is unnecessary to look far for the reasons.

Consideration of the rewards typically provided the worker for satisfying his needs through his employment leads to the interesting conclusion that most of these rewards can be used for satisfying his needs *only when he leaves the job*. Wages, for example, cannot be spent at work. The only contribution they can make to his satisfaction on the job is in terms of status differences resulting from wage differentials. (This, incidentally, is one of the reasons why small and apparently unimportant differences in wage rates can be the subject of so much heated dispute. The issue is not the pennies involved, but the fact that the status differences which they reflect are one of the few ways in which wages can result in need satisfaction in the job situation itself.)

Most fringe benefits—overtime pay, shift differentials, vacations, health and medical benefits, annuities, and the proceeds from stock purchase plans or profit-sharing plans—yield needed satisfaction only when the individual leaves the job. Yet these, along with wages, are among the major rewards provided by management for effort. It is not surprising, therefore, that for many wage earners *work is perceived as a form of punishment* which is the price to be paid for various kinds of satisfaction away from the job. To the extent that this is their perception, we would hardly expect them to undergo more of this punishment than is necessary.*

Under today's conditions management has provided relatively well for the satisfaction of physiological and safety needs. The standard of living in our country is high; people do not suffer major deprivation of their physiological needs except during periods of severe unemployment. Even then, the social legislation developed since the thirties cushions the shock.

But the fact that management has provided for these physiological and safety needs has shifted the motivational emphasis to the social and the egoistic needs. Unless there are opportunities *at work* to satisfy these higher-level needs, people will be deprived; and their behavior will reflect this deprivation. Under such conditions, if management continues to focus its attention on physiological needs, the mere provision of rewards is bound to be ineffective, and reliance on the threat of punishment will be inevitable. Thus one of the assumptions of Theory X will appear to be validated, but only because we have mistaken effects for causes.

People *will* make insistent demands for more money under these conditions. It becomes more important than ever to buy the mate-

---

* The implications of the long time lag between various fringe benefits and the point at which they are granted is an example of McGregor's documenting points that seem self-evident, but that are associated with persistent undercutting behavior by managers.

rial goods and services which can provide limited satisfaction of the thwarted needs. Although money has only limited value in satisfying many higher-level needs, it can become the focus of interest if it is the only means available.

The "carrot and stick" theory of motivation which goes along with Theory X works reasonably well under certain circumstances. The *means* for satisfying man's physiological and (within limits) safety needs can be provided or withheld by management. Employment itself is such a means, and so are wages, working conditions, and benefits. By these means the individual can be controlled so long as he is struggling for subsistence. Man tends to live for bread alone when there is little bread.

But the "carrot and stick" theory does not work at all once man has reached an adequate subsistence level and is motivated primarily by higher needs. Management cannot provide a man with self-respect, or with the respect of his fellows, or with the satisfaction of needs for self-fulfillment. We can create conditions such that he is encouraged and enabled to seek such satisfactions for himself, or we can thwart him by failing to create those conditions.

But this creation of conditions is not "control" in the usual sense; it does not seem to be a particularly good device for directing behavior. And so management finds itself in an odd position. The high standard of living created by our modern technological know-how provides quite adequately for the satisfaction of physiological and safety needs. The only significant exception is where management practices have not created confidence in a "fair break"—and thus where safety needs are thwarted. But by making possible the satisfaction of lower-level needs, management has deprived itself of the ability to use the control devices on which the conventional assumptions of Theory X has taught it to rely: rewards, promises, incentives, or threats and other coercive devices.

The philosophy of management by direction and control—*regardless of whether it is hard or soft*—is inadequate to motivate because the human needs on which this approach relies are relatively unimportant motivators of behavior in our society today. Direction and control are of limited value in motivating people whose important needs are social and egoistic.

People deprived of opportunities to satisfy at work the needs which are now important to them behave exactly as we might predict—with indolence, passivity, unwillingness to accept responsibility, resistance to change, willingness to follow the demagogue, unreasonable demands for economic benefits. It would seem that we may be caught in a web of our own weaving.

Theory X explains the *consequences* of a particular managerial strategy; it neither explains nor describes human nature although it purports to. Because its assumptions are so unnecessarily limiting, it prevents our seeing the possibilities inherent in other managerial strategies. What sometimes appear to be new strategies—decentralization, management by objectives, consultative supervision, "democratic" leadership—are usually but old wine in new bottles because the procedures developed to implement them are derived from the same inadequate assumptions about human nature. Management is constantly becoming disillusioned with widely touted and expertly merchandized "new approaches" to the human side of enterprise. The real difficulty is that these new approaches are no more than different tactics—programs, procedures, gadgets—within an unchanged strategy based on Theory X.*

In child rearing, in it recognized that parental strategies of control must be progressively modified to adapt to the changed capabilities and characteristics of the human individual as he develops from infancy to adulthood. To some extent industrial management

---

* As McGregor notes, assumptions are embedded not just in what we do, but also in how we do it—the implementation process must be aligned with the substantive strategy.

recognizes that the human *adult* possesses capabilities for continued learning and growth. Witness the many current activities on the fields of training and management development. In its *basic* conceptions of managing human resources, however, management appears to have concluded that the average human being is permanently arrested in his development in early adolescence. Theory X is built on the least common human denominator: the factory "hand" of the past. As Chris Argyris has shown dramatically in his *Personality and Organization*, conventional managerial strategies for the organization, direction, and control of the human resources of enterprise are admirably suited to the capacities and characteristics of the child rather than the adult.

This discussion further clarifies the earlier points about adults and adolescents on page 33. Note, however, the strong response elicited from Fred Stahl, a former executive with the Boeing Corporation who also served as the industry executive director of MIT's Lean Aerospace Initiative:

McGregor's* The Human Side of Enterprise *is a utopian polemic that had the unfortunate effect of fixing in the public mind the concept of abusive, inhumane management. Who exactly is this entity called "management" who has supposedly concluded that the average human being is permanently arrested in development at early adolescence? How many managers really hold these beliefs?

In one limited area—that of research administration—there has been some recent recognition of the need for selective adaptation in managerial strategy. This, however, has been perceived as a unique problem, and its broader implications have not been recognized. As pointed out in this and the previous chapter, changes in the population at large—in educational level, attitudes and values, motivation, degree of dependence—have created both the opportunity and the need for other forms of selective adaptation. However, so long as the assumptions of Theory X continue to influence managerial strategy, we will fail to discover, let alone utilize, the potentialities of the average human being.

REFERENCES

Allen, Louis A., *Management and Organization.* New York: McGraw-Hill Book Company, Inc. 1958.

Bendix, Reinhard, *Work and Authority in Industy.* New York: John Wiley & Sons, Inc., 1956.

Brown, Alvin, *Organization of Industry.* Englewood Cliffs, N.J.: Prentice-Hall, Inc., 1947.

Fayol, Henri, *General and Industrial Administration.* New York: Pitman Publishing Corporation, 1949.

Gouldner, Alvin W., *Patterns of Industiral Bureaucracy.* Glencoe, III.: Free Press, 1954.

Koontz, Harold, and Cyril O'Donnell, *Principles of Management.* New York: McGraw-Hill Book Company, Inc., 1955.

Maslow, A. H., *Motivation and Personality*. New York: Harper & Brothers, 1954.

Urwick, Lyndall, *The Elements of Administration.* New York: Harper & Brothers, 1944.

Walker, Charles R., *Toward the Automatic Factory*. New Haven, Conn.: Yale University Press. 1957.

Whyte, William F., *Money and Motivation*. New York: Harper & Brothers, 1955.

Zaleznik, A., C. R. Christensen, and F. J. Roethlisberger, *The Motivation, Productivity, and Satisfaction of Workers: A Prediction Study.* Boston: Division of Research, The Graduate School of Business Administration, Harvard University, 1958.

SELECTED REFERENCES TO THE ANNOTATED EDITION

Maslow, A., "A Theory of Human Motivation," *Psychological Review*, vol. 50, 1943, pp. 370–396.

Maslow, A., *Motivation and Personality*, New York: Harper & Brothers, 1943.

Taylor, F. W., *The Principles of Scientific Management*, New York: Harper & Brothers, 1911, pp. 5–29.

Walton, Richard, et al., *Strategic Negotiations: A Theory of Change in Labor-Management Relations*, Boston: Harvard Business School Press, 1994.

DISCUSSION QUESTIONS FOR CHAPTER 3

1. Can you name a workplace situation in which Theory X assumptions would be justified—either on the basis of being more effective or for other reasons? If so, please elaborate. If not, please explain why not.

2. McGregor argues that participative or consultative initiatives, such as decentralization, management by objectives, consultative supervision, and "democratic" leadership, are often flawed because they are implemented using Theory X approaches—authority, incentives, monitoring, control. Are there any situations in which a Theory X approach to implementation is justified?

3. Are competitive market models inherently based on Theory X assumptions? Or, is it possible to envision a competitive market system that is also rooted in Theory Y assumptions?

INTRODUCTION TO CHAPTER 4

THEORY Y: THE INTEGRATION OF INDIVIDUAL AND ORGANIZATIONAL GOALS

McGregor observes in Chapter 4 that management has "successfully striven to give more equitable and more generous treatment to its employees ... provid[ing] a generally safe and pleasant working environment, *but it has done all these things without changing its fundamental theory of management.*" This is, of course, the Theory X approach. He further rejects "soft" management, noting that "abdication is not a workable alternative to authoritarianism" and that "we have learned that there is no direct correlation between employee satisfaction and productivity" (a conclusion based on a set of studies conducted at the time at Ohio State University). Instead, McGregor offers Theory Y, which rests on these assumptions:

1. The expenditure of physical and mental effort in work is as natural as play or rest....
2. External control and the threat of punishment are not the only means for bringing about effort toward organizational objectives. Man will exercise self-direction and self-control in the service of objectives to which he is committed.
3. Commitment to objectives is a function of the rewards associated with their achievement....
4. The average human being learns, under proper conditions, not only to accept but to seek responsibility....

5. The capacity to exercise a relatively high degree of imagination, ingenuity, and creativity in the solution of organizational problems is widely, not narrowly, distributed in the population.

6. Under the conditions of modern industrial life, the intellectual potentialities of the average human being are only partly utilized.

Based on these assumptions, McGregor observes that "the limits on human collaboration in the organizational setting are not limits of human nature but of management's ingenuity in discovering how to realize the potential represented by its human resources." Even more pointedly, McGregor states that

> *Theory X offers management an easy rationalization for ineffective organizational performance: It is due to the nature of the human resources with which we must work. Theory Y, on the other hand, places the problems squarely in the lap of management. If employees are lazy, indifferent, unwilling to take responsibility, intransigent, uncreative, uncooperative, Theory Y implies that the causes lie in management's methods of organization and control.*

Importantly, McGregor observes that the organization is likely to suffer if it ignores the "personal needs and goals" of the workforce. He calls for "integration," which "demands that both the organization's and the individual's needs be recognized."

Over the past two decades, a broad range of studies have demonstrated the validity of McGregor's observations. Early studies documented work systems designed to foster high levels of worker commitment and the integration of social and technical principles.[1] Subsequent research documented the performance

---

[1] Richard Walton, "From Control to Commitment in the Workplace," *Harvard Business Review*, March–April 1985, pp. 77–84

advantages associated with bundles of participative and integrative practices.[2] However, most of these studies have focused on the visible practices, rather than the underlying assumptions. Just as we still don't know enough about the relative distribution

[2] In chronological order, scholarship in this domain includes Joel Cutcher-Gershenfeld, "The Impact on Economic Performance of a Transformation in Workplace Relations," *Industrial and Labor Relations Review*, vol. 44, no. 2, January 1991, pp. 241–260; Jeffrey B. Arthur, "Effects of Human Resource Systems on Manufacturing Performance and Turnover," *Academy of Management Journal*, vol. 37, 1994, pp. 670–687; J. A. Wagner, "Participation's Effects on Performance and Satisfaction: A Reconsideration of the Evidence," *Academy of Management Review*, vol. 19, 1994, pp. 312–330; Mark A. Huselid, "The Impact of Human Resource Management Practices on Turnover, Productivity, and Corporate Financial Performance," *Academy of Management Journal*, vol. 38, 1995, pp. 635–670; John Paul MacDuffie, "Human Resource Bundles and Manufacturing Performance: Organizational Logic and Flexible Production Systems in the World Auto Industry," *Industrial and Labor Relations Review*, vol. 48, 1995, pp. 197–221; Brian Becker and Barry Gerhart, "The Impact of Human Resource Management on Organizational Performance: Progress and Prospects," *Academy of Management Journal*, vol. 39, no. 4, 1996; Frits K. Pil and John Paul MacDuffie, "The Adoption of High Involvement Work Practices," *Industrial Relations*, vol. 35, 1996, pp. 423–455; Casey Ichniowski, Thomas A. Kochan, David Levine, Craig Olson, and George Strauss, "What Works at Work: Overview and Assessment," *Industrial Relations*, vol. 35, no. 3, 1996, pp. 299–333; Casey K. Ichniowski, Katherine Shaw, and G. Prennushi, "The Effects of Human Resource Management Practices on Productivity: A Study of Steel Finishing Lines," *American Economic Review*, vol. 97, no. 3, 1997, pp. 291–313; Rosemary Batt, "Work Organization, Technology and Performance in Customer Service and Sales," *Industrial and Labor Relations Review*, vol. 54, no. 4, 1999, pp. 539–564; Saul Rubinstein, "The Impact of Co-Management on Quality Performance: The Case of the Saturn Corporation," *Industrial and Labor Relations Review*, vol. 53, no. 1, 2000, p. 197; Eileen Appelbaum, Thomas Bailey, Peter Berg, and Arne L. Kalleberg, *Manufacturing Advantage: Why High-Performance Work Systems Pay Off*, Ithaca, N.Y.: ILR/Cornell University Press, 2002, pp. 779–801.

of Theory X assumptions in the working population, we also don't know enough about the relative distribution of Theory Y assumptions.[3]

[3] Naresh Khatri, who builds heavily on McGregor's work in his 2002 book *The Human Dimension of Organizations* (Spiro Press), comments, "Despite tremendous amounts of research effort since his work, the management theory has not advanced much. It is so strange that there [are not lots] of empirical studies examining Theory X and Theory Y directly. I can think of a number of theories/concepts that have received a lot of empirical attention but have not really added much to developing a relevant and valid management theory and practice."

CHAPTER 4

THEORY Y: THE INTEGRATION OF INDIVIDUAL AND ORGANIZATIONAL GOALS

To some, the preceding analysis will appear unduly harsh. Have we not made major modifications in the management of the human resources of industry during the past quarter century? Have we not recognized the importance of people and made vitally significant changes in managerial strategy as a consequence? Do the developments since the twenties in personnel administration and labor relations add up to nothing?

There is no question that important progress has been made in the past two or three decades. During this period the human side of enterprise has become a major preoccupation of management. A tremendous number of policies, programs, and practices which were virtually unknown thirty years ago have become commonplace. The lot of the industrial employee—be he worker, professional, or executive—has improved to a degree which could hardly have been imagined by his counterpart of the nineteen twenties. Management has adopted generally a far more humanitarian set of values; it has successfully striven to give more equitable and more generous treatment to its employees. It has significantly reduced economic hardships, eliminated the more extreme forms of industrial warfare, provided a generally safe and pleasant working environment, *but it has done all these things without changing its fundamental theory of management.* There are exceptions here and there, and they are important; nevertheless, the assumptions of Theory X remain predominant throughout our economy.

Management was subjected to severe pressures during the Great Depression of the thirties. The wave of public antagonism, the open warfare accompanying the unionization of the mass production industries, the general reaction against authoritarianism, the legislation of the New Deal produced a wide "pendulum swing." However, the changes in policy and practice which took place during that and the next decade were primarily adjustments to the increased power of organized labor and to the pressures of public opinion.*

Some of the movement was away from "hard" and toward "soft" management, but it was short-lived, and for good reasons. It has become clear that many of the initial strategic interpretations accompanying the "human relations approach" were as naïve as those which characterized the early stages of progressive education. We have now discovered that there is no answer in the simple removal of control—that abdication is not a workable alternative to authoritarianism. We have learned that there is no direct correlation between employee satisfaction and productivity. We recognize today that "industrial democracy" cannot consist in permitting everyone to decide everything, that industrial health does not flow automatically from the elimination of dissatisfaction, disagreement, or even open conflict. Peace is not synonymous with organizational health; socially responsible management is not coextensive with permissive management.

Now that management has regained its earlier prestige and power, it has become obvious that the trend toward "soft" management was a temporary and relatively superficial reaction rather than a general modification of fundamental assumptions or basic strategy. Moreover, while the progress we have made in the past quarter century is substantial, it has reached the point of diminishing returns. The tactical possibilities within conventional managerial strategies have been pretty completely exploited, and significant new developments will be unlikely without major modifications in theory.

---

* The limits of just changing policies and practices without changing underlying assumptions is highlighted here, a theme that is further developed by Ed Schein in *Organizational Culture and Leadership*, San Francisco: Jossey-Bass, 1988.

THE ASSUMPTIONS OF THEORY Y

There have been few dramatic break-throughs in social science theory like those which have occurred in the physical sciences during the past half century. Nevertheless, the accumulation of knowledge about human behavior in many specialized fields has made possible the formulation of a number of generalizations which provide a modest beginning for new theory with respect to the management of human resources. Some of these assumptions were outlined in the discussion of motivation in Chapter 3. Some others, which will hereafter be referred to as Theory Y, are as follows:

1. *The expenditure of physical and mental effort in work is as natural as play or rest.* The average human being does not inherently dislike work. Depending upon controllable conditions, work may be a source of satisfaction (and will be voluntarily performed) or a source of punishment (and will be avoided if possible).

2. *External control and the threat of punishment are not the only means for bringing about effort toward organizational objectives. Man will exercise self-direction and self-control in the service of objectives to which he is committed.*

3. *Commitment to objectives is a function of the rewards associated with their achievement.** The most significant of such rewards, e.g., the satisfaction of ego and self-actualization needs, can be direct products of effort directed toward organizational objectives.

4. *The average human being learns, under proper conditions, not only to accept but to seek responsibility.* Avoidance of responsibility, lack of ambition, and emphasis on security are generally consequences of experience, not inherent human characteristics.

---

* Subsequent work on "high-commitment work systems" illustrates how work systems centered on these assumptions might be organized. (See Richard Walton, "From Control to Commitment in the Workplace," *Harvard Business Review*, March–April 1985.)

5. *The capacity to exercise a relatively high degree of imagination, ingenuity, and creativity in the solution of organizational problems is widely, not narrowly, distributed in the population.*

6. *Under the conditions of modern industrial life, the intellectual potentialities of the average human being are only partially utilized.*

These assumptions involve sharply different implications for managerial strategy than do those of Theory X. They are dynamic rather than static: They indicate the possibility of human growth and development; they stress the necessity for selective adaptation rather than for a single absolute form of control. They are not framed in terms of the least common denominator of the factory hand, but in terms of a resource which has substantial potentialities.

Above all, the assumptions of Theory Y point up the fact that the limits on human collaboration in the organizational setting are not limits of human nature but of management's ingenuity in discovering how to realize the potential represented by its human resources. Theory X offers management an easy rationalization for ineffective organizational performance: It is due to the nature of the human resources with which we must work. Theory Y, on the other hand, places the problems squarely in the lap of management. If employees are lazy, indifferent, unwilling to take responsibility, intransigent, uncreative, uncooperative, Theory Y implies that the causes lie in management's methods of organization and control.

In reflecting on the way a Theory Y approach places the responsibilities "squarely in the lap of management," Larry Nirenberg, managing partner of the First Merchant Group, commented:

When I was first hired into the real estate industry, I was told that, if I was good enough to be hired, then the responsibility shifted to management. My boss at the time said that the first reaction if

something went wrong would not be to blame me, but to assume that it was somehow a failure of management. The result was that I was not looking over my shoulder afraid of being fired as I learned to do my job. Unfortunately, that approach changed when the company went through a hostile takeover and my boss left. I subsequently moved on in my career as well, but I took this lesson with me. It is something I always say when hiring new people, and it is how I run my business. I believe it has been central to our success.

The assumptions of Theory Y are not finally validated. Nevertheless, they are far more consistent with existing knowledge in the social sciences than are the assumptions of Theory X. They will undoubtedly be refined, elaborated, modified as further research accumulates, but they are unlikely to be completely contradicted.

On the surface, these assumptions may not seem particularly difficult to accept. Carrying their implications into practice, however, is not easy. They challenge a number of deeply ingrained managerial habits of thought and action.

These "habits of thought and action" were later codified in the organizational psychology literature on mental models, which (as was noted earlier) was widely popularized by Peter Senge in *The Fifth Discipline*, New York, Doubleday, 1990.

THE PRINCIPLE OF INTEGRATION

The central principle of organization which derives from Theory X is that of direction and control through the exercise of authority—what has been called "the scalar principle." The central principle which derives from Theory Y is that of integration: the creation of conditions such that the members of the organization can achieve their own goals *best* by directing their efforts toward the success of the enterprise. These two principles have profoundly different implications with respect to the task of managing human resources, but the scalar principle is so firmly built into managerial attitudes that the implications of the principle of integration are not easy to perceive.

Mary Parker Follett's analysis of integration is a key forerunner of these principles. In one of five lectures that she gave in 1933 to inaugurate the London School of Economics, she stated:

There are three ways of settling differences: by domination, by compromise and by integration. Domination, obviously, is a victory of one side over the other. This is not usually successful in the long run*[,] *for the side that is defeated will simply wait for its chance to dominate. The second way, that of compromise, we understand well, for that is the way we settle most of our controversies—each side gives up a little to have peace. Both of these ways are unsatisfactory. In dominating, only one* [side] *gets what it wants; in compromise neither side gets what it wants.... Is there any other way of dealing with difference?

There is a way beginning now to be recognized at least and sometimes followed, the way of integration.... The extraordinarily interesting thing about this is that the third way means progress. In domination, you stay where you are. In compromise likewise you deal with no new values. By integration something new has emerged, the third way, something beyond the either-or.

Someone once said that fish discover water last. The "psychological environment" of industrial management—like water for fish—is so much a part of organizational life that we are unaware of it. Certain characteristics of our society, and of organizational life within it, are so completely established, so pervasive, that we cannot conceive of their being otherwise. As a result, a great many policies and practices and decisions and relationships could only be—it seems—what they are.

Among these pervasive characteristics of organizational life in the United States today is a managerial attitude (stemming from Theory X) toward membership in the industrial organization. It is assumed almost without question that organizational requirements take precedence over the needs of individual members.* Basically, the employment agreement is that in return for the rewards which are offered, the individual will accept external direction and control. The very idea of integration and self-control is foreign to our way of thinking about the employment relationship. The tendency, therefore, is either to reject it out of hand (as socialistic, or anarchistic, or inconsistent with human nature) or to twist it unconsciously until it fits existing conceptions.

The concept of integration and self-control carries the implication that the organization will be more effective in achieving its economic objectives if adjustments are made, in significant ways, to the needs and goals of its members.

A district manager in a large, geographically decentralized company is notified that he is being promoted to a policy level position at headquarters. It is a big promotion with a large salary increase. His role in the organization will be a much more powerful one, and he will be associated with the major executives of the firm.

The headquarters group who selected him for this position have carefully considered a number of possible candidates. This man stands

---

* Today's growing attention to work-life issues further expands the scope of what might be meant by the "needs of individual members" of an organization. See Mona Harrington, *Care and Equality: Inventing a New Family Politics*, New York: Knopf, 1999; Joan Williams, *Unbending Gender: Why Family and Work Conflict and What to Do about It*, New York: Oxford University Press, 2000; and Rhona Rapoport, et al. *Beyond Work-Family Balance: Advancing Gender Equity and Workplace Performance*, San Francisco: Jossey-Bass, 2002.

out among them in a way which makes him the natural choice. His performance has been under observation for some time, and there is little question that he possesses the necessary qualifications, not only for this opening but for an even higher position. There is genuine satisfaction that such an outstanding candidate is available.

The man is appalled. He doesn't want the job. His goal, as he expresses it, is to be the "best damned district manager in the company." He enjoys his direct associations with operating people in the field, and he doesn't want a policy level job. He and his wife enjoy the kind of life they have created in a small city, and they dislike actively both the living conditions and the social obligations of the headquarters city.

He expresses his feelings as strongly as he can, but his objections are brushed aside. The organization's needs are such that his refusal to accept the promotion would be unthinkable. His superiors say to themselves that of course when he has settled in to the new job, he will recognize that it was the right thing. And so he makes the move.

Two years later he is in an even higher position in the company's headquarters organization, and there is talk that he will probably be the executive vice-president before long. Privately he expresses considerable unhappiness and dissatisfaction. He (and his wife) would "give anything" to be back in the situation he left two years ago.

Within the context of the pervasive assumptions of Theory X, promotions and transfers in large numbers are made by unilateral decision. The requirements of the organization are given priority automatically and almost without question. If the individual's personal goals are considered at all, it is assumed that the rewards of salary and position will satisfy him. Should an individual actually refuse such a move without a compelling reason, such as health or a severe family crisis, he would be considered to have jeopardized his future because of this "selfish" attitude. It is rare indeed for management to give the individual the opportunity to be a genuine and active partner in such a decision, even though it may affect his most important personal goals. Yet the implications following from Theory Y are that the organization is likely to suffer if it ignores these personal needs and goals. In making unilateral decisions with respect to promotion, management is failing to utilize its human resources in the most effective way.

The principle of integration demands that both the organization's and the individual's needs be recognized.* Of course, when there is a sincere joint effort to find it, an integrative solution which meets the needs of the individual *and* the organization is a frequent outcome. But not always—and this is the point at which Theory Y begins to appear unrealistic. It collides head on with pervasive attitudes associated with management by direction and control.

The assumptions of Theory Y imply that unless integration is achieved *the organization will suffer*. The objectives of the organization are *not* achieved best by the unilateral administration of promotions, because this form of management by direction and control will not create the commitment which would make available the full resources of those affected. The lesser motivation, the lesser resulting degree of self-direction and self-control are costs which, when added up for many instances over time, will more than offset the gains obtained by unilateral decisions "for the good of the organization."

In "A Leader Who Listens" by Hannah Beech in the June 27, 2005, issue of *Time*, Sun Chao, mayor of the Chinese city of Xuhui and a constitutional law expert who has instituted town-hall meetings on a wide range of issues in this city of over 1 million people, comments: "We shouldn't trust ourselves, even if we have the power. We should listen to others' opinions."

---

* Note that still more research is needed to fully explore the assumption that both the individual and the organization are better off when the needs of both are integrated.

One other example will perhaps clarify further the sharply different implications of Theory X and Theory Y.

It could be argued that management is already giving a great deal of attention to the principle of integration through its efforts in the field of economic education. Many millions of dollars and much ingenuity have been expended in attempts to persuade employees that their welfare is intimately connected with the success of the free enterprise system and of their own companies. The idea that they can achieve their own goals best by directing their effort toward the objectives of the organization has been explored and developed and communicated in every possible way. Is this not evidence that management is already committed to the principle of integration?

The answer is a definite no. These managerial efforts, with rare exceptions, reflect clearly the influence of the assumptions of Theory X. The central message is an exhortation to the industrial employee to work hard and follow orders in order to protect his job and his standard of living. Much has been achieved, it says, by our established way of running industry, and much more could be achieved if employees would adapt themselves *to management's definition* of what is required. Behind these exhortations lies the expectation that of course the requirements of the organization and its economic success must have priority over the needs of the individual.*

Naturally, integration means working together for the success of the enterprise so we all may share in the resulting rewards. But management's implicit assumption is that working together means adjusting to the requirements of the organization *as management perceives them*. In terms of existing views, it seems inconceivable that individuals, seeking their own goals, would further the ends of the enterprise. On the contrary, this would lead to anarchy, chaos, irreconcilable conflicts of self-interest, lack of responsibility, inability to make decisions, and failure to carry out those that were made.

---

* This is a nice illustration of bringing to the surface the underlying assumptions driving managerial actions.

All these consequences, and other worse ones, *would* be inevitable unless conditions could be created such that the members of the organization perceived that they could achieve their own goals *best* by directing their efforts toward the success of the enterprise. If the assumptions of Theory Y are valid, the practical question is whether, and to what extent, such conditions can be created. To that question the balance of this volume is addressed.

THE APPLICATION OF THEORY Y

In the physical sciences there are many theoretical phenomena which cannot be achieved in practice. Absolute zero and a perfect vacuum are examples. Others, such as nuclear power, jet aircraft, and human space flight, are recognized theoretically to be possible long before they become feasible. This fact does not make theory less useful. If it were not for our theoretical convictions, we would not even be attempting to develop the means for human flight into space today. In fact, were it not for the development of physical science theory during the past century and a half, we would still be depending upon the horse and buggy and the sailing vessel for transportation. Virtually all significant technological developments wait on the formulation of relevant theory.

Similarly, in the management of the human resources of industry, the assumptions and theories about human nature at any given time limit innovation. Possibilities are not recognized, innovating efforts are not undertaken, until theoretical conceptions lay a groundwork for them. Assumptions like those of Theory X permit us to conceive of certain possible ways of organizing and directing human effort, *but not others*. Assumptions like those of Theory Y open up a range of possibilities for new managerial policies and practices.* As in the case of the development of new physical science theory, some

* In the field of negotiations, the principle of focusing on underlying interests and options, rather than fixed positions, is a parallel illustration of the way in which alternative approaches can open up or limit possibilities.

of these possibilities are not immediately feasible, and others may forever remain unattainable. They may be too costly, or it may be that we simply cannot discover how to create the necessary "hardware."

There is substantial evidence for the statement that the potentialities of the average human being are far above those which we typically realize in industry today. If our assumptions are like those of Theory X, we will not even recognize the existence of these potentialities and there will be no reason to devote time, effort, or money to discovering how to realize them. If, however, we accept assumptions like those of Theory Y, we will be challenged to innovate, to discover new ways of organizing and directing human effort, even though we recognize that the perfect organization, like the perfect vacuum, is practically out of reach.

We need not be overwhelmed by the dimensions of the managerial task implied by Theory Y. To be sure, a large mass production operation in which the workers have been organized by a militant and hostile union faces management with problems which appear at present to be insurmountable with respect to the application of the principle of integration. It may be decades before sufficient knowledge will have accumulated to make such an application feasible. Applications of Theory Y will have to be tested initially in more limited ways and under more favorable circumstances. However, a number of applications of Theory Y *in managing managers and professional people* are possible today. Within the managerial hierarchy, the assumptions can be tested and refined, techniques can be invented and skill acquired in their use. As knowledge accumulates, some of the problems of application at the worker level in large organizations may appear less baffling than they do at present.

Ironically, McGregor found applications of Theory Y at the worker level to be the most baffling. Yet, there has, if anything, been more progress around mechanisms to value the ideas and

commitment of the front-line workforce, in the forms of employee involvement, quality circles, team-based work systems, and other such mechanisms. Many of these initiatives have been correctly criticized for failing to provide similar avenues for front-line and middle-level managers—the groups that McGregor thought were less of a challenge.

Perfect integration of organizational requirements and individual goals and needs is, of course, not a realistic objective. In adopting this principle, we seek that degree of integration in which the individual can achieve his goals *best* by directing his efforts toward the success of the organization.* "Best" means that this alternative will be more attractive than the many others available to him: indifference, irresponsibility, minimal compliance, hostility, sabotage. It means that he will continuously be encouraged to develop and utilize voluntarily his capacities, his knowledge, his skill, his ingenuity in ways which contribute to the success of the enterprise.[1]

---

* This is a key point—McGregor points out that integration will be preferred not because of its inherent merits (however worthy), but because it is likely to be preferred to the alternatives that he lists here.

[1] A recent, highly significant study of the sources of job satisfaction and dissatisfaction among managerial and professional people suggests that these opportunities for "self-actualization" are the essential requirements of both job satisfaction and high performance. The researchers find that "the wants of employees divide into two groups. One group revolves around the need to develop in one's occupation as a source of personal growth. The second group operates as an essential base to the first and is associated with fair treatment in compensation, supervision, working conditions, and administrative practices. *The fulfillment of the needs of the second group does not motivate the individual to high levels of job satisfaction and … to extra performance on the job.* All we can expect from satisfying [this second group of needs] is the prevention of dissatisfaction and poor job performance." Frederick Herzberg, Bernard Mausner, and Barbara Bloch Snyderman, *The Motivation to Work*. New York: John Wiley & Sons, Inc., 1959, pp. 114–115. (Italics mine.)

Acceptance of Theory Y does not imply abdication, or "soft" management, or "permissiveness." As was indicated above, such notions stem from the acceptance of authority as the *single* means of managerial control, and from attempts to minimize its negative consequences. Theory Y assumes that people will exercise self-direction and self-control in the achievement of organizational objectives *to the degree that they are committed to those objectives.* If that commitment is small, only a slight degree of self-direction and self-control will be likely, and a substantial amount of external influence will be necessary. If it is large, many conventional external controls will be relatively superfluous, and to some extent self-defeating. Managerial policies and practices materially affect this degree of commitment.

Authority is an inappropriate means for obtaining commitment to objectives. Other forms of influence—help in achieving integration, for example—are required for this purpose. Theory Y points to the possibility of lessening the emphasis on external forms of control to the degree that commitment to organizational objectives can be achieved. Its underlying assumptions emphasize the capacity of human beings for self-control, and the consequent possibility of greater managerial reliance on other means of influence. Nevertheless, it is clear that authority *is* an appropriate means for control under certain circumstances—particularly where genuine commitment to objectives cannot be achieved. The assumptions of Theory Y do not deny the appropriateness of authority, but they do deny that it is appropriate for all purposes and under all circumstances.

In reflecting on the interdependence between people and technology, Larry Prusak, executive director of IBM's Institute for Knowledge Management and coauthor of *Working Knowledge: How Organizations Manage What They Know*, made the following observation:

It has been argued "technology's most valuable role in knowledge management is extending the reach and enhancing the speed of knowledge transfer." Information technology is indeed very useful in capturing, storing, and distributing structured and codified knowledge, therefore enabling other individuals in the organization to have access to it. However, IT plays a much more limited role in knowledge creation, which is very much a social process involving the exchange of hard-to-codify knowledge and personal experiences. Also, IT, by itself, cannot create a knowledge-based environment that promotes knowledge use and sharing. For any technology to be optimized, it must be augmented by strategy, process, culture, and behavior that support knowledge sharing and knowledge-based work.

Many statements have been made to the effect that we have acquired today the know-how to cope with virtually any technological problems which may arise, and that the major industrial advances of the next half century will occur on the human side of enterprise. Such advances, however, are improbable so long as management continues to organize and direct and control its human resources on the basis of assumptions—tacit or explicit—like those of Theory X. Genuine innovation, in contrast to a refurbishing and patching of present managerial strategies, requires first the acceptance of less limiting assumptions about the nature of the human resources we seek to control, and second the readiness to adapt selectively to the implications contained in those new assumptions. Theory Y is an invitation to innovation.

REFERENCES

Brown, J. A. C., *The Social Psychology of Industry*. Baltimore: Penguin Books, Inc., 1954.

Cordiner, Ralph J., *New Frontiers for Professional Managers.* New York: McGraw-Hill Book Company, Inc., 1956.

Dubin, Robert, *The World of Work: Industrial Society and Human Relations.* Englewood Cliffs, N.J.: Prentice-Hall, Inc., 1958.

Friedmann, Georges, *Industrial Society: The Emergence of the Human Problems of Automation.* Glencoe, Ill.: Free Press, 1955.

Herzberg, Frederick, Bernard Mausner, and Barbara Bloch Snyderman, *The Motivation to Work.* New York: John Wiley & Sons, Inc., 1959.

Krech, David, and Richard S. Crutchfield, *Theory and Problems of Social Psychology.* New York: McGraw-Hill Book Company, Inc., 1948.

Leavitt, Harold J., *Managerial Psychology.* Chicago: University of Chicago Press, 1958.

McMurry, Robert N., "The Case for Benevolent Autocracy," *Harvard Business Review*, vol. 36, no. 1 (January–February), 1958.

Rice, A. K., *Productivity and Social Organizations: The Ahmedabad Experiment.* London: Tavistock Publications, Ltd., 1958.

Stagner, Ross, *The Psychology of Industrial Conflict.* New York: John Wiley & Sons, Inc., 1956.

SELECTED REFERENCES TO THE ANNOTATED EDITION

Fisher, Roger, and Ury, William, *Getting to Yes: Negotiating Agreement without Giving In*, New York: Houghton Mifflin, 1981.

Graham, Pauline (ed.), *Mary Parker Follett, Prophet of Management: A Celebration of Writings from the 1920s*, Boston: Harvard Business School Press, 1995.

Senge, Peter, *The Fifth Discipline: The Art and Practice of the Learning Organization*, New York: Doubleday, 1990.

DISCUSSION QUESTIONS FOR CHAPTER 4

1. What are examples of managerial practices that reflect Theory Y assumptions? Review all six of McGregor's core assumptions and indicate which assumptions are most relevant to a given management practice.

2. In the integration of individual and organizational objectives, must the result always be evenly balanced? If not, how far can the balance tilt toward individual or organizational objectives without things becoming unstable?

3. Must developing nations first organize work on the basis of Theory X assumptions and then gradually evolve toward Theory Y assumptions? Or, is it possible to build new work systems in developing economies around Theory Y assumptions from the outset?

PART TWO

THEORY Y IN PRACTICE

MANAGEMENT BY INTEGRATION AND SELF-CONTROL

Extending the theme of integration in Chapter 5, McGregor's focus is "to create a situation in which a subordinate can achieve his own goals *best* by directing his efforts toward the objectives of the enterprise." Toward these ends, McGregor urges a highly interactive dialogue between superiors and subordinates that is oriented around

1. The clarification of the broad requirements of the job
2. The establishment of specific "targets" for a limited time period
3. The management process during the target period
4. Appraisal of the results

The key to this process is that each step does not involve an imposed answer from the superior, but an interactive dialogue such that the subordinate assumes responsibility for each step. As McGregor notes with respect to a case example of this process, "The critically significant factor in these discussions was not their content, but the redefinition of roles which took place." In this context, McGregor points out that "the acceptance of responsibility (for self-direction and self-control) is correlated with commitment to objectives. Genuine commitment is seldom achieved when objectives are externally imposed." He also rejects simple forms or the "selling" of a management program oriented around these four steps. That, he notes, "is the surest way to *prevent* the development of management by integration and self-control." McGregor adds, "The manager who finds the underlying assumptions of Theory Y congenial will invent his own tactics provided he has a conception of the strategy involved. The manager whose underlying assumptions are those of Theory X cannot manage by integration and self-control no matter what techniques or forms are provided him."

The strategic importance of coaching as a core component of management and leadership is now a staple of the business press and an important area of organizational research.[1] Although McGregor's focus in this chapter is primarily on the managerial workforce, a key characteristic of high-performance work systems involves a similar process of dialogue, clarification, and coaching of front-line teams and work groups.

---

[1] See, for example, Arthur X. Deegan, *Coaching: A Management Skill for Improving Individual Performance*, Reading, Mass.: Addison-Wesley, 1979.

CHAPTER 5

MANAGEMENT BY INTEGRATION AND SELF-CONTROL

Let us now consider in some detail a specific illustration of the operation of a managerial strategy based on Theory Y. The concept of "management by objectives" has received considerable attention in recent years, in part due to the writings of Peter Drucker. However, management by objectives has often been interpreted in a way which leads to no more than a new set of tactics within a strategy of management by direction and control.

The strategy to be illustrated in the following pages is an application of Theory Y. Its purpose is to encourage integration, to create a situation in which a subordinate can achieve his own goals *best* by directing his efforts toward the objectives of the enterprise. It is a deliberate attempt to link improvement in managerial competence with the satisfaction of higher-level ego and self-actualization needs. It is thus a special and not at all a typical case of the conventional conception of management by objectives.

This strategy includes four steps or phases:*

1. The clarification of the broad requirements of the job
2. The establishment of specific "targets" for a limited time period
3. The management process during the target period
4. Appraisal of the results

---

* The key aspect of this model is that each step is voluntary—positional authority is not imposed.

In this chapter, McGregor offers a detailed case example of integration and self-control. Here is a related vignette from Dennis Dabney, director for human relations, DTE Energy, who describes a personal experience in a prior company where he had worked:

Our new plant manager at the Detroit Plant was very different. He walked the plant floor every day looking for employees doing things right and then complimented them on what they were doing. He made a deal with the employees each quarter of the year. He would set goals and measures around performance and then agree to reward employees with a celebration if they achieved the goals for the quarter. After the first quarter we stopped work 30 minutes early and there was a carnival-like celebration—hot dogs, candy, and games right on the shop floor. Our employees were laughing, enjoying, and having big fun. But more importantly, production output, efficiency, and quality started to rise. At each quarterly celebration the management team planned more fun and activities—involving the workforce and their families—with ever greater increases in performance each time. The plant manager stated that the increased performance only cost the company genuine attention and concern for the employees. But the news of managers in dunk tanks and fun in the plant traveled to our corporate office. Word came back that they would not have a carnival in our shops. The new plant manager was removed from the position, and shortly thereafter our performance declined to the precelebration levels.

Harry Evans is Vice President, Staff Services, for a manufacturing company with twenty plants throughout the Middle West and the South. The company is aggressively managed and financially successful; it is growing fairly rapidly through acquisition of smaller companies and the development of new markets for its products.

Evans was brought into the company three years ago by the President, who felt that the staff functions of the organization needed strengthening. One of the President's concerns was the personnel department, which had been something of a stepchild since it was established in the early forties. He felt that the management needed a lot of help and guidance in order to fulfill its responsibilities in this field.

Tom Harrison has been Director of Personnel Administration for a little less than a year. Evans selected him from among a number of candidates. Although he is not as well trained professionally as some of his colleagues, he appeared to have good promise as an administrator. He is in his young forties, intelligent, ambitious, personable, a hard worker with ten years of practical experience in personnel administration.

After Harrison had been on the job a few months, Evans had formed the following impressions about him:

1. He is overly anxious to make a good impression on top management, and this interferes with his performance. He watches too carefully to see which way the wind is blowing and trims his sails accordingly. He accepts even the most trivial assignments from any of the top management group, which makes a good impression but does little to strengthen the personnel function. He has done nothing to change the rather naïve top management expectation that personnel administration can be delegated to a staff department ("You take care of the personnel problems and we'll run the business.").

2. Harrison is a poor manager, somewhat to Evans's surprise, since he appeared to function well with more limited supervisory responsibilities. He uses his subordinates as errand boys rather than as resources, and he is much too ready to impose upon them his own practical and common-sense views of what should be done, brushing aside their specialized professional knowledge. He is anxious to reorganize the department, giving key responsibilities to men like himself who have practical experience but limited professional training.

These things added up, in Evans's eyes, to an inadequate conception of the nature of the personnel job and the proper role of the department within the company. He recognized the value of management's acceptance of Harrison's practical orientation, but he felt that the real needs of the company would not be met unless management acquired a quite different point of view with respect to the function. He was not at all inclined to replace Harrison, since he believed he had the capacity to perform effectively, but he recognized that Harrison was not going to grow into the job without help. His strategy involved the four steps listed below.

STEP 1. DETERMINING THE MAJOR REQUIREMENTS OF THE JOB. Evans suggested to Harrison that he would like him to give some intensive thought to the nature of his job in the light of his experience so far. He asked him to list what he felt to be his major responsibilities, using the formal position description in his possession if he wished, but not limiting himself to it. He said, "I'd like to discuss with you at some length *your* view of your job after being on it for the past eight months."

The list of requirements which Harrison subsequently brought in for discussion with Evans was as follows:

1. Organization of the Department
2. Services to top management
   a. Awareness of company problems and provision of programs and policies for solving them
3. Productivity of the Department
   a. Efficient administration of personnel programs and services
   b. Definite assignments of projects to staff with completion dates and follow-up
   c. Periodic appraisals of the performance of department members, with appropriate action
4. Field relations
   a. Providing the field units with advice, adequate programs, information
   b. Periodic visits to assure the adequacy of field personnel units

Harrison and Evans had several lengthy discussions of this list of responsibilities. Evans began by saying, "Tom, I asked you to bring to this meeting a written statement of the major requirements of your job as you see them. Perhaps you expected me to define your job for you, to tell you what I want you to do. If I were to do so, it would not be your job. Of course, I don't expect that I will necessarily see eye to eye with you on everything you have written down. I do take it for granted that we have a common purpose: We both want yours to be the best damned personnel department anywhere.

"The difficulty we are likely to have in discussing your ideas is that if I disagree with you, you'll feel you have to accept what I say because I'm your boss. I want to help you end up with a list that we are both completely satisfied with, but I can't help if you simply defer to my ideas or if I don't express them for fear of dominating you. So try to think of me as a colleague whose experience and knowledge are at your disposal—not as your boss. I'm certain we can resolve any differences that may come up."

In the course of the discussion Evans did bring up his concerns, but he put major emphasis on encouraging Harrison to examine his own ideas critically. Evans talked quite frankly about the realities of the company situation as he saw them, and he discussed his conception of the proper role for a personnel department. He tried to persuade Harrison that his conception of the personnel function was too limited, and that his own subordinates, because of their training and experience, could help him arrive at a more adequate conception. Harrison held a couple of meetings with his own department staff to discuss this whole question, and after each of them he had further conversations with Evans.

The critically significant factor in these discussions was not their content, but the redefinition of roles which took place. Evans succeeded, by his manner more than by his specific words, in conveying to Harrison the essential point that he did not want to occupy the conventional role of boss, but rather, to the fullest extent possible, the role of a consultant who was putting all of his knowledge and experience at Harrison's disposal in the conviction that they had a genuine common interest in Harrison's doing an outstanding job.

As he began to sense this, and to believe it, Harrison's whole perception of his own role changed. Instead of seeking to find out, as would be natural under conventional circumstances, how Evans wanted him to define his job, what Evans wanted him to do, what Evans would approve or disapprove, Harrison began to think for himself. Moreover, with this greater sense of freedom about his own role (and with Evans's open encouragement) he began to perceive his own subordinates not as "hands," but as resources, and to use them thus.*

The result, unrealistic as it may seem at first glance, was a dramatic change in Harrison's perception of himself and of his job. The true nature of the change that took place during these discussions with Evans and with his subordinates was revealed in his final statement of his responsibilities as he now perceived them:

1. Organization of the Department
2. Continuous assessment of both short- and long-run company needs through:
   a. Exploration in the field
   b. General awareness of management's problems
   c. Exploration of the views of members of the Department
   d. Knowledge of external trends

3. Professional help to all levels of management
   a. Problem solving
   b. Strategy planning

---

* By Evans treating Harrison in ways in which Harrison might then treat others, this interaction involves both modeling of behavior and a particular form of reciprocity. It is an exchange in that Harrison might take the same approach and pass it along in his treatment of others. There is, of course, a vast literature on reciprocity. A nice early codification of the sociological literature can be found in Alvin W. Gouldner, "The Norm of Reciprocity: A Preliminary Statement," *American Sociological Review*, vol. 25, 1960, pp. 161–178. This is also a major focus of modern anthropology.

   c. Research studies
   d. Effective personnel programs and policies
   e. Efficient administration of services

4. Development of staff members
5. Personal development

In new research published in their paper "Managing the Employment Relationship: The Role of Managers' Attachment Beliefs in How Workers are Managed" (MIT, 2005), Diane Burton and Matthew Bidwell build on McGregor's work to document the ways in which managers' beliefs come to shape employees' behavior. They write:

In his seminal work on Theory X and Theory Y, McGregor (1960) argued that differences in managers' theories about workers' behavior give rise to very different management systems.... A long line of literature in both high performance work systems (e.g., Cutcher-Gershenfeld, 1991; MacDuffie, 1995; Huselid, 1995; Ichniowski, Prennushi & Shaw, 1997; Becker and Huselid, 1998) and psychological empowerment (e.g., Koberg et al, 1999; Liden et al, 2000; Seibert, 2004) has explored McGregor's theory that participatory management could benefit both firms and workers. However, very little work has addressed McGregor's insight that managers' implicit theories of their subordinates' behavior are a key determinant of the nature of the employment relationship.

Researching managers' beliefs about subordinates' behavior has the potential to broaden our understanding of the employment relationship in two important ways. First, it can help us to move beyond formal practices in understanding what it is that managers do. Second, it has the potential to explain variation in management practices within firms. We test the impact of managers' beliefs on how workers are managed through a matched survey of engi-

neers and managers in a high-tech firm. Drawing on extensive qualitative research and prior literature, we created a set of scales to measure managers' beliefs, and tested how these beliefs affected the practices that managers used in managing workers and the subsequent outcomes for workers.

We find that managers' attachment beliefs directly and indirectly affect subordinate job satisfaction. The findings therefore support the idea that managers' beliefs may be an important factor in shaping employment relationships for workers, providing an alternative view to the current focus on formal human resource management practices.

This first step in Evans's managerial strategy with Harrison is thus consistent with his commitment to Theory Y. He believes that Harrison must take the major responsibility for his own development, but he believes he can help. He conceives of integration as an active process which inevitably involves differences of opinion and argument. He recognizes the likelihood that Harrison may accede too readily to his views without real conviction, and he does not want this to happen. Consequently he attempts to establish a relationship in which Harrison can perceive him as a genuine source of help rather than as a boss in the conventional sense. He knows that the establishment of this relationship will take time, but it is the long-term results which he considers important. Since he does not expect that Harrison will grow into his job overnight, he is prepared to accept a definition of Harrison's job which is considerably short of perfection. He is confident that it will be improved six months hence when they discuss it again.

If Harrison is going to learn and grow in competence, and if he is going to find opportunities to satisfy his higher-level needs in the process, it is essential that he find a genuine challenge in his job. This is unlikely if the job is defined for him by a formal position description or by a superior who simply tells him what he wants done. Thus, the principle of integration is important right at the start. It is not necessary in applying it to ignore the work of the organization planning staff. The necessity for a logical division of responsibilities within any organization is obvious. However, a position description is likely to become a strait jacket unless it is recognized to be a broad set of guidelines within which the individual literally makes his own job. The conception of an organization plan as a series of predetermined "slots" into which individuals are selectively placed denies the whole idea of integration.

The process involved at this step is similar, although more limited in scope, to the one so aptly described by Drucker as discovering "what business we are in." In the case of top management looking at the organization as a whole, this frequently is a highly instructive experience. The same thing can be true even in a limited setting such as this, especially if the superior can, by doing something like Evans is doing, encourage the subordinate to think creatively about his job.

STEP 2. SETTING TARGETS. When Evans and Harrison finished their discussion of the major requirements of Harrison's job, Evans suggested that Harrison think about some specific objectives or targets which he might set for himself and his department during the following six months. Evans suggested that he think both about improving the over-all performance of his unit and about his own personal goals. He asked him further to consider in broad terms what steps he proposed to take to achieve these targets. Evans said, "I don't want to tell you how to do your job, but I would like you to do some careful thinking about how you are going to proceed. Perhaps I can be helpful when we discuss your ideas." Finally, Evans asked Harrison to consider what information he would require, and how he might obtain it, in order to know at the end of the period how well he had succeeded in reaching his targets. He suggested that they get together to talk further when Harrison had completed his thinking and planning along these lines.

This is the planning phase, but again the process is one in which the subordinate is encouraged to take responsibility for his own performance. The conventional process is one in which objectives are conceived by higher levels and imposed on lower levels of the organization. The rationale is that only the higher levels have available the broader knowledge necessary for planning. To some extent this is true, but there is an important difference between the kind of planning in which a central group determines in detail what each division or department will do, and that in which the central group communicates what are believed to be the desirable over-all objectives and *asks* each unit to determine what it can contribute.

Even when general objectives are predetermined, they can usually be limited to certain aspects of performance such as production goals, costs, and profit margin. There are other aspects which are subject to local determination, as is, of course, the planning with respect to personal objectives.

The important theoretical consideration, derived from Theory Y, is that the acceptance of responsibility (for self-direction and self-control) is correlated with commitment to objectives. Genuine commitment is seldom achieved when objectives are externally imposed. Passive acceptance is the most that can be expected; indifference or resistance are the more likely consequences. Some degree of *mutual* involvement in the determination of objectives is a necessary aspect of managerial planning based on Theory Y. This is embodied in Evans's suggestions to Harrison.

In the discussion of targets, the superior again attempts a helping role rather than an authoritative one. His primary interest is in helping the subordinate plan his own job in such a fashion that both personal and organizational goals will be achieved. While the superior has a veto power by virtue of his position, he will exercise it only if it becomes absolutely necessary.

To be sure, subordinates will sometimes set unrealistic goals, particularly the first time they approach a task like this. Experience has indicated that the usual problem is that the goals are set too high, not too low. While the superior can, through judicious advice, help the subordinate adjust unrealistic goals, there may often be greater long-run advantages in permitting the subordinate to learn by experience than in simply telling him where his planning is unrealistic or inadequate.

The list of targets which Harrison brought for discussion with Evans was this:

1. Determination of major company needs, long and short range, by:
   a. Field visits and discussions with local management
   b. Intensive discussions with top management
   c. Exploration of the views of the personnel department staff

   A plan, with assignments of responsibility, and a time schedule will be worked out for this. I expect we can complete the study within six months, but a report and subsequent plans will probably not be completed by September.

2. Joint determination with department staff of current projects
   This will involve planning such as you and I are doing.
3. Development of departmental staff members
   Items 1 and 2 can be a vehicle for this. I need help in learning how to work better with my subordinates, and particularly on how to eliminate the friction between the old-timers and the college-trained youngsters.

4. Self-development
   a. I'd like to do some reading to improve my own thinking about personnel administration—or maybe take a university course. I'd like your advice.
   b. I guess I haven't gained as much skill as a manager as I need. I hear rumblings that some of my staff are not happy with me as a boss. I'd like to do something about this, but I'm not sure what is the best way to proceed.

5. Development of a good plan of organization for the department
   In working through some of the above projects, I think I'll get some good ideas about how we ought to be set up as a department.

Since the working relationship between the two men had been quite well established during their earlier discussions, there was a comfortable give and take at this stage. Evans saw the first target as a crucial one which could become the basis for an entirely new conception of the department's role. He felt also that it could be extremely educational for Harrison provided he tackled it with sensitivity and an open mind. Accordingly he spent several hours helping Harrison to think through his strategy for determining the needs of the company with respect to personnel administration. Harrison began to see that this project was a means by which he could work toward all the other targets on his list.

Evans had little difficulty after Harrison's earlier experiences in persuading him to involve his subordinates in developing plans for the project. He suggested that Harrison continue to meet with him to discuss and evaluate this process for a couple of months. He felt—and said—that this might be the best method for Harrison to begin improving his own managerial skills.

They agreed that Harrison would explore possible university programs during the next few months to see if some one of these might meet his needs a little later. Meanwhile, they worked out a reading list and a plan for an occasional session when Harrison could discuss his reading.

In view of the nature of the personnel function, and the particular problems facing Harrison, the targets did not lend themselves to quantitative measurement such as might have been possible in a production operation. Nevertheless, Harrison, under Evans's tutelage, worked out a fairly detailed plan with specific steps to be accomplished by the end of six months. Evans's interest was that Harrison would have a basis for evaluating his own accomplishments at the end of the period.

Evans brought into the discussion the question of their relationship during the ensuing period. He said, "I don't want to be in a position of checking up on you from week to week. These are your plans, and I have full confidence that you will make every effort to reach your targets. On the other hand, I want you to feel free to seek help if you want it. There are ways in which I believe my experience can be useful to you. Suppose we leave it that we'll get together on your initiative as often as you wish—not for you to report how you are doing, but to discuss any problems which you would like my help on, or any major revisions in your plans." Thus Evans helped Harrison still further to perceive the role that he wanted to occupy as a superior, and thus also to clarify his own responsibilities as a subordinate.

STEP 3. THE ENSUING PERIOD. Since this is a managerial strategy rather than a personnel technique, the period between the establishment of targets and the evaluation of accomplishment is just as important as the first two steps. What happens during this period will depend upon the unique circumstances. The aim is to further the growth of the subordinate: his increased competence, his full acceptance of responsibility (self-direction and self-control), his ability to achieve integration between organizational requirements and his own personal goals.

In this particular situation Evans's primary interests were two: (1) the emergence throughout the company of a more adequate conception of the personnel function, and (2) the development of a competent department which would provide leadership and professional help to all levels of management with respect to this function. He felt that, as a result of steps 1 and 2 of his strategy, Harrison too was committed to these objectives. Moreover, he was persuaded that Harrison's project for assessing company needs in the field of personnel administration—as now conceived—was a highly promising means to these ends. He warned himself that he must be careful on two counts. First, he must not expect too much too fast. The company situation was in no sense critical and there was no need for a crash program. Harrison's project was certain to be a valuable learning experience for him and his staff.

Second, Evans recognized that if the best learning was to occur, he must curb his natural tendency to step in and guide the project. Harrison would make mistakes; at his present level of sophistication he would quite possibly fail to appreciate the full scope of the task. Nevertheless, Evans decided more would be gained if he limited his influence to those occasions when Harrison sought his help.

This is what he did. His confidence in Harrison proved to have been justified. He and his staff tackled the project with more ingenuity and sensitivity than Evans would have imagined possible and began rather quickly to understand the true dimensions of the problem. Harrison came in one day to tell him that they had decided to extend their explorations to include visits to several university centers in order to take advantage of the point of view of some top-flight academic people. Also, they planned to test some of their emerging ideas against the experience of several other companies.

After this discussion, and the evidence it provided concerning the expansion of Harrison's intellectual horizons and the use he was making of the resources represented by his subordinates, Evans stopped worrying. He would bail them out if they got into trouble, but he anticipated no such necessity.

STEP 4. SELF-APPRAISAL. At the end of August, Harrison reminded Evans (not vice versa!) that the six months was up. "When do you want a report?" was his question. Evans responded that a report was not what he wanted, but Harrison's own evaluation of what he had accomplished with respect to the targets he had set six months earlier. Said Evans, "This can give you a basis for planning for the next six months."

A week later Harrison brought the following notes to a discussion with Evans.

Appraisal, September 1

1. Determination of major company needs:
   a. The field work is completed.
   b. My staff and I are working on a proposal that will involve a new conception of personnel administration in this company. We will have a draft for discussion with you within thirty days, and we want you to take a full day to let us present our findings and proposals to you.
   c. The results of our work make it clear that we have an educational job to do with top management, and I want to include a plan along these lines in my next set of targets.

2. Joint determination with staff of current projects. I am now conducting a set of target-setting meetings with my department staff as a whole in which we are laying our plans for the next year. All major projects—individual or group—are being discussed out in detail there. These department meetings will be followed by individual planning sessions.

3. Development of department staff members
   a. The major project we have been carrying out has changed my ideas about several of my subordinates. I'm learning how to work with them, and it's clear they are growing. Our presentation to you next month will show you what I mean.
   b. I've appreciated how much your target-setting approach has helped my development, and I'm attempting to use it with each of my subordinates. Also, I think the departmental planning mentioned under 2 above is a developmental tool. I've been talking with some people in the B ___________ Company who do this and I'm excited about its possibilities in our own company.

4. Self-development

   All I can say is I've learned more in the past six months than in the previous five years.

5. Departmental organization

   I haven't done a thing about it. It doesn't seem very important right now. We seem to be able to plan our work as a department pretty well without developing a new setup. Perhaps we'll need to come back to this during the next six months, but there are more important things to be done first.

6. General comment

   I would rate myself considerably lower than I would have six months ago in terms of how well I'm filling the responsibilities of my job. It's going to take me a couple of years to measure up to what you have a right to expect of the man in this spot, but I think I can do it.

The discussion of this self-appraisal went into considerable detail. Evans felt that Harrison had acquired quite a little insight into his own strengths and weaknesses, and they were able to discuss objectively where he needed to give thought to improving his competence further. Harrison, for example, opened up the whole problem of his "yes-man" attitude in dealing with top management and pointed out that his exploratory interviews with some of these men had resulted in increased self-confidence. He said, "I think maybe I can learn to stand up for my ideas better in the future. You have helped me to realize that I can think for myself, and that I can defend myself in an argument."

They agreed to postpone Harrison's discussion of plans for the next six months until after the one-day session at which Evans would meet with the whole department. "Then," said Harrison, "I want to talk over with you a new statement of my responsibilities which I'm working on."

MANAGERIAL STRATEGY VERSUS PERSONNEL TECHNIQUES

The most important point with respect to management by integration and self-control is that it is a strategy—a way of managing people. The tactics are worked out in the light of the circumstances. Forms and procedures are of relatively little value. I stress this point because it has been my frequent experience, ever since some of my colleagues and I began to talk publicly about target setting, to have people send or bring me *forms* (often with the heading "self-appraisal") with the request that I tell them whether "this is all right" as a means of installing a new program.

"Selling" management a program of target setting, and providing standardized forms and procedures, is the surest way to *prevent* the development of management by integration and self-control. The manager who finds the underlying assumptions of Theory Y congenial will invent his own tactics provided he has a conception of the strategy involved. The manager whose underlying assumptions are those of Theory X cannot manage by integration and self-control no matter what techniques or forms are provided him.

McGregor's critique of "forms" that aim to force people to follow a constructive approach is well taken. However, this fails to anticipate the important role of standardization as a necessary foundation for continuous improvement. This is at the core of lean, Six Sigma, and other related systems change initiatives. It should be noted, however, that the power of standardization is achieved only when it is led on a voluntary basis by the front-line workforce. (See W. Edwards Deming, *Out of Crisis*, Cambridge, Mass.: MIT Press, 1986 and Maasaki Imai, *Kaizen: The Key to Japan's Competitive Success*, New York: McGraw-Hill, 1986.)

If a staff department is interested in the potential values of target setting, the approach will be to devise means of getting management to examine its assumptions, to consider the consequences of its present strategy and to compare it with others. The tools for building this managerial philosophy are attitudes and beliefs about people and about the managerial role, not manuals and forms.

Often such a development of management by integration and self-control begins with an individual who develops his own strategy and discovers its value. Soon, his subordinates are following his example, and before long others around him are asking questions and considering their own applications of the idea. If the initial steps are taken by a manager toward the top of the organization, the growth of the idea may be more rapid, but the process can start anywhere. As interest begins to be shown by others, the staff will often face the problem of persuading management that this is not a new gimmick and of fending off demands for the formal machinery which is so often seen as the only requirement for a new personnel program.

In "She Took Everything but the Blame: The Bad Boss Is Back" in his "On Managing" Column for *LA&M Journal* (Summer, 2002), John Lubans, an expert in library administration writes:

In one of my workshops I give participants a self-test on "Theory X" and "Theory Y."

Participants take the test twice, for how they supervise others and for how they want to be supervised. Then the participants arrange themselves around the room by their scores for how they supervise. There's usually a wide distribution from extreme X to extreme Y.

They re-arrange themselves—this time by the score for how they want to be supervised. There's usually a total shift to the theory Y side of the room. Those with a strong theory X inclination in supervising others find themselves wondering "Why am I the boss that I would not want?"

Managers who have undertaken to manage by integration and self-control report that the strategy is time-consuming. Roles cannot be clarified, mutual agreement concerning the responsibilities of a subordinate's job cannot be reached in a few minutes, nor can appropriate targets be established without a good deal of discussion. It is far quicker to hand a subordinate a position description and to inform him of his objectives for the coming period. If, however, the strategy is perceived as a way of managing which requires less policing of subordinates and which is accompanied by growth in managerial competence, the expenditure of time will be accepted as natural.

This approach does not tack a new set of duties on top of the existing managerial load. It is, rather, a different way of fulfilling existing responsibilities—of "running the job." I have yet to meet a manager who has made effective use of this managerial strategy who is critical of the time required. Several have said, "If this isn't the primary job of the manager, what is?"

SELECTED REFERENCES TO THE ANNOTATED EDITION

Deming, W. Edwards, *Out of Crisis*, Cambridge, Mass.: MIT Press, 1986.

Imai, Maasaki, *Kaizen: The Key to Japan's Competitive Success*, New York: McGraw-Hill, 1986.

DISCUSSION QUESTIONS FOR CHAPTER 5

1. In what ways is management goal setting different when the goals are imposed as compared to when the goals are reached through mutual dialogue? Are there ever situations in which mutual dialogue is just not possible?

2. Analyze the case example in the chapter involving "Harry Evans" and "Tom Harrison." What forms of influence are involved? Are there other forms of power embedded in this case example?

3. In discussing structured programs for goal setting, McGregor asserts that the "manager whose underlying assumptions are those of Theory X cannot manage by integration and self-control no matter what techniques or forms are provided him." Does that mean that we should just give up on these managers? If not, what do you recommend?

A CRITIQUE OF PERFORMANCE APPRAISAL

At the beginning of Chapter 6, McGregor notes that performance appraisal is not just a technique of personnel administration. "Where it is used for administrative purposes," he observes, "it becomes part of a managerial strategy." He further points out that the implicit logic is that "in order to get people to direct their efforts toward organizational objectives, management must tell them what to do, judge how well they have done, and reward or punish them accordingly." Focusing on the underlying assumptions, McGregor also notes that "appraisal programs are designed not only to provide more systematic control of the behavior of subordinates, but also to control the behavior of superiors." "Position descriptions," McGregor observes, "do not often produce the clarity of understanding they are designed to provide." He elaborates by noting that "the chief values of position descriptions are (1) to satisfy the needs of organization planners for order and systematization, and (2) to provide reassurance to top management that everyone has a piece of paper which tells him what to do. The danger is that both these groups will make the mistake of assuming that the descriptions represent reality." In noting that these methods of control are "not particularly appropriate for controlling human behavior in the setting of industry today," McGregor concludes that "it appears to be something of a tribute to the adaptability of human beings that these procedures work at all."

Dr. Deming listed performance appraisal as one of his 12 deadly sins for the precise reasons articulated by Douglas McGregor. Nonetheless, most large and midsize organizations feature performance appraisal systems, which are regularly redesigned with the help of large numbers of consultants. Douglas McGregor would be no more patient with today's state of affairs than was Dr. Deming (who was brutal in his critiques). After a decade of working with Dr. Deming in work systems where performance appraisal programs were eliminated and more integrative mechanisms established for feedback, career planning, and other matters, Mary Jenkins joined Thomas Coens to write *Abolishing Performance Appraisals: Why They Backfire and What to Do Instead*, which is a book-length treatment of the themes brought out by McGregor back in 1960.

Although the limits of performance appraisal are clear, as are the viability of alternative methods for personal feedback and career planning, there is still a need to better understand the role of core values and assumptions in these processes of personal development. If an organization is indeed persuaded that Theory X assumptions need to be challenged and Theory Y or related assumptions fostered, what are the best mechanisms for doing so (without re-creating the "gimmick" forms and procedures of which McGregor was rightly critical)?

CHAPTER 6

A CRITIQUE OF PERFORMANCE APPRAISAL

It will be instructive to contrast the strategy of management by integration and self-control with a more familiar one utilizing performance appraisals. Performance appraisal is often perceived simply as a technique of personnel administration, but where it is used for administrative purposes it becomes part of a managerial strategy, the implicit logic of which is that in order to get people to direct their efforts toward organizational objectives, management must tell them what to do, judge how well they have done, and reward or punish them accordingly. This strategy varies in detail from company to company, but in general it includes the following steps:

1. A formal position description, usually prepared by staff groups, which spells out the responsibilities of the job, determines the limits of authority, and thus provides each individual with a clear picture of what he is supposed to do.

2. Day-by-day direction and control by the superior within the limits of the formal position description. The superior assigns tasks, supervises their performance and, of course, is expected to give recognition for good performance and criticize poor performance, correct mistakes, and resolve difficulties in the day-to-day operation.

3. A periodic, formal summary of the subordinate's performance by the superior, using some kind of a standardized rating form. Typically, the rating will include judgments concerning the quantity and quality of the subordinate's work; his attitudes toward his work and toward the company (loyalty, cooperativeness, etc.); such personality characteristics as his ability to get along with

others, his judgment, and his reactions under stress; and over-all judgments of his "potential" and of his readiness for promotion.

4. A session in which the superior communicates his judgments to the subordinate, discusses the reason for them, and advises the subordinate on ways in which he needs to improve.

5. The subsequent use of the formal appraisal by others in the administration of salaries, promotions, management development programs, etc.

Variations of these procedures are utilized to improve the objectivity of the superior's judgments, to increase comparability of judgment among different superiors, and to improve the fineness of discrimination. For example, some plans utilize multiple judgments obtained independently from several superiors or developed in a group setting; some utilize the "forced choice" method in which a series of quite specific judgments are translated into general scores (the superior does not know the weighting of individual items and presumably does not know how he has evaluated the subordinate until the results are calculated). Many companies conduct programs for training superiors in rating procedures and in counseling techniques.

Appraisal programs are designed not only to provide more systematic control of the behavior of subordinates, but also to control the behavior of superiors. For example, it is believed that an appraisal program will force the superior to face up to problems of poor performance and deal with them, that it will force him to communicate to his subordinates his judgments of their performances, etc.*

A considerable amount of experience has accumulated with respect to the way in which this general strategy tends to work out in practice. How well does it achieve its purposes? Let us see.

---

* This highlights the all-pervasive nature of Theory X assumptions, even affecting higher managers' assumptions about lower-level managers.

THE POSITION DESCRIPTION

First, formal position descriptions provide management with an orderly picture of the organization and the comfortable conviction that people know what they are supposed to do. They establish formal chains of command and they delimit authority so that people will not interfere with each other. Position descriptions are a basis for an equitable salary classification scheme, provided it is recognized that at best they yield only a rough picture of reality. However, they are not a particularly realistic device for telling people what to do. Within the managerial hierarchy it is doubtful that any job is performed the same by two successive incumbents, or by the same incumbent over any long period of time. Not only do conditions change, but so do skills and relative abilities, and perceptions of priorities. Companies would utilize less of their human resources than they now do if managers were to adjust to their position descriptions rather than the other way around.

Management at middle and lower levels makes little actual use of position descriptions. Typically, they are glanced over when they are received in order to determine whether they coincide with commonsense preconceptions, and then they are filed away and forgotten. Many research studies show up substantial differences in the perceptions of subordinates and superiors concerning the requirements and priorities of the positions of the former. Position descriptions do not often produce the clarity of understanding they are designed to provide.

Organizations which really attempt to use position descriptions for control purposes (government agencies, for example) stimulate a substantial amount of managerial behavior the primary purpose of which is to defeat the system. The juggling of position descriptions by mangers to enable them to do what they want to do—hire a particular person who does not fit a classification, make a salary adjustment, legitimize a promotion—is a common phenomenon in such organizations. The neat systems are often rendered ineffective by these countermeasures.*

Organization planning groups sometimes attempt to eliminate these difficulties by a participative approach in which individual incumbents of jobs are encouraged to help the staff by contributing their own knowledge to the writing of the job description. While this process undoubtedly reduces the resistance to the whole idea, it is doubtful whether it results in greater use of the position descriptions themselves for direction and control of behavior.

The dimensions of a managerial position can be precisely defined only for a particular incumbent in a particular set of circumstances at a given point in time. Among the variables which affect the "shape" of the position are the following:

1. The way in which superiors, subordinates, and colleagues are performing their jobs. The position of a sales vice president, for example, will be vastly different if the president of the organization has had his major exprience in sales than it will if the president's experience has been in research or in manufacturing.

2. The individual's qualifications. These include his experience and competence which change over time and thus lead him to perceive the requirements of his position differently and to perform differently.

3. The individual's personal interests. These are related to, but not identical with, his qualifications.

4. The individual's assumptions about his role as a manager. His position will be different depending upon the degree to which he delegates responsibility, for example.

---

* Lean/Six Sigma systems change initiatives depend on standardized work descriptions as a baseline for continuous improvement efforts. McGregor's point here is key—if these same work descriptions are used for control purposes, it will undercut their effectiveness for continuous improvement efforts.

5. The constantly changing requirements of the external situation. Economic conditions, peculiarities of the market, political circumstances, competitive conditions, and a host of other variables require changes in performance which affect the nature of the job.

At two different points in time, perhaps a year apart, a given position might change from being like Figure 1 to being like Figure 2. Meanwhile, the formal position description is likely to continue to look like the rectangle in the figures. Even when there are attempts to keep position descriptions up to date and to relate them closely to the incumbents' views of their responsibilities, the variations in the real dimensions of the jobs are rarely captured.

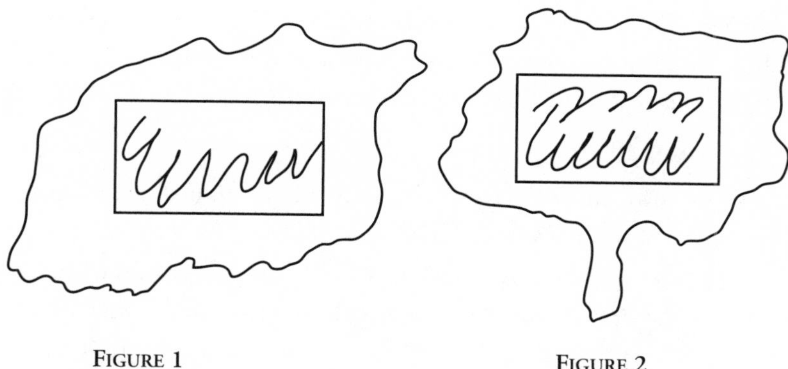

FIGURE 1　　FIGURE 2

Apart from providing guides for salary administration and some help in hiring and placement, the chief values of position descriptions are (1) to satisfy the needs of organization planners for order and systematization, and (2) to provide reassurance to top management that everyone has a piece of paper which tells him what to do. The danger is that both these groups will make the mistake of assuming that the descriptions represent reality.*

---

* This challenge to the utility of position descriptions highlights how attention to underlying assumptions helps us to see the way a work practice ends up failing to accomplish its stated objectives.

APPRAISAL: THE ADMINISTRATIVE PURPOSE

Let us consider now how well the appraisal process itself achieves its purposes. One of these purposes is administrative: the results of appraisal are used for salary administration, promotion, transfer, demotion, and termination. There are difficulties here, too.

In the first place, the problem of variation in the standards of different judges has never been completely solved, nor have we succeeded in eliminating the effects of bias and prejudice in making appraisal judgments. These variations among judges will be greater or smaller depending upon the particular method of appraisal used (whether it involves multiple judgments, for example) and the amount of training given in its use, but they remain substantial nevertheless. The answer given by an appraisal form to the question: "How has *A* done?" is as much a function of the superior's psychological make-up as of the subordinate's performance.

In the introduction to their book *Abolishing Performance Appraisals: Why They Backfire and What to Do Instead*, (San Francisco: Berrett-Koehler Publishers), Tom Coens and Mary Jenkins quote Timothy D. Schellhardt from the *Wall Street Journal*, who wrote: "If less than 10% of your customers judged a product effective and seven out of 10 said they were more confused than enlightened by it, you would drop it, right? So, why don't more companies drop their annual job-performance reviews?"

In their book, Coens and Jenkins expand on these limitations of performance appraisal and argue that the entire practice should be eliminated, saying:

Abolish performance appraisal. Yes, it feels uncomfortable to say that. Appraisal represents the conventional wisdom. We've grown accustomed to it, in spite of its inevitable flaws. Letting go of it

feels like we're going on a course to abandon people and their needs—the need for feedback, good coaching and development, the need for a measuring stick so people and the organization can know where people stand.

...Abolishing appraisal does not mean abandoning its good intentions. It is diametrically the opposite—it is about getting serious about those intentions and finding pathways that can deliver without bringing on the perennial problems of appraisal.

If we then take these somewhat questionable data and attempt to use them to make fine discriminations between people for purposes of salary administration and promotion, we can create a pretty picture, but one which has little relation to reality. Using fairly simple procedures, and some safeguards against extreme bias and prejudice, it is probably fair to say that we can discriminate between the outstandingly good, the satisfactory, and the unsatisfactory performers. When, however, we attempt to use the results of appraisal to make discriminations much finer than this, we are quite probably deluding ourselves. The fact is that many salary administration and promotion plans use appraisal results to make discriminations considerably smaller than the margin of error of the original judgments.

The problem of judging performance for administrative purposes is further complicated by the fact that any individual's performance is, to a considerable extent, a function of how he is managed.* For example, the individual who operates best when he is given quite a bit of freedom may find himself under a superior who provides close and detailed supervision. Under these conditions, even the most objective measures of his performance will provide a better basis for judging his boss than him!

---

* If the other aspects of McGregor's critique were not enough, here the responsibility for performance comes right back to the manager and the system as a whole.

Finally, it is relatively easy to find evidence that the judgments which managers make of their subordinates' performances differ depending upon whether they are used for administrative purposes.

One company used formal appraisals for several years simply as a basis for consultation between the superior and his subordinates. The appraisal forms were kept in a central file, but with the understanding that they would not be used for any administrative purpose.

As a result of certain changes in top management, a concern developed that there was too much "deadwood" in the managerial organization of this company. The staff were instructed to go through the appraisal forms in the central file in order to locate individuals who had, over a period of time, showed no particular improvement in performance, and the managers of these individuals were instructed to do something to change this behavior or terminate the relationship. It was further announced that the periodic appraisals would henceforth be used for administrative purposes.

The next set of appraisals showed a drastic revision upward. Most of the "deadwood" had disappeared from the distribution, although not from the organization. Thus, top management's attempt to control through the appraisals brought about a change, but not quite the one that had been intended.

It would seem to be a fair generalization that performance appraisals are something less than a perfect tool for administering salaries, promotions, transfers, and terminations. What about their value in achieving their informative purpose? Are they an adequate means for letting the subordinate know where he stands?

APPRAISAL: THE INFORMATIVE PURPOSE

It is characteristic of human beings that they find it difficult to hear and accept criticism. Judgments which are positive can perhaps be communicated effectively, but it is rather difficult to communicate critical judgments without generating defensiveness.

This difficulty with the appraisal interview is well illustrated by a common dilemma. If the superior attempts to communicate his criticism in the form of abstractions and generalities, he is likely to be asked to be more specific, to give illustrations. The subordinate feels that the generalizations do not give him a sufficient basis for correcting his behavior. If, on the other hand, the superior attempts to communicate in terms of concrete illustrations, he is likely to find himself on the defensive as the subordinate attempts to show that there were extenuating circumstances surrounding any illustration which he brings up.

In attempting to communicate criticisms to a subordinate the superior usually finds that the effectiveness of the communication is inversely related to the subordinate's need to hear it. The more serious the criticism, the less likely is the subordinate to accept it. If the superior is insistent enough, he may be able to convey his negative judgments to a subordinate, but when this happens he often finds that he has done serious damage to the relationship between them. Since the appraisal interview is an important occasion during which the attempt is made to give the subordinate a rather complete evaluation, it carries substantial overtones for him. It accentuates his dependence and thus readily arouses latent anxieties and hostilities. Critical judgments in this setting mean far more than when they are made with respect to specific incidents in the day-to-day relationship. Criticism of the latter type does not threaten the person himself as do the more general evaluative judgments communicated in connection with a formal appraisal, and thus they are easier to hear and respond to.*

It is an open question whether subordinates in general really want to know where they stand. It is true that when asked, the great majority will insist that they do want to know. However, it is possible to

---

* New scholarship on coaching and mentoring further reinforces the importance of feedback that is timely and specific.

interpret this expressed desire in several ways. It may mean, for example, "I don't know whether my boss feels I am doing an adequate job because he says so little about my performance in our day-to-day relationship. I feel I am doing well, and I would certainly like to know whether he feels the same way." This is not necessarily the desire for a cold-blooded, objective evaluation. It may be an expression of anxiety and of a need for reassurance. If, in fact, the individual is doing well, and the evaluation involves only minor criticisms, the appraisal interview may fill the need. If the individual is not doing well, the interview will intensify the anxiety and make it extremely difficult for him to react realistically.

The expressed desire to know where he stands may, for another individual, mean, "I know that I am doing a relatively poor job in some respects, but I hope the boss is not aware of it. I would like to be sure this is the case." Still another meaning might be, "I know I am doing an outstanding job, and I would like more recognition for it from the boss. He doesn't seem to be aware of how good I am."

These and many other attitudes are the natural consequence of the situation in which the responsibility for evaluation rests, not on the individual himself, but on the boss. If our managerial strategy emphasizes this childlike dependence, this schoolboy reliance on teacher's grade, we should not be surprised if the reactions to an objective appraisal are sometimes immature.

There is still another aspect of the appraisal interview as a communications device. Since most appraisals involve the superior's evaluation of attitudes and personality traits, in addition to objective performance, there is an invitation inherent in the situation to invade the personality of the subordinate. Recognizing the delicacy of this situation, many managements encourage the superior to use the interview for "counseling" purposes.

It can be stated categorically that few managers are competent to practice psychotherapy. Moreover, the situation of the appraisal interview, in which the superior is in the role of a judge, is the poorest possible one for counseling. The effective counseling relationship is one in which the counselor is a neutral party who neither criticizes nor praises, and whose concern is solely for the health and well-being of the client. To attempt to counsel in a formal appraisal interview is as much a travesty as to attempt bribery of a victim during a holdup. The manager, in making judgments about a subordinate, is implying that he needs to change his behavior in certain ways, and clearly in the minds of both is the recognition that the superior is in a position to punish him if he does not change. Surely this is not a situation for effective counseling, even if the superior is skilled in psychotherapy. The role of judge and the role of counselor are incompatible.

APPRAISAL: THE MOTIVATIONAL PURPOSE

Finally, consider the motivational purpose of appraisal. The common-sense assumption is that telling an individual where he is falling down will provide effective motivation to get him to change. Clearly it will not do so unless he accepts the negative judgment and agrees with it. We have already seen that this is not too likely a possibility. Contrast the situation in which a subordinate is evaluating his own performance relative to specific targets which he set a few months ago with the situation in which he is listening to his superior evaluate his performance against the superior's standards and objectives. In the latter case, the stage is set for rationalization, defensiveness, inability to understand, reactions that the superior is being unfair or arbitrary. These are not conditions conducive to effective motivation.

The semiannual or annual appraisal is not a particularly efficient stimulus to learning for another reason: It provides "feedback" about behavior at a time remote from the behavior itself. People do learn and change as a result of feedback. In fact, it is the only way they learn. However, the most effective feedback occurs immediately after the behavior. The subordinate can learn a great deal from a mistake, or a particular failure in performance, provided it is analyzed while all the evidence is immediately at hand. Three or four months later, the likelihood of effective learning from that experience is small. It will be still smaller if the superior's generalized criticism relates to several incidents spread over a period of months.

Finally, it is common experience that managers tend to resist and avoid the task of making formal appraisals, and particularly of conducting appraisal interviews when critical judgments are involved. Somehow, the task is an onerous one. Many managers recognize the difficulties described above, and their resistance is due to a realistic skepticism about the whole procedure. Whatever the reasons, it is unlikely that the superior will perform a disliked task in a manner which will motivate and encourage the subordinate to become more effective. Once more, it seems that a means of control—in this instance control of the superior—through the procedure of the formal appraisal and interview is inappropriate. It does not represent selective adaptation to human nature.

It should be pointed out that many managers, guided by assumptions like those of Theory Y, have invented adaptations of conventional appraisal procedures which avoid some of the difficulties discussed above.

As one simple and relatively effective example, a chief engineer in a large manufacturing organization which has a typical appraisal program distributes copies of the appraisal form to his subordinates every six months with this comment: "Why don't you fill this out on yourself from your knowledge of how you have performed during these few months. I'll fill one out on you independently. If we agree, we won't need to worry about much of an appraisal interview. If we disagree, we can get together and thrash out our differences."

Of course this "gimmick" in the hands of an exponent of Theory X could be a devastating weapon! As used by this man in the light of his philosophy of management, however, it is a rather effective countermeasure to the impact of the appraisal machinery as it is administered in his company.

The theoretical assumptions of Theory X lead quite naturally to a strategy of telling people what to do, judging their performance, and rewarding or punishing them, and to procedures such as those involved in performance appraisal. It appears to be something of a tribute to the adaptability of human beings that these procedures work at all. The main point, however, is that the managerial strategy underlying them is not particularly appropriate for controlling human behavior in the setting of industry today. Certainly, the strategy of management by integration and self-control is more appropriate for intelligent adults and is more likely to be conducive to growth, learning, and improved performance.

REFERENCES

Drucker, Peter F., "Integration of People and Planning, *Harvard Business Review*, vol. 33, no. 6 (November–December), 1955.

Foundation for Research on Human Behavior, *Performance Appraisal and Review*. Ann Arbor, Mich.: 1958.

Kelly, Philip R., "Reappraisal of Appraisals," *Harvard Business Review*, vol. 36, no. 3 (May–June), 1958.

Mahler, Walter R., and Guyot Frazier, "Appraisal of Executive Performance: The 'Achilles Heel' of Management Development," *Personnel*, vol. 31, no. 5, 1955.

Maier, Norman R. F., *The Appraisal Interview*. New York: John Wiley & Sons, Inc., 1958.

Rowland, Virgil K., "From the Thoughtful Businessman," *Harvard Business Review*, vol. 35, no. 5 (September–October), 1957.

Whisler, Thomas L., "Performance Appraisal and the Organization Man," *The Journal of Business*, vol. 31, no. 1 (January), 1958.

SELECTED REFERENCES TO THE ANNOTATED EDITION

Coens, Tom, and Mary Jenkins, *Abolishing Performance Appraisals: Why They Backfire and What to Do Instead*, San Francisco: Berrett-Koehler Publishers, 1990.

DISCUSSION QUESTIONS FOR CHAPTER 6

1. McGregor observes that performance appraisal systems not only control the behavior of subordinates, but also control the behavior of superiors. In what ways might this be the case?
2. In this chapter, McGregor could be read as suggesting that there is little or no use for position descriptions. Do you agree or disagree—and why?
3. If, as McGregor suggests, feedback is best when it occurs immediately after the behavior, what sort of workplace system might you establish to help enable such timely and specific feedback to take place?

ADMINISTERING SALARIES AND PROMOTIONS

At the outset of Chapter 7, McGregor acknowledges that his approach raises core questions concerning the administration of salaries, promotions, transfers, and terminations. In this context, he points out that Theory X views money as "the major motivator of human behavior in the organizational setting." Stated even more directly, "The employment contract is perceived as an agreement to accept direction in return for economic rewards." Although various formal methods of wage determination such as market surveys, cost-of-living indices, and policies of paying "equal to or better than" the average are all recognized as helpful in achieving some equity in pay, McGregor notes that, within a framework of measurement, it is "collective and individual bargaining" that will "become the ultimate determinants [of pay levels]." He is then critical of merit pay, noting a situation where employees variously receive 3 percent, 6 percent, and 10 percent merit increases. In this case, he states that "it is likely that the probable error of measurement of most merit rating plans is several times the magnitude of the differentiations that are made in their administration." Ultimately, McGregor concludes:

1. Individual pay differentials might be made for the small number of individuals whose performance "can be directly tied to objective criteria of accomplishment such as profit and loss."
2. For the balance of the workforce, he recommends "time-service" increments "so long as performance is not unsatisfactory."

3. He reserves merit increases for "the small proportion of individuals ... whose performance is clearly *outstanding.*"
4. Finally, he calls for "group rewards for departmental, or divisional, or company-wide achievement of objectively measured economic results."

In reaching these conclusions, McGregor points to research by Herzberg, Mausner, and Snyderman that finds that "salary has more potency as a job dissatisfier than as a job satisfier." The goal is to minimize the degree to which pay is a de-motivator, rather than to increase the degree to which it is attempted to be used as a motivator.

Promotions and placements, McGregor notes, will necessarily rely on "subjective judgments by superiors of their subordinates." In this process, he rejects highly structured or "scientific" ways of matching the fit of individual qualifications to the job, since it would be sharply contrary to Theory Y to hold that "the individual must be adapted and molded to the requirements of the organization." Instead, he calls for "*active and responsible participation of the individual in decisions affecting his career.*" Finally, McGregor provides an addendum in which he makes a careful distinction between psychological tests that assess aptitude for a job and personality tests. He states flatly that management does not have any "moral right to invade the personality," and he predicts that future advances in personality testing will intensify the ethical challenges.

Today, approaches to pay and performance are still dominated by a view of pay as a motivator, and the use of various personality tests as a predictor of job performance has expanded in all the ways that McGregor anticipated. Though the use of psychological tests is regulated to some degree by legal constraints around avoiding discrimination, the ethical dilemmas that McGregor anticipated are today's challenges.

CHAPTER 7

ADMINISTERING SALARIES AND PROMOTIONS

It will not be surprising if the reader is saying at this point: "Yes, but what about the practical problems connected with administering salaries and promotions? It is all very nice to be informal and to encourage managers to avoid the difficult task of making judgments about their subordinates. How are the necessary decisions going to be made concerning problems, transfers, terminations? How are we to decide who gets a salary increase, or an executive bonus, and how much? Does self-appraisal mean self-determination of income and self-placement?"

These are legitimate questions. In order to see that they have at least partial answers, it will be necessary to examine the conventional approach to wage and salary administration and to promotion and placement.

WAGE AND SALARY ADMINISTRATION

Within the framework of Theory X, the ability to provide or withhold economic rewards is the prime means by which management exercises authority in industry. Money is perceived as the major motivator of human behavior in the organizational setting. Money is a means for satisfying many needs. This fact enables management to use it to obtain acceptance of direction and control. The employment contract is perceived as an agreement to accept direction in return for economic rewards.*

As we have seen, the existence of a situation of full employment, the relatively high standard of living, the considerable mobility of the population, and the presence of various forms of social legislation all tend to lessen somewhat the degree of dependence of employees today. Money *is* essential for satisfying many needs, but the individual is less dependent upon a single employer for obtaining it than he once was.

At the time that McGregor was writing, he assumed that increased job mobility would increase an employee's ability to advance his or her own interests beyond just financial rewards. During the 1990s, this was highly evident in regions dominated by new-technology industries, though more recent experience also points to limits on the bargaining power of individuals in tight labor markets, regardless of mobility.

The more important question, however, is *how much* money is necessary to make the employment contract effective? This, of course, is a relative matter in several respects. The necessary amount is first of all relative to the competition of the labor market and to general economic conditions including the cost of living, the tax structure, etc. Second, it is relative to the importance of the job in question within the hierarchy of jobs in the organization. Third, it is relative to the contribution of the individual because the "productivity" of individuals on the same job varies.

---

* The "employment contract" has become the focus of renewed attention as it devolves into what is seen as an even more market-based set of arrangements than was the case in McGregor's time. (Peter Capelli, *The New Deal at Work: Managing the Market-Driven Workforce*, Boston: Harvard Business School Press, 1999; Thomas Kochan, "Building a New Social Contract at Work," Presidential Address, Industrial Relations Research Association Proceedings, IRRA, 2000.)

ESTABLISHING THE WAGE AND SALARY STRUCTURE. Two major considerations determine the nature of managerial policy and practice with respect to wage and salary administration. The first is the consideration of equity: whether the amount of money provided is perceived to be fair relative to the market, economic conditions, the importance of the job, and the individual's contribution. If it is not, either the individual will not take the job, or, having taken it, he will not perform in a satisfactory manner (he will restrict his output, be indifferent or antagonistic to organizational objectives, engage in countermeasures which interfere with management's attempts to direct and control his behavior).

The second consideration is that of incentive (in the broad sense, including all types of economic rewards): the use of differential increments of money to yield differential increments of effort. In general it is assumed that more money will result in more effort.

In this field of wage and salary administration there is a strong emphasis on measurement because it is recognized that a systematic determination of economic rewards is more equitable than one based on arbitrary decisions, personal considerations, pressure ("the squeaky wheel"), and individual opinion. Arguments, friction, and countermeasures are reduced to the extent that economic rewards can be determined by impersonal and objective methods. Measurement is, therefore, the key to equity in administering economic rewards.

Management's success in achieving equity through the use of measurement varies, depending upon the nature of the problems involved. In the determination of general levels of wages and salaries relative to economic conditions, we encounter some difficult problems which are reduced, but not solved, by systematic approaches. Market surveys, cost-of-living indices, and policies such as that of providing economic benefits "equal to or better than" the average, certainly increase the degree of acceptance. However, questions of the company's "ability to pay" and of the employee's "fair share of the fruits of enterprise" do not lend themselves to determination by formula. Collective and individual bargaining, within a framework of measurement, become the ultimate determinants.*

Within the organization, determination of differential wages and salaries for particular jobs is generally accomplished today by wage and salary classification plans which rest on systematic attempts to measure job importance. Management has been reasonably successful in this area. There are, however, some inequities which seem to be impossible to eliminate with present classification methods. For example, the differential between top worker job rates and the rates for the lowest levels of supervisory jobs is a constant source of trouble. Certain kinds of jobs, such as that of the research scientist or the top-level executive, are difficult to evaluate. Market conditions sometimes create insurmountable inequities (the current inflation of the market price for technically trained college graduates puts a severe strain on the salary structure).

By and large, however, it has proved possible to achieve a reasonable equity by means of job evaluation and salary classification plans. It has become clear that attempts to achieve ever more precise measurement in this field are not particularly rewarding. The specialists are so enamored of the intricacies of measurement itself that the plans tend to become unintelligible, and suspicion of their adequacy is generated. Equity hinges on acceptance, and relatively simple classification plans appear to be more readily accepted than some of the more elaborately "scientific" ones.

REWARDING INDIVIDUAL DIFFERENCES IN PRODUCTIVITY. The most difficult problems in wage and salary administration arise when we turn to the measurement of individual contributions within the framework of general wage levels and of wage and salary classification. Variations in performance among individuals on any job are substantial, and management continually seeks ways of relating eco-

---

* It is important to note that collective and individual bargaining have proved to be far less stable foundations for employment relations in the United State than McGregor anticipated.

nomic rewards to these variations. The major concern is, of course, the motivational one, but it is inextricably tangled with problems of equity.*

The wage incentive field yields some instructive insights if we are willing to perceive them. An incredible amount of effort and ingenuity have been directed toward the problem of measuring worker output in order to relate economic rewards to it. Nevertheless, individual incentive plans have never provided the motivation which might be expected on logical grounds. Problems of equity plague management continually, and the costs involved in trying to alleviate them are so high that many managements have abandoned incentive plans in favor of measured day work. It has been impossible so far to prove conclusively which approach is better, but it is clear that the gains for the organization from individual incentive plans are modest even under the best conditions.

For salaried employees (including managers), merit rating plans take the place of incentive plans as a method of providing differential economic rewards for individual contributions. Measurement here becomes an even more difficult matter. Except in the limited number of instances where direct measures of profit and loss can be utilized, the criterion for the individual's contribution is uncertain.

The most carefully designed systematic attempts at measurement of individual contribution (and these are few and far between!) are usually based on over-all subjective ratings or rankings of performance. These are then correlated with specific characteristics of performance which can be judged, and a rating form is developed, utilizing the items which correlate best with the over-all rankings.

---

* There is now a large literature and an even larger array of consultants advocating various forms of "pay for performance." Although leading texts on this subject do recognize many complexities of establishing such systems, there is still an underlying set of assumptions centered on pay as a motivator for individual performance that is the opposite of McGregor's recommendations. (See George T. Milkovich and John W. Boudreau, *Human Resource Management*, 8th ed., New York: Irwin, 1996.)

The correlations are rarely high enough to account for more than half the variance in performance, even when many items are combined. Moreover, even if the correlations are high, they are correlations with a criterion of performance which is itself subjective (the original ranking).

Few merit rating plans even attempt this degree of scientific precision. Normally, the rating form is a series of variables which are simply assumed without any test whatever to correlate with over-all contribution to the enterprise. They are rated by the individual's superior, weighted (or not) according to arbitrary rules, and combined in some fashion to give a general "measure" of performance. It requires no more than a cursory examination of most such plans to raise serious questions about their validity.

As one illustration, consider a rating form which includes a factor of "loyalty." While it is probably true that active disloyalty is negatively correlated with contribution to the enterprise, does it follow that maximum loyalty represents a positive contribution? Is it not possible that the blindly loyal individual would never even perceive policies or practices or decisions which were poor and sorely needed correction? Does management value most the individual who puts loyalty to the organization above loyalty to his own highest principles?*

Similar naïve assumptions are revealed when, for example, "quality" and "control of costs" are rated as independent factors with no recognition that in some sense they are reciprocal.

---

* "Whistle-blower" legislation and a growing focus on ethics in management point to the importance of enabling individuals to honor their own "highest principles," even if doing so looks to be disloyal to the organization. For example, Joseph A. Petrick and John F. Quinn connect ethics with the principle of integration when they state, "This book is devoted to enhancing managerial performance by integrating managerial and ethical competence" in *Management Ethics: Integrity at Work* (SAGE Series on Business Ethics), Thousand Oaks, Calif.: Sage, 1997.

The problems with merit rating plans are compounded by another consideration, namely, the widespread policy of strict secrecy with respect to individual managerial salaries. Equity—that is, acceptance of the fairness of decisions—cannot rest *alone* on confidence in a system of measurement. It rests also on perceptions of how fairly the system is administered. But here we have a situation in which the plan itself is usually subject to serious questions concerning the adequacy of measurement, and there is an additional requirement of secrecy concerning the results of its administration.

A final complication results from the fact that merit plans are used to make not gross but fine differentiations between individuals. One may receive a 3 per cent increase, another 6 per cent, another 10 per cent. As previously suggested, it is likely that the probable error of measurement of most merit rating plans is several times the magnitude of the differentiations that are made in their administration. Perhaps it is just as well that management attempts to maintain secrecy with respect to the results of its administration of such plans!

In the light of considerations such as these, let us ask some questions: Given an adequate base salary structure, is it in fact likely that small increments of salary provide genuine motivation for increased effort? In view of our earlier consideration of motivation, is it likely that such kinds of limited economic rewards have a fraction of the incentive value that opportunities for increased satisfaction of social, ego, and self-actualization needs would have? Within the present income tax structure, what is the real significance, motivationally speaking, of a 5 or even a 10 per cent salary increase to an individual making $15,000 or $20,000 a year? Is it possible that the assumptions of Theory X have led to reliance on the least appropriate among several alternative methods of influence? To be sure, management can provide or withhold salary increments authoritatively, while it can only create conditions (or fail to) for individuals to achieve satisfaction of their higher-level needs. However, would it not seem that emphasis on the principle of integration in contrast to authoritative control of relatively minor increments of economic reward, might merit exploration?*

CONCLUSIONS. The conclusions which seem to me reasonable with respect to salary administration are these:

1. The problems of equity with respect to economic rewards can be reasonably solved by systematic market survey, attention to the cost of living, policies such as paying salaries "equal to or better than" average, well-conceived position classification plans, and the processes of collective and individual bargaining. In this fashion the individual can be assured of a general level of economic reward which he will accept as fair.
2. The problems of motivation will be solved in part by the provision of equitable rewards in the form of base salaries and in part by providing opportunities for achieving satisfaction of higher-level needs through efforts directed toward organizational objectives (the principle of integration).
3. Four categories of increments of economic reward above base salaries are realistic:
   a. Those that can be directly tied to objective criteria of accomplishment such as profit and loss. These will necessarily be limited to a few people in the total population if they are administered on an individual basis. Moreover, they will, potentially, be large enough to have genuine motivational value.
   b. Those that are administered as "time-service" increments, received automatically at intervals so long as performance is not unsatisfactory. Such increments will be small, and will have as their chief value the maintenance of equity (on the

* Alfie Kohn and others have argued that it is better to ensure that pay is not a de-motivator than it is to try to use rewards to motivate behavior. (See Alfie Kohn, *Punished by Rewards: The Trouble with Gold Stars, Incentive Plans, A's, Praise, and Other Bribes*, Boston: Houghton Mifflin, Marinar Books, 1993.)

assumption that time on a job brings some increase in competence and in contribution).

c. Merit increases to the small proportion of individuals in a given salary classification whose performance is clearly *outstanding*. These will require only gross differentiations of performance in which the probable error of measurement will be small, and they will also involve large enough salary increments to have genuine motivational value.

d. Group rewards for departmental, or divisional, or companywide achievement of objectively measurable economic results. These would be shared within the group in terms of an equal percentage of base salary. (The Scanlon Plan, to be considered in Chapter 8, utilizes this method of motivating performance.)

When a pay system following these attributes was implemented for the 7,000 managers and engineers in the GM Powertrain Division during the decade of the 1990s, the result was some of the best performance in the history of that organization. Four successive attempts by a sequence of senior managers to shift back to a more traditional "pay-for-performance" system centered on performance appraisals were strongly and successfully resisted by the workforce. This case story is presented by Tom Coens and Mary Jenkins in *Abolishing Performance Appraisals: Why They Backfire and What to Do Instead*, San Francisco: Berrett-Koehler Publishers, 1990. Mary Jenkins was the human resource director for GM Powertrain during this time and led this effort in consultation with Dr. W. Edwards Deming.

4. Conventional programs for providing large numbers of people with differential and relatively small merit salary increases, in the light of our present ability to measure managerial contributions

> to the enterprise, are not very realistic. The absence of objective criteria of performance and the problems involved in measurement are such that equity cannot be achieved through such methods. Moreover, there is reason to doubt that such rewards have much motivational value relative to other opportunities which can be provided through applications of the principle of integration.[1]

Thus the question about salary administration raised at the beginning of this chapter is answered: *It is unnecessary for the superior to make the judgments we have customarily relied upon to administer economic rewards* (except possibly with respect to a few individuals whose performance is outstanding). For some, these conclusions will appear defeatist. They are, if one stays within the framework of Theory X. From the point of view of Theory Y, they suggest simply that we have been relying on inappropriate methods of control. Conventional merit plans of salary administration do not represent selective adaptation to the conditions we face. The challenge is to find other ways to motivate people. Management by integration and self-control offers one such method.

There is no implication in this conclusion that economic rewards are unimportant. The implication is that an equitable salary struc-

---

[1] The previously mentioned study of Herzberg, Mausner, and Snyderman supports the conclusion in this paragraph. The writers point out that when salary was a factor in producing dissatisfaction, it was associated with "the unfairness of the wage system within the company, and this almost always referred to increases in salaries rather than the absolute levels. It was the system of salary administration that was being described, a system in which wage increases were obtained grudgingly, or given too late, or in which the differentials between newly hired employees and those with years of experience on the job were too small." On the other hand, salary increases were a source of satisfaction primarily as they accompanied job achievements. They conclude: "It would seem that as an affector of job attitudes salary has more potency as a job dissatisfier than as a job satisfier." Herzberg, Mausner, and Snyderman, *The Motivation to Work*, pp. 82–83.

ture furnishes the major economic rewards, but that our attempts to get greater "productivity" *through the use of small increments of economic reward within such a structure* have not been particularly effective.

THE ADMINISTRATION OF PROMOTIONS AND PLACEMENT

Unfortunately, it does not seem possible to solve the problems involved in promotion by eliminating the necessity for subjective judgments by superiors of their subordinates. Moreover, in addition to considerations of equity and motivation, there are considerations of qualifications involved. What experience and training, what abilities and skills are required to perform a given job, and how can we determine which individual among several candidates possesses these to the greatest degree?

It is tempting to assume that these problems would be solved if we could develop adequate methods for measuring (1) jobs and (2) individual qualifications (in contrast to individual contributions to the enterprise). Much time and effort has been and is being devoted to the pursuit of this objective. Many staff specialists have the dream of a system which would involve a set of punched cards carrying the detailed requirements of every job and another set carrying the qualifications of every member of the organization. Filling openings would then require only a mechanical process of matching. However, as in the case of measuring merit, there are formidable obstacles.

We noted in the previous chapter that jobs—and particularly managerial jobs—do not consist of fixed receptacles whose detailed dimensions can be measured. They are embedded in complex organizational and external relationships which change substantially over time. In addition, it is simply not true that one and only one pattern of qualifications of the incumbent will yield the best performance of a given job. Variations in personal qualifications will result in the job being performed *differently*, but several such patterns could lead to equivalent results as far as the achievement of organizational objectives is concerned.

Conventional organization theorists usually lay great stress on defining the job and then fitting an individual to it. They are concerned to prevent the "square peg in the round hole." Such an idea may have the merit of logical simplicity, but the fact that this rule is so rarely followed in practice should warn us that the problem is considerably more complex than this. Moreover, the principle of integration is sharply contradictory to the conception that the individual must be adapted and molded to the requirements of the organization.

Further, while progress is being made, we are still a long way even from knowing what the qualifications for managerial success in most jobs may be, let alone from being able to measure them. Finally, since personality characteristics and factors of emotional adjustment are thought to be as important as factors of experience, training, skill, and intellectual capacity, we must face the ethical problem which was briefly mentioned in Chapter 1. There is a real question concerning the ethics of using private and personal data (in contrast to "public" data on performance, educational achievement, etc.) in administering promotions and placement.

Certainly the dream of a mechanical matching of job characteristics and personal qualifications has no more than very limited possibilities. For the foreseeable future, managerial judgments of a subjective kind are going to play a large part in administering promotions and placements.

A ROLE FOR MEASUREMENT. Research groups in several companies have developed methods of measurement for selection and for promotion with respect to a limited number of positions which have given management substantial help. A rather elaborate procedure is necessary for each position, and hence the method is useful only when there is continuing need for numbers of candidates. It does not lend itself to the situation where replacements on a given job are infrequent, or where the number of incumbents is small.

The research involves the determination by statistical means of a large number of "items" (aspects of experience, attitude, ability, personality) which discriminate between present incumbents of the position who are ranked by management on the basis of over-all value to the company. These items are combined in a test (with weights determined by their discriminative value) which is then used to help screen applicants.

There is evidence that this procedure can improve selection and promotion practices materially *provided*:

1. Management becomes actively involved in the research leading to the development of the tests (and thus acquires a real understanding both of the values and the limitations of the instruments).

2. The tests are used as an aid to selection and not as the sole basis for judgment. (It is easy to obtain lip service to this principle, but hard to maintain it in practice because the tendency is to rely on the test scores. This is one reason why management participation in the research is important.)

3. The conception of "good" and "poor" performance remains unchanged. (Since the whole approach hinges on management's original ranking of incumbents, the tests discriminate *only in terms of that criterion.* If the requirements of the job change, or if management acquires a different idea of what constitutes "good" performance, the tests become useless and the research must be repeated.)

Even this rather elaborate research method does not eliminate managerial judgment in the administration of promotion and placement. Nevertheless, the use of standardized tests and procedures (without such custom-tailored methods) as the primary basis for selection in filling complex managerial jobs is not uncommon today. Many commercial firms offer services of this kind. The evidence for the validity of such methods is dubious, to say the least. (This is one more reason for concern with the ethics of managerial practices in this field. The manager is likely to feel some responsibility in making subjective judgments which affect the career of a fellow human being. Most of us are a little hesitant about "playing God." When, however, one can let the decision rest on a "scientific" determination, it is all too easy to slough off the responsibility.)

Whether or not tests are utilized, there are safeguards in the form of procedures which can help to improve the validity of managerial judgments and which will help to protect the individual against the consequences of prejudice, poor judgment, and the like. Carefully designed methods for utilizing group judgments represent the best of these.

THE ROLE OF THE INDIVIDUAL. Perhaps the biggest change required in current practices with respect to promotion and placement—if we desire to utilize the principle of integration—has to do with the relation of the "candidate" to the process. Today he tends to be a pawn on the organizational chessboard. Plans are frequently made with respect to his career which may have profound effects upon his most important goals and needs. Yet he is likely to have no voice in these plans and to remain in complete ignorance of them until after the decision has been reached. Moreover, the organization's needs are given priority almost without consideration of his needs. If his goals and needs are considered at all, it is likely to be in the paternalistic sense of deciding "what is good for him."

An assistant chief engineer, aged thirty-eight, in a large organization, has for several years desired some line experience. He has expressed a strong interest in a job where he could have a reasonable autonomy and be judged by "the p. and 1. statement." He has shown considerable administrative ability in the various engineering jobs he has held. He is regarded by those above him as outstanding, and a likely prospect some day for vice president of engineering.

In a discussion with a manager two levels above him who has had both interest and influence on this man's career, I asked if he had ever been considered for a line job. The answer was emphatic: "Oh, no! His forte is engineering."

The principle of integration requires active and responsible participation of the individual in decisions affecting his career. However radical this may be, however impractical it may seem in the light of traditional practice, it is requirement if we would create conditions such that the individual can achieve his own goals best by directing his efforts toward organizational objectives. No amount of scientific evidence concerning his qualifications, no safeguards to ensure sound and unprejudiced judgments, no rationalizations about the disappointment of unsuccessful candidates can justify excluding the individual from a process which is so important to him.*

A beginning can be made in target-setting sessions. Here it is feasible to discuss the individual's career interests, to consider needed experiences and training, kinds of opportunities which would be relevant, questions of timing. Here, too, personal considerations which might affect his desire to move from his present job or to stay on it can be discussed.

One company has had a practice for several years of asking each member of management, periodically: "Is your hat in the ring?" If his answer is yes, he is considered for relevant openings which may occur. If it is no, he is excluded from such considerations *without prejudice*. Of course, the question will be asked again in a year or two, and he may feel differently then. The decision, however, is his.

Data about the individual's interests, his relevant experience, and even his capacities as measured by tests can, with his full knowledge and agreement, be included in the central personnel file for possible reference as openings occur. The results of personality tests and

---

* The field of career development has advanced just as McGregor suggests—focusing on the match between personality and career choice, as well as the integration of broader organizational factors (see Arthur, Michael B., et al., *Handbook of Career Theory*. Cambridge, England: Cambridge University Press, 1989). Pay-for-performance scholarship, by contrast, retains a strong Theory X flavor.

clinical evaluations, *provided they are kept confidential between the psychologist and the individual*, can be a basis on which he plans his career and decides whether to be a candidate for particular openings.

A few companies have developed procedures which make it possible for individuals to submit their names as candidates for particular openings. This enables the individual to take a responsible role with respect to his own career development. There are problems involved, of course, but it is possible to find a middle ground between administrative practices which treat the individual as a pawn and those sometimes found at the worker level which involve direct "bidding" for jobs.

In the context of management by integration and self-control, both the superior and the subordinate can furnish data for the administration of promotions. If the superior's judgments differ sharply from those developed by the subordinate's self-appraisals, there will be the need for discussion and resolution of the differences. There is reason to expect, however, that such differences can usually be reconciled during the course of a series of target-setting and self-appraisal discussions.

While I was President of Antioch College, we worked out a review procedure under which any promotional decision made by me which was felt by the faculty member to be unfair could be taken to a faculty board for a hearing and a final decision. Since I was not a member of the review board, this meant that my decision could be overruled.

In the course of about four years during which this system was in operation, only two cases went to the review board. I was upheld on one of these, overruled on the other. My feeling was that this mechanism provided a valuable check against the fallibility of administrative judgments; odd as it may seem, the decision which went against me served to strengthen rather than weaken my position with my faculty. Certainly the very presence of this procedure, even though it was rarely used, lessened the feelings of dependence in the relationships and made it easier for me to deal with difficult situations.*

CONCLUSIONS. Some general conclusions with respect to the administration of promotions and placement within the context of Theory Y are:

1. The matching of individuals of jobs—at least at managerial levels—cannot be a mechanical process because:
   a. Job requirements are dynamic rather than static; they change as a function of many variables in the situation.
   b. Individuals with different patterns of qualifications, although they may perform a given job differently, can achieve organizational objectives equally well.
   c. We do not have adequate knowledge of the characteristics associated with managerial success, nor very precise methods for measuring those that are considered important.

2. Hence, a considerable element of subjective judgment remains—regardless of the use that is made of measurement—in decisions concerning the placement of individuals. Careful, systematic research can provide tools that will aid judgment, but such tools cannot replace judgment. Exclusive reliance on the results of tests is completely unwarranted at the present stage of development of such tools.

3. The principle of integration demands an active rather than a passive role for the individual in the administration of promotions and placement. At the very least, data which he can provide concerning his interests, goals, and qualifications can be utilized to permit him to become an active candidate for promotional opportunities under most circumstances. His goals and needs—

* This vignette nicely illustrates the connection between institutional arrangements and underlying values and assumptions.

as perceived by him and not simply by others—can influence decisions affecting his career.

4. Judgments of the superior about his subordinates, developed within a strategy of management by integration and self-control, are likely to be based upon data and experience which will improve their quality.

In the administration of promotions, therefore, we face a situation in which it is unrealistic to relinquish the use of authority. The decisions need not be completely unilateral, but they must be made. In the absence of truly objective criteria of performance, there is a substantial degree of dependence of the individual upon those above him. Given this dependence, the exercise of authority is an appropriate means of control *provided we are aware of the negative consequences if equity is not preserved.* Under some conditions it may be feasible to establish review procedures which will serve as a check against arbitrary decisions and thus increase the likelihood of achieving equity.

The answer to the questions raised at the beginning of this chapter is that unilateral direction and control with respect to the administration of salaries and promotions can be reduced but not eliminated (1) by the use of measurement *where it is appropriate*, (2) by eliminating differentiations between individuals when the error of measurement is large and the motivational value of the differentiations is small, and (3) by giving individuals greater opportunities to play an active part in decisions affecting their careers.

ADDENDUM

I can offer no easy solution to the ethical problems involved in the use of test data and clinical personality diagnoses for administrative purposes. The issues are exceedingly complex, but a few comments may be in order.

First, it seems to me that a distinction can be made between test data concerning intellectual aptitudes and capacities on the one hand, and those concerning personality characteristics on the other. Certainly measurement of the latter is still quite primitive, but the critical point is whether management has any moral right to invade the personality. Management's legitimate concern is with performance. Obviously performance is affected by personality characteristics and adjustment, but the question is whether management has a right to go behind the performance to the diagnosis of its causes *when those causes are personal and private.**

The difficulty, of course, is that the restriction imposed by this protection of the individual severely limits the data which can be used for prediction of success or failure on the job. The real reason for management interest in information about the personality is the possibility of improving such predictions. We are interested in an individual's inferiority feelings, or anxieties, or neurotic tendencies because of what they lead us to expect about his performance in given situations. It can even be argued that such knowledge would enable us to protect him from failure and unhappiness, and to protect others from harmful consequences of his personal adjustment.

Yet the use of such knowledge in these ways seems to me to be manipulative in the worst sense of the word. It is permitting the organization to step into the private domain of the person and make decisions for him which only he has the right to make. (Note that, except under the most extreme conditions, a surgeon does not make the final decision to operate, even to save a patient's life. This is felt to be the inviolate right of the person.)

---

* Case law under the Equal Employment Opportunity Act, the Americans with Disabilities Act, and other legislation has developed around ensuring that such tests can be shown to be appropriately related to job requirements, but adherence to these legal provisions does not mean that the underlying assumptions have changed.

For the clinical psychologist to share his diagnosis with the individual *on a confidential basis*, advising him concerning the possible consequences for him and others if he attempts certain types of responsibilities, raises no problems. If it were left to the individual in consultation with the psychologist to decide what use to make of personality measurements and diagnoses, we would have a situation comparable to that which obtains between managers and medical departments in many large companies today. We have come to accept the idea that it is the individual's own responsibility, not that of his superiors, to decide how health considerations should affect his career decisions, except in cases like those of the airplane pilot and the locomotive engineer where the public safety is directly involved. The parallel with "mental health" seems to me a fairly good one.

Tests of capacity—intelligence tests, for example—seems somehow to be different in nature, and the implications with respect to their use don't present the same difficulties. A measure of intelligence is less personal and private than a diagnosis of emotional adjustment. It is more like a measurement of height or of job knowledge. The test is composed not of questions about personal habits and private attitudes, but of impersonal problems to be solved. It is a measurement based on *performance*.

Many personality characteristics and aspects of adjustment are subject to modification through individual effort, certain types of education, and psychotherapy. It seems unjust to predict behavior on the basis of measures and diagnoses of such characteristics, and therefore to deny the individual the opportunity to change. If we limit ourselves to the statement that a given form of behavior or aspect of his performance is unsatisfactory, we leave open to him the possibility that he can do something about it.

In the end, I can only confess to a degree of disquiet over the possibilities for manipulation and exploitation of my fellow human beings inherent in the administrative use of personality tests and clinical diagnoses of adjustment for purposes of placement. I view with even greater concern the probability that the predictive value of such instruments will be increased substantially during the next decade or two. The issues involved will then be intensified. This whole field of selection, promotion, and placement presents a substantial challenge to the ethical values of professional management. We cannot afford to dismiss the issues by defending unilaterally the needs of the organization, or to look the other way in the hope that they will go away. If we do either, we run the risk that a growing public concern will lead one day to legislative restrictions further curtailing management's freedom of action. More importantly, we put materialistic economic considerations ahead of ethical ones and thus place ourselves as managers in a position few of us would care to defend.

REFERENCES

American Management Association, *Handbook of Wage and Salary Administration*. New York: 1950.

Belcher, David W., *Wage and Salary Administration*. Englewood Cliffs, N.J.: Prentice-Hall, Inc., 1955.

Employee Relations Department, Esso Standard Oil Company, *Made to Measure*. New York: 1953.

Foundation for Research on Human Behavior, *Assessing Managerial Potential*. Ann Arbor, Mich.: 1958.

Jacques, Elliot, *Measurement of Responsibility*. London: Tavistock Publications, Ltd., 1956.

National Industrial Conference Board, Inc., *Employee Salary Plans in Operation*, Studies in Personnel Policy, no. 100, 1949.

Whyte, William H., Jr., *The Organization Man*. New York: Simon & Schuster, Inc., 1956.

SELECTED REFERENCES TO THE ANNOTATED EDITION

Arthur, Michael B., Barbara Lawrence, and Douglas T. Hall, *Handbook of Career Theory*. Cambridge, England: Cambridge University Press, 1989.

DISCUSSION QUESTIONS FOR CHAPTER 7

1. McGregor depended on "collective and individual bargaining, within a framework of measurement" to be the ultimate determinants of fair pay and promotional procedures. Is this still valid today, and, if not, what are the alternatives?

2. Given an adequate base salary, McGregor argued that small incremental distinctions in pay are not likely to provide genuine motivation. Yet, today we see that the vast majority of pay systems are dominated by these small incremental distinctions. Why do you think this is the case?

3. Does management have a moral right to administer personality and intelligence tests to job applicants and employees and then use the data to guide decisions on hiring and promotion?

THE SCANLON PLAN

In devoting all of Chapter 8 to the Scanlon plan, McGregor risks being seen as advocating one of the management "gimmicks" of which he is so critical. Thus, he emphasizes at the outset that it "is not a formula, a program, or a set of procedures." Instead, he states that the Scanlon plan "is a way of industrial life—a philosophy of management—which rests on theoretical assumptions entirely consistent with Theory Y." McGregor first highlights the way the Scanlon plan is designed to share "economic gains from improvements in performance," which are derived from "a ratio between the total manpower costs of the organization and a measure of output such as total sales or value added by manufacture." He notes that sharing gains at the level of the business has the effect of "promoting collaboration within an interdependent system. Competition is minimized within the organization and maximized with respect to other firms in the industry." Also, because the payments are made on a monthly basis, there is a "psychologically meaningful cause-and-effect connection" between "the behavior and the reward." In these respects, the Scanlon plan connects to McGregor's third assumption for Theory Y, stated in Chapter 4, that "commitment to objectives is a function of the rewards associated with their achievement." Still, McGregor cautions that, based on these features alone, the Scanlon plan would "simply be another example of the many varieties of incentive and profit-sharing plans found in industry today."

What distinguishes the Scanlon plan is the emphasis on the participation of the entire workforce, or, as McGregor puts it, "a formal method providing the opportunity for every member of the organization to contribute his brains and ingenuity as well as his physical effort to the improvement of organizational effectiveness." Structurally, the Scanlon plan features a network of departmental committees of workers and lower-level supervision, combined with a "'screening committee' consisting of representatives of the work force and of higher management."[1] "The mechanics of the participation," McGregor notes, "are relatively unimportant; the underlying assumptions about human beings which are reflected are crucial." He is referring, of course, to the reliance that is placed on the "know-how, the ingenuity, the innovativeness of all the human resources in the organization," which stands in contrast to the "narrow and insulting conception" that "if ... people would only do more of what they are told to do, productivity would rise and the economy would be better off."

McGregor's interest in Scanlon plans led to an enduring legacy at MIT, where companies involved in Scanlon plans and other participative gain-sharing programs would regularly meet, and each year an MIT doctoral student was awarded a Scanlon Plan fellowship. In reflecting on this legacy, Robert McKersie comments:

> *McGregor's endorsement of the Scanlon plan spurred considerable interest on the part of labor and management—*

[1] Note that McGregor indicates throughout the book that it will be unions who are the representatives of the workforce. In fact, such a representative structure is limited under U.S. law in the absence of a union.

leading to its adoption in scores and scores of organizations during the '50s and '60s. For many years Scanlon Plan Associates—a grouping of companies and unions using the plan—met annually at MIT to share experiences. Other gain-sharing plans came on the scene during the '60s and '70s with names such as Rucker and Improshare. By the turn of the century, however, gain sharing could be seen as having gone "generic," with companies tailoring programs to their special circumstances, but in all cases emphasizing the themes of participation, achievement, and rewards—and in so doing giving tangible form to the precepts of Theory Y.

One individual closely associated with Joe Scanlon during his days at MIT was George Shultz, who found great value in the practical advice of Joe Scanlon: "Share the problems with all members of the organization, give them a stake in improving performance, and review and learn from experience." These guidelines would characterize Shultz's leadership as his career unfolded after MIT, as dean of the University of Chicago's Graduate School of Business and culminating in four cabinet posts during the Nixon and Reagan years, including service as secretary of state during the 1980s, when the world witnessed historic changes in relations between the USSR and the United States.

Although McGregor was careful to distinguish gain sharing from other incentive and profit-sharing plans, research on all of these arrangements has unambiguously demonstrated that more participative approaches outperform simple incentive programs.[2] While this concept has been codified as part of what might be termed "best practice" when it comes to gain-sharing, goal-sharing, and profit-sharing plans, there are still a remarkably high number of these various plans that are instituted primarily as incentive programs, without a robust mechanism for employee participation.

[2] Denis Collins, *Gainsharing and Power: Lessons from Six Scanlon Plans*, Ithaca, N.Y.: Cornell University Press, 1998; Jeffrey B. Arthur and Lynda Aiman-Smith, "Gainsharing and Organizational Learning: An Analysis of Employee Suggestions over Time," *Academy of Management Journal*, vol. 44, pp. 737–754, August 2001; Jeffrey Arthur and Dong One Kim, "The Effect of Employee Suggestions and Union Support on Plant Performance under Gainsharing" *IRRA Proceedings*, Champaign-Urbana, Ill.: IRRA, 2002, P. 16; Kenneth Mericle and Dong-One Kim, *Gainsharing and Goalsharing: Aligning Pay and Strategic Goals*, New York: Praeger, 2004; Corey Rosen and Ed Carberry, *Ownership Management: Building a Culture of Lasting Innovation*, Washington, D.C.: National Center for Employee Ownership, 2002; Patrick McHugh, Joel Cutcher-Gershenfeld, and Diane Bridge, "Examining Structure and Process in ESOP Firms: Employee Influence, Plan Design, and Information Sharing," *Personnel Review*, vol. 34, no. 3, March 2005, pp. 277–293.

CHAPTER 8

THE SCANLON PLAN

Management by integration and self-control can take many forms. One of the most unusual of these is the Scanlon Plan. Out of his deep interest in union-management cooperation, the late Joseph Scanlon evolved a collaborative strategy which has achieved solid results, in both economic and human terms, in a number of industrial companies. Scanlon died in 1956. His work is being ably carried on at MIT today by his close friend and successor, Frederick Lesieur.

The Scanlon Plan is not a formula, a program, or a set of procedures. it is a way of industrial life—a philosophy of management—which rests on theoretical assumptions entirely consistent with Theory Y. The Scanlon Plan differs from target setting in that it is applied to the whole organization rather than to superior-subordinate pairs or to small groups. However, the underlying strategic considerations are very similar.

On the site www.scanlonleader.org, Robert Sligh, president of Sligh Furniture, comments:

The Scanlon Plan is a fabric that becomes interwoven into the organization. It's not a book. It's not a bonus plan. It's more than the Principles. Perhaps the essence of it is the Equity triangle: a fair and balanced return for customers, employees, and owners.

The plan embodies two central features which in their operation bring about profound changes in organizational relationships, attitudes, and practices. Scanlon's discovery that these two features would encourage the development of a different set of managerial assumptions about organized human effort represents a social invention of considerable significance. Neither of these features alone would be likely to bring about a major change; linked together, however, they represent a powerful system of organizational "control."

COST-REDUCTION SHARING

The first feature is a means of sharing the economic gains from improvements in organizational performance. It is not profit sharing in the conventional sense at all, but a unique kind of cost-reduction sharing. It is not a substitute for a normal, competitive wage and salary structure, but is built on top of it.

This method for sharing cost-reduction savings utilizes a ratio between the total manpower costs of the organization and a measure of output such as total sales or value added by manufacture. The latter index in the ratio can only be derived after considerable study and analysis of the particular company, and it is relatively unique to the situation. Allowances are made, of course, for product mix, inventory, work in process, etc. In most companies a ratio can be developed which turns out to have been relatively stable for considerable periods of time. Sharp fluctuations can usually be traced to major technological or economic changes.

This ratio is not seen as an exact, infallible, permanent measure. Careful study of the company's financial records, a good deal of common sense, and a lot of mutual discussion enter into its determination. It is subject to change from time to time, as circumstances warrant, and the history of Scanlon companies indicates that these changes are made without difficulty when the need arises.

Improvement of the ratio represents an over-all economic gain for the organization. Some portion of the resultant savings (sometimes 50 per cent, often 75 per cent, occasionally 100 per cent) are paid to participants in the Plan on a monthly basis as a percentage of their base wages or salaries. Normally, all members of the organization except possibly the very top management group participate in this economic reward for improvement. Such a reward, properly developed, gains genuine acceptance (it is perceived to be equitable) and, in addition, provides genuine motivation. It is a means for promoting collaboration within an interdependent system. Competition is minimized within the organization and maximized with respect to other firms in the industry.

This is a key underlying assumption—maximizing external competition, while minimizing internal competition. Seth G. Atwood, founder of Atwood Vacuum Machine Company, connects business success to this orientation around internal and external competition on www.scanlonleader.org:

The adoption of the Scanlon Plan was the most important business decision made in over 50 active years. I'm totally convinced that the money spent, as a result of the plan was a fraction of the money saved. Furthermore, the total reorientation of all employees was profound. All employees participated in trying to improve the success of the company. Instead of viewing management as the enemy, the company employees were able to work together with management towards the goal of outperforming the competition.

An important characteristic of this method of measurement is that it is directly related to the success of the members in improving the over-all economic success of the organization. The ordinary profit-sharing plan lacks this direct relationship. Profits may reflect circumstances and factors almost completely irrelevant to the efforts of the members of the organization. I knew of an instance a few years ago, for example, where nearly three-quarters of the profits of the enterprise over a period of several years resulted from the manipulations of the treasurer in the raw material market. The profit-sharing bonus paid to the employees of this company had little connection with their contribution to the success of the enterprise.

Employees under a Scanlon Plan, on the other hand, are able to trace directly the results of various changes and innovations, stimulated by their efforts, upon the bonus, and thus to see the connection between their behavior and organizational achievement. The result is a very real and quite sophisticated understanding of the economics of the firm, gained through direct experience. Economic education of the work force is never a problem in a Scanlon factory.

There are many examples in Scanlon companies of profitable orders for products obtained after the employees had persuaded management to bid for the business at prices which appeared initially to be ridiculously low. Given a full understanding of the competitive situation and a knowledge of existing costs, the members of the organization were willing to exercise their ingenuity to help management put itself in a strong competitive position. Commitment to the economic objectives of the enterprise is clearly evident at every level and in every function of these companies.

A third feature of the economic reward is that it is reasonably well related temporally to the behavior which produced it. An annual profit-sharing bonus is a reward which has little relationship to daily behavior. A monthly payment carries with it a psychologically meaningful cause-and-effect connection because the behavior and the reward are reasonably close together in time.*

EFFECTIVE PARTICIPATION

If the Scanlon Plan consisted of nothing but this measure of organizational effectiveness and the bonus, there would be some reason for singling it out for special attention because of the features mentioned

---

* Although the lack of a close cause-and-effect relationship between behavior and reward may be less effective, this concern with behavior and rewards is, in itself, a bit jarring given McGregor's dominant focus on intrinsic rewards.

above, but fundamentally it would simply be another example of the many varieties of incentive and profit-sharing plans found in industry today. The distinguishing feature of the Scanlon Plan is the coupling of this incentive with a second feature: a formal method providing an opportunity for every member of the organization to contribute his brains and ingenuity as well as his physical effort to the improvement of organizational effectiveness. This is the integrative principle in operation. It is the means by which rich opportunities are provided every member of the organization to satisfy his higher-level needs through efforts directed toward the objectives of the enterprise.

Dick Ruch, retired chairman of the board at Herman Miller and author of *Leaders and Followers*, states:

Participative management is fundamental to the Scanlon Process … it has the potential of using all of our minds, imaginations, and talents rather than just those of a few (www.scanlonleader.org).

Even the repetitive worker at the bottom of the hierarchy is potentially more than a pair of hands. He is a human resource. His know-how and ingenuity, properly utilized, may make a far greater difference to the success of the enterprise than any improvement in his physical effort, although of course his effort is not unimportant. Moreover, he achieves recognition and other important social and ego satisfactions from this utilization of his capacities.

We hear a great deal of talk about improved productivity and its significance in our total economic picture. Many of those who talk the loudest conceive of productivity solely in terms of the physical output of production and clerical workers. If such people would only do more of what they are told to do, productivity would rise and the economy would be better off. This message is to be heard on every hand today. It is a true virtue of the Scanlon Plan that it scraps completely this narrow and insulting conception of the worth of the human being in the industrial enterprise. Productivity is seen in terms of the over-all effectiveness of the organization, and everything that contributes to it is valued. The distinctive potential contribution of the human being in contrast to the machine, *at every level of the organization*, stems from his capacity to think, to plan, to exercise judgment, to be creative, to direct and control his own behavior. In contrast to the philosophy of traditional incentive plans and the conventional practices of industrial engineering, the Scanlon Plan encourages *and rewards* the distinctively human contribution.

The mechanics of the second feature of the Scanlon Plan consists in a series of committees whose purpose is to receive, discuss, and evaluate every means that anyone can think of for improving the ratio, and to put into effect those that are considered to be workable. Representatives from every group and function in the organization serve on these committees. Departmental committees of workers and lower-level supervision are empowered to put into effect ideas appropriate to their level. Those suggestions which have broader implications are referred to a higher level "screening committee" consisting of representatives of the work force and of higher management.

While this machinery provides channels for evaluation and action, the formalities of its operation are minimal. The committees may meet at regular intervals, but at the departmental level, at least, a committee "meeting" may consist of a five-minute discussion between three or four people on the factory floor, which is followed by adoption of an idea. Minutes of formal meetings are kept to ensure that ideas are not lost and that the screening committee is aware of all actions that are taken anywhere in the organization.

In this fashion the concept of participation is given a meaning which everyone can understand. The fact of interdependence is accepted; reliance is placed on the know-how, the ingenuity, the innovativeness of all the human resources of the organization. The mechanics of the participation are relatively unimportant; the underlying assumptions about human beings which are reflected are crucial.

Participation in Scanlon companies is greatly different from that obtained with conventional suggestion plans. There are no forms to fill out, no impersonal "suggestion boxes," no remote committees to evaluate the merits of the idea in secret. The individual in his own work setting, or at a meeting of the screening committee, discusses his idea, participates in the evaluation of it, obtains recognition if it is a good idea or encouragement to work further on it if it is promising but still impractical. Moreover, he is in a situation which encourages him to seek and obtain help anywhere in the organization in developing the idea rather than one which encourages secrecy in order to prevent someone from stealing his idea and cheating him out of an award. The focus is not on competing for awards but on improving the effectiveness of the enterprise. The economic gains are shared, but the social and ego satisfactions are his alone.

The evidence for the significance of these differences is readily observable in any Scanlon company. There is no need for periodic propaganda campaigns to keep suggestions coming in. Companies which have had suggestion programs for years before the advent of the Scanlon Plan find themselves flooded with economically significant ideas which never appeared before. The proportion of suggestions which get a $5 award, not because they contribute anything to the success of the enterprise but because nobody knows what else to do about them, shrinks to zero. Carefully contrived and intelligently developed collaborative studies of organizational problems are common.

In one company the possible savings to be obtained through the use of fork-lift trucks came up for discussion at a department meeting. Out of this discussion there emerged three months later a complete study by a self-appointed group of employees of the savings which could be effected, and a recommendation for purchase based on a penetrating examination of initial and maintenance costs of the various types of lift trucks available. The president of the company commented that he would have had to pay a couple of thousand dollars to an outside consultant for an analysis which would have been as thorough and as competent.*

EFFECTS ON RELATIONS

There are literally hundreds of examples in Scanlon Plan companies of improvements in the relationship between functional groups which occur once the Plan gets under way. A single illustration will serve to indicate the kind of thing that happens.

In one company there was a substantial amount of friction and antagonism between the work force and the engineering department. When workers would discover what they believed to be an error in design, and would call the engineers to bring it to their attention, the stock answer was: "Follow the blueprint."

Since engineers, like all other human beings, are fallible, mistakes did occur. The workers took malicious pleasure in following the blueprint exactly, even though they knew they were making a costly mistake for the company. A common expression among the work force when a piece of equipment went out the door en route to the customer was: "There she goes; she'll be back." The complete lack of confidence either way between workers and engineers led to a considerable amount of behavior inimical to the organization as a whole.

Since the advent of the Scanlon Plan, this relationship has changed. Both groups have a stake in a common objective; they recognize that collaboration toward that objective is to their mutual interest. As a result, a question raised by a worker concerning the correctness of a detail in a blueprint will bring an engineer to the work

---

* The subsequent literature on worker participation, knowledge-driven work, and related topics features countless additional examples of employee initiative enabled by participative systems. (See Thomas Kochan, Harry Katz, and Nancy Mower, *Worker Participation and American Unions: Threat or Opportunity?* Kalamazoo, Mich.: W. E. Upjohn Press, 1984.

floor immediately. The engineers have gained considerable respect for the know-how of the work force, and the latter have come to regard the engineers as a genuine source of help.

The changed relationship was evidenced a couple of years after the plan went into effect. The company's business was off, general economic conditions were poor, and there had been some layoffs. A substantial new order was received in the late spring, but the design work on it would take several months. If the normal company practice of shutting down the plant for summer vacation were to be followed, the result would be additional lost time for the work force until the completion of the design work on the new order. Accordingly, the suggestion was made to the screening committee that the engineers change their vacation plans (which naturally included travel reservations, arrangements for renting cottages, etc.) to work on the design through the normal vacation period. The screening committee reaction was that it was a fine idea but that the engineers would never agree to the disruption in their plans. The answer from the group of workers who had submitted the idea was simple and direct: "Oh, we have already talked with the engineers, and they have agreed to shift their plans if you will approve the idea."

The atmosphere in a Scanlon Plan company is not always a peaceful one. There are arguments, disagreements, hot discussions. The distinctive feature of these, however, is that they are almost always centered around the problems of improved performance. Individuals at every level have a stake in the success of the enterprise, and it is a stake which goes well beyond the straight economic rewards that are involved. There is genuine integration, genuine commitment to organizational objectives, because it represents the best way for members to achieve their individual goals, whether these are related to basic biological needs, social needs, egoistic or self-actualization needs. The linking of the two central features of the Scanlon Plan provides a wealth of opportunity for achieving satisfaction of all kinds of human needs. But because human beings differ in their goals and in their perceptions of how best these may be achieved, one finds a normal, healthy disagreement about ways and means. The participative feature of the Plan helps managers to discover the true value of the organization's human resources and in time generates a degree of confidence "downward" which is amazingly different from what one finds in the ordinary company.

These changes in managerial attitude do not always come easily. There is often some tough learning involved, particularly for lower levels of line management. It is not easy for the foreman or the superintendent to adjust to what may seem to him to be a severe loss of power. He is faced squarely with his actual dependence downward and laterally.

As pointed out above, the Plan in operation tends to resolve many of the typical problems of staff-line relationships. While there is frequently a fair amount of initial wear and tear, mutual confidence and collaboration between staff and line eventually develop. Staff groups become resources to the organization rather than policemen. The Plan makes no distinction between "productive" groups and "burden" groups.

The Scanlon Plan cannot be operated on the basis of formulas, gimmicks, or packaged programs. It is truly a way of life, with infinite variations appropriate to the circumstances of the individual company. Scanlon companies reveal the presence of underlying assumptions about human behavior similar to those of Theory Y. The principle of integration receives daily confirmation in practice.

SOME QUESTIONS

There are several unanswered questions concerning the wider applicability of this philosophy of management which deserve consideration. In the first place, the Plan has so far been applied almost entirely in relatively small companies of a few hundred employees. The largest example is a company of 8,000 employees. Consideration of the way in which the Plan operates indicates that there would be obvious difficulties in applying it to a big organization. The possibility does exist, however, of utilizing the Scanlon approach in the context of divisional "profit centers" which are popular among decentralized big companies today.

A more critical question concerns the applicability of the Scanlon philosophy in situations which are highly automated, and where the technology is of a kind that leaves little room for improvement and change originating anywhere but in engineering or research. Some of us who have watched the development of the Scanlon Plan are optimistic about its applicability even under such conditions. The influence of human behavior upon organization success—in maintenance, in construction, in the clerical force, in management generally—even though the operation is highly automated, is more substantial than most people recognize. Sooner or later, an opportunity will come to test this optimism in a real situation. To date, the managements of such companies or divisions have been too skeptical to give the idea a try.

Another question concerns the relation of the Scanlon Plan to general economic conditions. Some of the earlier developments of Scanlon's ideas took place in the depths of the Depression in companies which were either in or on the verge of bankruptcy. Critics of the philosophy were quick to point out that the highly collaborative efforts they observed were a function of the strong motivation of employees to protect their jobs. The conclusion they drew was that the Scanlon Plan might operate under severely depressed economic conditions, but that it would certainly not be successful in boom times. Since the war the Plan has flourished in companies experiencing boom conditions. The critics have argued that, of course, the Plan should be expected to operate successfully when the financial rewards are large, but that it would not operate successfully in a depression!

The point is, of course, that the motivation is different under different economic conditions. This experience of Scanlon companies provides interesting evidence in support of the motivational ideas presented in Chapter 3. There are psychological gains to be realized, regardless of the economic situation of the company. There is an important contrast here again between the Scanlon Plan and the typical profit-sharing plan. Many profit-sharing plans have gone by the board when the economic conditions were such that the profit-sharing bonus was materially reduced or eliminated. In contrast, a number of Scanlon companies have gone through both boom and depression times without losing their underlying commitment. Since the Scanlon Plan is a way of life rather than a particular form of financial incentive plan, one would expect exactly this result.

The point is often raised that successful, efficiently operated companies would be ill-advised to adopt a Scanlon Plan because the possibilities for improving a properly developed ratio would be infinitesimal. It has come as a distinct shock to the top managements of such companies who have adopted the plan that substantial—not minor—improvements have occurred. In one instance the President simply refused to believe that a 20 per cent improvement had occurred until he reexamined in detail all the data on which the ratio had been based. He had been absolutely sure that his company was so efficiently managed that a two or three percent improvement would be maximal.

Another question concerns the problem of "selling" this philosophy to an organization. Many people believe that the success of the Plan is directly attributable to the remarkable personality of Joseph Scanlon, and that the philosophy could not have been sold and would not have been workable if it had not been for his direct influence. There are today a number of Scanlon companies the members of which never met Joe Scanlon. The plans were installed during Joe's last illness or since his death. Fred Lesieur is indeed a remarkable personality also, but he is a different personality than Joe, and he operates in his own fashion.

A recent analysis of failed incentive plans in a set of Hewlett-Packard facilities illustrates the continued relevance of the basic principles underlying the Scanlon plan. In commenting on the analysis, MIT Professor Thomas Kochan summarized four lessons about Scanlon plans and other pay-for-performance plans that were developed by Fred Lesieur, a protégé of Joseph Scanlon. Kochan notes that Lesieur would frequently present in MIT Sloan School classes and remind students that, for performance plans to be successful and sustainable, they must

1. Provide for an independent employee voice and participation in (*a*) the decision to initiate a new plan, (*b*) its design, (*c*) the generation of suggestions for continuous improvement, and (*d*) the plan's administration and adjustment.

2. Cover all employees in a facility so as to encourage cross-occupational and cross-level cooperation, not competition.

3. Build on, and not substitute for, fair base wages and benefits.

4. Recognize that the Achilles heel of any performance-sharing formula lies in the challenges posed to it by changes in technology, market conditions, product mix, or organizational strategies and leadership.

As Professor Kochan notes, these principles pretty much account for what Beer and Cannon report happened in these Hewlett-Packard (HP) cases and point to the limitations of many pay-for-performance plans that are not aligned with these principles.*

---

* Martha Lagace, "Pay-for-Performance Doesn't Always Pay Off," (featuring the work of Michael Beer, Nancy Katz, and Mark Connon), *Harvard Business School Working Knowledge for Business Leaders*, April 14, 2003.

It does require a forceful personality somewhere in the situation to help bring about the initial willingness to undertake the risks involved in establishing this new managerial philosophy. Obviously, such a broad shift in managerial philosophy will not occur without skillful leadership. The usual experience has been that such a personality was present inside the organization and that he provided the leadership, while Scanlon or Lesieur has filled the roles of catalyst, teacher, consultant, and sometimes severe critic.

The Scanlon philosophy has been successful in both unionized and nonunionized plants. The presence of an effective union appears to be a positive factor in the success of the Plan. It provides a formal means for communication and discussion during the early stages, particularly in the development of the ratio. It provides a somewhat more organized pressure to keep management "on its toes" as the Plan gets under way. It ensures that there will be no tendency to try to substitute bonus earnings for a competitive wage structure. While there has been an occasional private expression of thought that perhaps successful operation of such a plan would obviate the necessity for collective bargaining, experience has not borne out this prediction. On the contrary, the managements of unionized Scanlon companies tend to be rather more positive about the values of a sound collective bargaining relationship than are many managements in other unionized firms.

One rather significant thing is the complete absence of concern on the part of Scanlon managements over the problem of managerial prerogatives. The protection of their authority is not a central preoccupation. Their confidence in their own employees is such that they feel no defensiveness about their "right to run the business." Given the kind of integration which is characteristic of these companies, the question of control, in the traditional sense, simply ceases to be a meaningful issue.

During discussions which take place in Scanlon Plan Conferences at MIT, managers from companies contemplating adoption of the Plan regularly raise questions about the possible disasters that could occur *if* economic or technological changes dictated a change in the ratio and the employees would not agree to it, or *if* employees took advantage of their access to information about the economic situation of the company, or *if* a variety of other possibilities of employee infringement on managerial prerogatives were to arise.

Charles Conrad, founder of Thermatron, reinforces McGregor's observations:

The Scanlon Plan or philosophy is not something to only give lip service to. It must be a dedicated belief by the company founders, owners, and the management people that this is the way to operate a company. It will not function in a dictatorship style operation (www.scanlonleader.org).

The fascinating aspect of these discussions is the sheer inability of Scanlon company managements to understand what is worrying the questioners. *Of course* they run their businesses, *of course* they make the essential managerial decisions. Where did the idea originate that the Scanlon Plan weakens management? At the same time they reveal by their examples as well as their attitudes that authority in the conventional sense is not the method of control upon which they rely. Persuasion, logical argument, professional help, the joint recognition of the objective requirements of the situation—these are the influences which determine their behavior and that of the members of their organizations.

In conclusion, it is interesting to note that the issue of individual differentials in economic rewards tied to individual contributions to the success of the company is simply not an issue in these organizations. Many of them have abandoned individual incentive plans in the process of adopting the Scanlon philosophy. In some cases fears were expressed that the high producers would lower their performance under the new arrangements. Not only has this not occurred, but the general level of productivity, measured in the industrial engineer's terms, has almost always increased. The proverbial task of selling refrigerators to Eskimos would be easy compared to the task of selling a traditional incentive plan or a merit rating plan in most Scanlon companies. Both equity and motivation are achieved by more appropriate means.

REFERENCES

Krulee, Gilbert K., "The Scanlon Plan: Cooperation through Participation," *The Journal of Business*, vol. 28, no. 2, 1955.

Lesieur, Frederick G. (ed.), *The Scanlon Plan*. Cambridge, Mass., and New York: Technology Press and John Wiley & Sons, Inc., 1958.

DISCUSSION QUESTIONS FOR CHAPTER 8

1. Although both are important, which aspect of a Scanlon plan is *more* important, (1) the sharing of gains from cost-reduction ideas or (2) the principle of worker participation in the process?

2. McGregor was drawn to the way Scanlon plans minimize internal competition in an organization, while maximizing external competition. Is this approach still valid today?

3. Research unambiguously finds that more participative gain-sharing programs outperform simple incentive schemes that lack a participative component. Why is it, then, that so many gain-sharing programs—perhaps a majority—lack a robust participative component?

PARTICIPATION IN PERSPECTIVE

In the beginning of Chapter 9, McGregor observes that "participation is one of the most misunderstood ideas that have emerged from the field of human relations." Although a vast volume of scholarship on this subject has been produced since he wrote these lines, there is still a great deal of misunderstanding about the concept of participation. Knowledge has advanced on some of the issues highlighted in this chapter, such as the different degrees to which individuals and groups can participate in a decision—from awareness to consultation to consensus to delegation. But there is still confusion today between, as McGregor put it, "making people *feel* important and *making* people important."

McGregor deftly points out that many of the concerns about participation are, in fact, Theory X assumptions in disguise. For example, he notes that some managers fear that employees who are "given the opportunity to influence decisions affecting them ... will soon want to participate in matters which should be none of their concern." In fact, if there is a reciprocal interest in employee growth and development, McGregor notes, there should be the "expectation that employees will become involved in an increasing range of decision-making activities." When examples are brought up to illustrate how employees intrude on what should be management prerogatives, McGregor notes that this "reverses cause and effect." "This suspicious, almost paranoid, attitude of management," McGregor points out, "actually tends to *promote* interference with management prerogatives."

Participation is not and should be seen as "a panacea, a manipulative device, a gimmick, or a threat," McGregor notes. Instead, it should be seen as "a natural concomitant of management by integration and self-control."

The analysis in this chapter barely scratches the surface of what has become a broad range of related literature on participation in decision making that spans many fields of study. McGregor's unique contribution remains centered on bringing to the surface the underlying assumptions about people that motivate the participative efforts.

CHAPTER 9

PARTICIPATION IN PERSPECTIVE

Participation is one of the most misunderstood ideas that have emerged from the field of human relations. It is praised by some, condemned by others, and used with considerable success by still others. The differences in point of view between its proponents and its critics are about as great as those between the leaders of Iron Curtain countries and those of the Free World when they use the term "democracy."

Some proponents of participation give the impression that it is a magic formula which will eliminate conflict and disagreement and come pretty close to solving all of management's problems. These enthusiasts appear to believe that people yearn to participate, much as children of a generation or two ago yearned for Castoria. They give the impression that it is a formula which can be applied by any manager regardless of his skill, that virtually no preparation is necessary for its use, and that it can spring full-blown into existence and transform industrial relationships overnight.

Some critics of participation, on the other hand, see it as a form of managerial abdication. It is a dangerous idea that will undermine management prerogatives and almost certainly get out of control. It is a concept which for them fits the pattern of "soft" management exclusively. It wastes time, lowers efficiency, and weakens management's effectiveness.

Benjamin Schneider, professor of psychology (emeritus) at the University of Maryland, comments that

As a young Ph.D. student in industrial psychology, finding McGregor (through Ed Schein's little 1965 book called Organizational Psychology*) was a very significant event in my academic life. I have benefited ever since. McGregor's book, along with those by Likert and Argyris, literally made organizational behavior. The book framed the organization-employee-manager relationship in stark terms that made it clear to everyone that worker psychology was a function of the implementation of the manager's philosophy (or cosmology, as he later called it). The book is still central to the field today because it simultaneously deals with how managers should think about employees as adult humans (see Argyris, too) and how such an approach to employees in no ways diminshes the responsibility managers retain for effectiveness in the workplace. My favorite quote from the book is "Participation is not co-equivalent with the abdication of responsibility." This balancing act is still the major management challenge, and McGregor did the best job early on of presenting it in ways that offered the possibility of achieving it.*

A third group of managers view participation as a useful item in their bag of managerial tricks. It is for them a manipulative device for getting people to do what they want, under conditions which delude the "participators" into thinking they have had a voice in decision making. The idea is to handle them so skillfully that they come up with the answer which the manager had in the first place, but believing it was their own. This is a way of "making people feel important" which these managers are quick to emphasize as a significant motivational tool of management.* (It is important to note the distinction between making people *feel* important and *making* people important.)

---

* McGregor nicely illustrates the importance of underlying assumptions in explaining the intent behind managerial behavior—as well as the central importance of distilling the intent from the behavior.

Naturally, there are severe critics of this manipulative approach to participation, and they tend to conceive of all participation as taking this form.

A fourth group of managers makes successful use of participation, but they don't think of it as a panacea or magic formula. They do not share either the unrestrained enthusiasm of the faddists or the fears of the critics. They would flatly refuse to employ participation as a manipulative sales device.

Among all of these groups is a rather general but tacit agreement—incorrect, I believe—that participation applies to groups and not to individuals. None of them appears to view it as having any relationship to delegation. After all, it has a different name! Many of the strong proponents of delegation have no use whatever for participation.

In the light of all this it is not surprising that a fair number of thoughtful managers view this whole subject with some skepticism.

The effective use of participation is a consequence of a managerial point of view which includes confidence in the potentialities of subordinates, awareness of management's dependency downwards, and a desire to avoid some of the negative consequences of emphasis on personal authority. It is consistent with Theory Y—with management by integration and self-control. It consists basically in creating opportunities under suitable conditions for people to influence decisions affecting them. That influence can vary from a little to a lot.

It is perhaps most useful to consider participation in terms of a range of managerial actions. At one end of the range the exercise of authority in the decision-making process is almost complete and participation is negligible. At the other end of the range the exercise of authority is relatively small and participation is maximum. There is no implication that more participation is better than less. The degree of participation which will be suitable depends upon a variety of factors, including the problem or issue, the attitudes and past experience of the subordinates, the manager's skill, and the point of view alluded to above.*

Let us suppose that a manager has made a decision which will affect his subordinates. The circumstances are such that he feels that he cannot permit them to share in making this decision, but he is concerned to have them accept it with the best grace possible. He might hold a discussion in which he would inform them of the decision and reasons for it, and give them an opportunity to raise questions about it. His purpose would be to test the decision to see if it is acceptable. If he finds that it is strongly resented, he may be tempted to modify it rather than to risk the possibilities that it may be sabotaged. If it is not strongly resisted, his subordinates have at least had an opportunity to understand why he has made the decision and to clarify any aspects of it which are obscure. Such a discussion as this—when held under circumstances that permit genuine interaction—involves a limited degree of participation.

A slightly different situation might arise when a superior, having made a decision, would discuss with his subordinates the best way of implementing it. Often the implementation of a decision can occur in various ways, and it may make relatively little difference to the superior which of these alternatives is chosen, so long as the decision is carried out. The subordinates can have a voice in this matter which under some circumstances can be quite important to them. Such a situation involves somewhat more participation.

A third example involving still more participation would be the situation in which the superior discussed a pending decision with his subordinates before making it final. Under these conditions he would

---

* This spectrum from highly authoritarian to highly participative decision making is at the core of scholarship in a wide range of fields, from political science to sociology to decision science to industrial relations. [See, for example, David E. Bell, Howard Raiffa, and Amos Tversky (eds.), *Decision Making: Descriptive, Normative, and Prescriptive Interactions*, Cambridge: Cambridge University Press, 1988; Jeff Hyman and Robert Mason, *Managing Employee Involvement and Participation*, Thousand Oaks, Calif.: Sage, 1995.]

be ready to consider modifying his proposed decision or substituting another for it, depending upon the considerations which arose in discussion. The decision would still be his to make, but he would make it in the light of the discussion.

A still greater degree of participation would be involved if the superior were to present to his subordinates a problem facing him with the request that they help him find the best solution to it. He would not necessarily commit himself in advance to accepting any solution agreeable to them, but the understanding would be that if they could find a solution which he felt to be workable he would accept it.

Finally, there are some situations in which it is a matter of relative indifference to the superior which of several alternative decisions are made. These may be ones in which management has only a small stake and subordinates have a large one. Under these conditions the superior might say to his subordinates, "I will accept any decision which is agreeable to you."

Any of the above examples could occur at any level of an organization. Participation is not confined to the relationship between a first-line supervisor and his workers. It can occur between a president and his executive committee. Moreover, since there are many managerial decisions which affect a single subordinate, it is equally applicable to the individual or to the group. The kind of participation which will be utilized will vary depending upon the level of the organization as well as upon the other factors mentioned above.

The superior who is considering the use of participation will examine his strategy and the reasons for it in advance. If his subordinates are unaccustomed to having any influence on decisions affecting them, he will be unlikely to present a major issue to them on the first occasion, or to give them complete freedom of choice. He will be careful to indicate clearly the limits within which he is prepared to have them influence the decision. In making use of participation under these circumstances, he recognizes that he is beginning what may be a lengthy process of growth and learning for his subordinates, and for himself as well. He will plan to have them learn to crawl before they attempt to walk or run.

Since one of the major purposes of the use of participation is to encourage the growth of subordinates and their ability to accept responsibility, the superior will be concerned to pick appropriate problems or issues for discussion and decision. These will be matters of some significance to subordinates; otherwise they will see little point in their involvement. Some managers have limited their use of participation to subjects of so little concern to subordinates that there is no opportunity for growth. It may be fine to begin a participative approach at lower levels of the organization by asking employees to deal with such questions as car pools, United Fund drives, and the like. If the process stops here, however, the subordinates will soon recognize that management has no intention of permitting them to influence decisions of any moment, even though such decisions may have important consequences for them. The reaction then is likely to be a negative one to the whole idea, and the managerial conclusion that employees are not interested in accepting responsibility will be entirely correct.

Of course, there are some risks connected with the use of participation. All significant managerial activities involve risk, and this is no exception. The usual fear is that if employees are given an opportunity to influence decisions affecting them, they will soon want to participate in matters which should be none of their concern. Managements who express this fear most acutely tend to have a very narrow conception of the issues which should concern employees. If management's concern is with the growth of employees and their increasing ability to undertake responsibility, there will of course be an expectation that employees will become involved in an increasing range of decision-making activities.*

---

* Work redesign to foster increased participation is an important legacy of the points introduced here. (See, for example, J. Richard Hackman and Greg R. Oldham, *Work Redesign*, Reading, Mass.: Addison-Wesley, 1980.)

As pointed out in Chapter 8, the experience in companies that have acquired the point of view toward participation described above—some of the Scanlon Plan companies, for example—has not supported this fear. Perhaps the significant point is that management itself changes its attitude and becomes increasingly willing to have employees influence decisions of wider significance. As mentioned earlier, the Scanlon company managers seem completely unable to comprehend the anxieties of others about the loss of management prerogatives. They feel that they have full control over the management of the business, and yet at the same time they are quite willing to have employees discuss and influence almost any managerial decision. Many non-Scanlon managers, on the other hand, cannot conceive of such a situation except in terms of a severe weakening of managerial control.

In *Employee Participation and Company Performance: A Review of the Literature* (Joseph Rowntree Foundation, York, England: 2005), Juliette Summers and Jeff Hyman found that

The effects of participation schemes vary with the environment into which they are introduced. An insecure workplace environment may induce employees' compliance with participation measures, but may not achieve the commitment needed for attitude changes.

I am led to wonder what is cause and what is effect in this matter. Those managements who are most worried about their prerogatives seem, in general, to have the greatest difficulty in protecting them. It is at least possible that this suspicious, almost paranoid, attitude of management actually tends to *promote* interference with management prerogatives, to create targets which employees promptly shoot at. The chain of events in some companies amounts to a self-fulfilling prophecy: Management expects certain things to happen, and it behaves in such a fashion that they do happen. Then management reverses cause and effect in its interpretation of what has taken place.

In any event, there are now so many instances of the successful use of participation which has not in any discernible way weakened management's ability to manage that I can see little basis for anxiety over the issue of management prerogatives. The only conclusion I would draw is that the managements who are primarily concerned to protect their power and authority had better leave the whole matter alone.*

It is apparent that participation in the terms discussed above is quite consistent with the general theoretical approach of this whole volume. In view of the interdependence characteristic of industrial organizations there is reason for modifying the typical unilateral nature of the decision-making process. Participation, used judiciously, and in many different ways, depending upon the circumstances, offers help along these lines. It is a process which differs very little from delegation in its essential character. In fact, participation is a special case of delegation in which the subordinate gains greater control, greater freedom of choice, with respect to his own responsibility. The term participation is usually applied to the subordinate's greater influence over matters within the sphere of his superior's responsibilities. When these matters affect him and his job—when interdependence is involved—it seems reasonable that he should have

---

*Sally Payne, Program Manager for the International Brotherhood of Teamsters, Education Department, further sharpens the challenge for managers in these comments: "I have used McGregor's Theory X/Theory Y concepts in Teamster education programs for over 10 years and still find the discussion relevant. For Teamster members, these theories play out daily at worksites throughout the country. The incongruity between what Theory Y assumptions propose and what corporate America truly embraces is the right to belong to a union. We believe union membership merely institutionalizes Theory Y. If Theory Y creates a more effective and high-performing organization, then Corporate America would be in agreement with the principles of free unionism."

the opportunity to exert some influence. Thus, for example, the target-setting approach discussed in Chapter 5 involves both delegation and participation. The ideas involved in these two concepts are not mutually exclusive but complementary.

In the book *Creativity, Inc: Building an Inventive Organization*, (Boston: Harvard Business School Press, 2003), Jeff Mauzy and Richard Harriman further discuss the importance of managers' designing work systems to engage the full workforce:

Corporate leaders emerging from today's business schools have been encouraged to value McGregor's Theory Y management approach—employees want and need to excel and in the right organizational climate will do so. But despite Theory Y, hierarchical, paternalistic attitudes still permeate many businesses of every size today. Management's approach continues to be that position equals knowledge and intelligence and power, that the higher the position the better the ideas, that only someone with formal authority can responsibly handle decisions.

The effect of this management approach is to reduce the creative power of a 30,000-person organization to the top 100 leaders, a power reduction of 300 to 1. To install systemic creativity, leaders must engage the other 29,900 employees. In sum, leaders need to confer the responsibility and capability of creative leadership on every employee. When each employee can engage with the creative process, when each employee feels the need and the chance to perform as a creative leader in the course of his or her work, the company as a whole has begun to reach systemic creativity.

Participation which grows out of the assumptions of Theory Y offers substantial opportunities for ego satisfaction for the subordinate and thus can affect motivation toward organizational objectives.

It is an aid to achieving integration. In the first place, the subordinate can discover the satisfaction that comes from tackling problems and finding successful solutions for them. This is by no means a minor form of satisfaction. It is one of the reasons that the whole do-it-yourself movement has grown to such proportions in recent years. Beyond this there is a greater sense of independence and of achieving some control over one's destiny. Finally, there are the satisfactions that come by way of recognition from peers and superiors for having made a worth-while contribution to the solution of an organizational problem. At lower levels of the organization, where the opportunities for satisfactions like these are distinctly limited, participation in departmental problem solving may have considerable significance in demonstrating to people how they can satisfy their own needs best by working toward organizational objectives.

Viewed thus, participation is not a panacea, a manipulative device, a gimmick, or a threat. Used wisely, and with understanding, it is a natural concomitant of management by integration and self-control.*

REFERENCES

Argyris, Chris, "Organizational Leadership and Participation in Management," *The Journal of Business*, vol. 28, no. 1, 1955.

Coch, Lester, and John R. P. French, Jr., "Overcoming Resistance to Change," *Human Relations*, vol. 1, no. 4, 1948, pp. 512–532.

Maier, Norman R. F., *Psychology in Industry*, 2d ed. New York: Houghton Mifflin Company, 1955.

Tannenbaum, Robert, and Warren H. Schmidt, "How to Choose a Leadership Pattern," *Harvard Business Review*, vol. 36, no. 2 (March–April), 1958.

---

* It is interesting to note that participation was, for McGregor, a complement to what he viewed as the core of Theory Y, namely "integration and self-control." In fact, the subsequent literature and attention by practitioners to participation far exceeds the scholarship and practical focus on integration and self-control.

SELECTED REFERENCES TO THE ANNOTATED EDITION

Bell, David E., Howard Raiffa, and Amos Tversky (eds.), *Decision Making: Descriptive, Normative, and Prescriptive Interactions,* Cambridge: Cambridge University Press, 1988.

Hackman, J. Richard, and Greg R. Oldham, *Work Redesign,* Reading, MA: Addison-Wesley Publishing Co., 1980.

Mauzy, Jeff, and Richard Harriman, *Creativity, Inc: Building an Inventive Organization,* Boston: Harvard Business School Press, 2003.

Summers, Juliette, and Jeff Hyman, *Employee Participation and Company Performance: A Review of the Literature,* York, England: Joseph Rowntree Foundation (Work and Opportunity series), 2005.

DISCUSSION QUESTIONS FOR CHAPTER 9

1. Employee participation in organizational decision making was, as McGregor reports, viewed with skepticism at the time he was writing. Is it now more widely valued and utilized? If so, why? If not, why not?
2. To what degree should the focus of employee participation be allowed to emerge from the front-line workforce and to what degree should managers provide direction or guidance concerning the areas where participation is most needed?
3. Is participation in decision making in front-line operations (service or manufacturing) different from participation in decision making at the executive level?

THE MANAGERIAL CLIMATE

The managerial climate is a product, McGregor notes in Chapter 10, not so much of individual policies or statements, but of the "day-by-day behavior of the immediate superior and of other significant people in the managerial organization." What they do, McGregor reminds us, communicates their assumptions much more than what they say. He cites the example of a hard-driving manager who was like a "bull of the woods," but who also was scrupulously fair, was genuinely interested in people's welfare, was never patronizing, and would "go to bat "when higher management treated his people unfairly. The management climate may not have been a carefully constructed, consistent set of attributes, but the underlying sense of respect and fairness was far more important to organizational success. Workforce demands for increased security, McGregor notes, happen only "when they feel threatened, when they fear arbitrary action, favoritism, discrimination." He cites the case of a union that negotiated contract language guaranteeing that promotions be made only on the basis of plantwide seniority. Suspecting that the motivation for this demand was a perception that front-line supervisors were seen as treating people unfairly, the industrial relations staff embarked on what ended up being a three-year effort to improve the quality of front-line leadership. Illustrating the way patterns of behavior can change a management climate, McGregor notes that the union subsequently agreed to shift back to an arrangement where all promotions were made on the basis of merit. Thus, the management climate does not "spring from the air"; it is a product of people's observations of managers' daily behavior, which is evidence regarding their underlying assumptions about human nature. Where there is evidence that the workforce is generally held in low esteem, McGregor notes, "they will have relatively limited expectations concerning the possibilities for achieving their own goals" and so reciprocate by holding management in low esteem. At the beginning of the chapter, McGregor observes that Theory X focuses attention on the "techniques of direction and control," while Theory Y focuses attention on the "*nature of relationships.*" Management climate, we learn, doesn't just reflect the tone of these relationships; it is a direct product of these daily patterned interactions.

Although McGregor was not the first scholar to focus on the "managerial climate," his attention to the construction of climate through daily interactions is a key contribution. Today's literature on organizational culture has direct roots in this approach.[1] Almost all of McGregor's focus (and the focus of some of the subsequent literature on organizational culture) is inward-looking—focusing on people within organizations interacting with others in the same organization. More recent research (at micro and macro levels) is focused on the interactions that span boundaries across organizations—through strategic partnerships, joint ventures, and even what scholars have come to term "enacted environments" (where firms shape the context in which they operate).[2]

---

[1] Edgar Schein, *Organizational Culture and Leadership*, San Francisco: Jossey-Bass, 1988.

[2] This is a theme first identified by Warren Bennis in "Chairman Mac," *Harvard Business Review*, vol. 50, no. 4, September–October 1972, p. 140.

CHAPTER 10

THE MANAGERIAL CLIMATE

Theory X leads naturally to an emphasis on the tactics of control—to procedures and techniques for telling people what to do, for determining whether they are doing it, and for administering rewards and punishments. Since an underlying assumption is that people must be made to do what is necessary for the success of the enterprise, attention is naturally directed to the techniques of direction and control.

Theory Y, on the other hand, leads to a preoccupation with the *nature of relationships*, with the creation of an environment which will encourage commitment to organizational objectives and which will provide opportunities for the maximum exercise of initiative, ingenuity, and self-direction in achieving them.

Roger Komer, internal organizational development resource (retired) for UAW-Ford and now consultant with WorkMatters, LLC, comments:

McGregor provided a common language and framework for all OD practitioners that truly is a key element of systems thinking. In my own work, I constantly point to the importance of understanding the underlying values and assumptions about people and organizations.

Up to this point, we have been looking primarily at strategies and tactics of management—at methods of influence and control, target setting, performance appraisal, the administration of salaries and promotions, and the Scanlon Plan. Let us now turn to an examination of relationships and their significance.*

In considering the psychological environment of people at work, one thinks first of the relationship between superior and subordinate. This relationship has been the subject of intensive research for several decades, and a good deal is known about it today.

As we have already seen, a central characteristic of this relationship is the interdependence of the parties. Since each of the parties in an interdependent relationship affects to some degree the other's ability to achieve his goals or satisfy his needs, major difficulties are likely to arise unless both have positive expectations that the relationship will further these purposes. Taking first the point of view of the subordinate, let us ask what determines his expectations?

A quick answer might be company policies and procedures, such as those that are usually described in a handbook for new employees. These are important, of course, but the correlation between the quality of the relationship and any particular set of personnel policies is relatively low. Companies having all the standard programs and practices may have excellent relations or very poor ones. Particular programs and practices in some companies may be a constant target for attack and a continuous source of friction. Essentially the same procedures in other companies may be completely accepted.

Since the subordinate is dependent on the superior, he is sensitive to a wide range of clues which influence his prediction of the success he will have in achieving his goals. More important than the existence of particular policies or the formal statements concerning them are evidences of how they are administered. The day-by-day behavior of the immediate superior and of other significant people in the managerial organization communicates something about their

* Although Theory Y is presented as rooted in a set of assumptions about individuals, there is a parallel set of underlying assumptions about interdependent relationships that is the focus here.

assumptions concerning management which is of fundamental significance.*

THE CLIMATE OF THE RELATIONSHIP

Many subtle behavioral manifestations of managerial attitude create what is often referred to as the psychological "climate" of the relationship. During childhood, when we were all in relationships involving extreme dependence, each of us acquired a high level of skill in perceiving aspects of parental behavior which told us whether everything was "all right" with the relationship. Even very small children are amazingly sensitive to quite unconscious manifestations of parental attitudes of acceptance or rejection. It is understandable that this should be so because of the extreme dependence of infancy and early childhood. In the psychological sense, survival is at stake.

Granted that the subordinate's dependence is far less in the employment relationship, it remains true that his ability to achieve his goals is materially affected by the attitudes of his superiors. He will make constant use of his ability to perceive the climate of the relationship in forming judgments about the opportunities for achieving his goals. The climate is more significant than the type of leadership or the personal "style" of the superior. The boss can be autocratic or democratic, warm and outgoing or remote and introverted, easy or tough, but these personal characteristics are of less significance than the deeper attitudes to which his subordinates respond.

The mechanical superintendent in a small manufacturing company was the prototype of the "bull of the woods" manager. He swore at his men, drove them, disciplined them, behaved superficially like a Napoleon. He was the despair of the staff group who were carrying on a program of supervisory training in human relations Yet, oddly, his subordinates appeared to have high regard for him. They

* This core point, that people will focus more on what managers do than on what they say, is not new; the way in which actions reveal underlying assumptions is the key additional thought.

said, "Oh, his bark is worse than his bit." Morale and productivity in his department were both high.

Probing revealed some significant facts. He was known as a "square shooter" who dealt with his men with scrupulous fairness. Despite his superficial toughness he was sincerely and warmly interested in his subordinates. When they were in trouble—whether it was a simple matter of a few dollars to tide a man over until payday, or a family crisis—he helped out in a matter-of-fact way that left no uncomfortable feeling of being patronized.

Most important of all, he was known to be ready to go to bat for his men on any occasion when he felt they had not been accorded a fair break by higher management. The men spoke with awe of two occasions during a ten-year period when he had stormed into the office of the big boss to demand that a decision be altered because it was unfair to "his boys." When he was refused in one of these instances, he resigned on the spot, put on his hat, and left. His superior actually followed him out to the gate and capitulated.

While perhaps this man left something to be desired with respect to current conceptions of good management, he was, nevertheless, successful in developing and maintaining his subordinates' confidence in him. His managerial attitude cut across authoritarianism, permissiveness, paternalism, firmness and fairness, and all the other "styles" of management to create a deep and satisfying emotional certainty of fair treatment.

CONFIDENCE IN A FAIR BREAK

The research studies of the superior-subordinate relationship have pointed to a number of variables in the behavior and attitude of the superior which correlate both with high productivity and with the morale of subordinates. Many of these have to do with the subordinate's expectation that he will receive a fair break in attempting to achieve his own goals. The studies by the staff of the Institute for

Social Research at the University of Michigan, for example, have stressed "employee-centered supervision." They find a positive correlation between this managerial attitude of genuine concern for the welfare of subordinates on the one hand and morale and productivity on the other.

This attitude, as the Michigan researchers have pointed out, is necessary but not sufficient. It is important also that the superior himself have influence upward in the organization. It is not enough for the subordinate to be liked by his superior, the latter must be able to do something about it. If the boss cannot carry substantial influence with respect to decisions on salary increases, promotion, or working conditions, his subordinates will have little confidence in him no matter what his attitude may be.

There is also the necessity for the boss to be competent—not that he is necessarily familiar with the details of every job under him, but that he is a capable manager. Subordinates cannot be confident that they will get a fair break from a manager who is incompetent.

It is sometimes thought that *security*, rather than the expectation of receiving the fairest possible break, is what is required. However, in these adult relationships it does not appear that the guarantees implied by the usual meaning of the term security are necessary. In fact, there are successful relationships—characterized by high morale and high productivity—in which security is literally zero. These conditions are found, for example, in certain military units on the battlefield.

Subordinates demand security when they feel threatened, when they fear arbitrary action, favoritism, discrimination. They ask only for a fair break when they have genuine confidence in their superiors.

An interesting illustration of this point occurred in a defense plant during World War II. The president of this company was absent on an assignment in Washington. The union, during the annual negotiations, demanded that the principle of plant-wide seniority be applied to all promotions within the worker ranks. The president, unwilling to take a strike, instructed his management to accede to this demand, and they did so.

The industrial relations staff of this company was persuaded that the fundamental reason for the intensity of the demand for seniority was a lack of confidence on the part of the workers in the way promotions were being administered. The workers believed—and with some justification—that many supervisors were playing favorites with liked and discriminating against disliked individuals.

The staff persuaded the management to undertake a series of actions designed to improve the leadership of supervision. These activities were carried on for about three years. There were indications that they were reasonably effective.

At the close of the war the president returned and prepared to carry on the union negotiations himself for the first postwar contract. The industrial relations manager suggested that since he was prepared to make substantial economic concessions, he might expect something in return. He urged the president to seek modifications in the seniority clause.

The president was unconvinced. His belief was that once a concession of this kind had been made it was next to impossible to withdraw it. Nevertheless, he was persuaded to make the attempt. When he did so, toward the close of the negotiations, he was considerably surprised to have the union agree, almost without argument. A new promotion clause was negotiated which gave merit 100 per cent of the weight in the determination of promotions. Seniority remained a factor along with merit only in the administration of layoffs. That clause, negotiated in 1946, remains in the union contract today.

A plausible interpretation of this situation is that the workers, threatened by the arbitrary and unfair administration of promotion policies, demanded the only form of protection that made sense to them: strict seniority (a purely objective measure which is not subject to personal judgment). However, when the conditions were altered so that these same workers had genuine confidence that they would receive a fair break from their bosses, they were quite willing to accept a policy in which this form of security was eliminated.

Confidence thus rests heavily on the subordinates' belief in the integrity of the superior, When one is dependent, any suspicion that the superior cannot be fully trusted arouses anxiety. It is obvious that neither techniques nor formulas, nor any particular leadership style, will *in themselves* fulfill this requirement. Techniques which are used as "gimmicks" can, on the other hand, readily destroy confidence.

The superior, for example, who utilizes "participation" as a manipulative device to trick subordinates into accepting his predetermined decisions or problem solutions runs a great risk of undermining their belief in his integrity. If his technique is recognized, as it likely will be, he will lose far more than he had hoped to gain by "making them feel important."

Another formula is that of displaying a "personal interest" in the worker. Some managers pride themselves on their skill in this technique, simply as a technique, when in fact their interest is negligible.

Bill Jaeger, director of the Harvard Union of Clerical and Technical Workers (HUCTW), comments:

In the American workplace of 2005, we still see many examples of Theory X thinking. When managers treat job training as a boondoggle or scrutinize medical leave requests with a magnifying glass, it is clear that Theory Y has not achieved the same prominence in the day-to-day workplace that it enjoys in business school classrooms. At the same time, positive influences of the Theory Y framework appear and grow steadily. Once the relationship between our union and management shifted to focus in a genuine way on improving the way work takes place, many leaders on both sides have been able to step forward and be part of work redesign initiatives that improve productivity and worker satisfaction. As the battle of assumptions about human behavior rages on in the work-

place, Doug McGregor's book is still relevant and powerfully instructive—as it probably will be for decades to come. It really is one of my favorite books!

I remember accompanying a production manager through his plant some years ago and watching him show off his memory by his first-name greetings and questions about their families to several dozen workers. Despite its hearty quality, the whole performance had a ring of insincerity,* but the verification of my suspicions came a week later when the plant voted by an overwhelming majority to be represented by a militant union, and I learned from the union organizer that a prime factor influencing the vote was the violent hostility toward this manager.

CONFIDENCE DOWNWARD

These characteristics of daily behavior and attitude to which subordinates respond with such sensitivity do not spring from the air. They are manifestations of the superior's conception of the managerial job and his assumptions about human nature. Consider a manager who holds people in relatively low esteem. He sees himself as a member of a small elite endowed with unusual capacities, and the bulk of the human race as rather limited. He believes also that most people are inherently lazy, prefer to be taken care of, desire strong leadership. He sees them as prepared to take advantage of the employment relationship unless they are closely controlled and firmly directed. In short, he holds to Theory X.

---

* Critics of worker participation from the left have argued that it doesn't go far enough, and those from the right have argued that it overly intrudes on managerial authority. This point is different, however, which is that it is too often not genuine and, consequently, risks undermining the very integrity of managers. Although there is a large and growing interest in managerial ethics, this is an issue that is worthy of further exploration.

It is obvious that this theoretical orientation will reflect itself in a variety of ways in this manager's daily behavior toward his subordinates. It is equally obvious that, perceiving his attitudes, they will have relatively limited expectations concerning the possibilities for achieving their own goals in a relationship where they are dependent on him.

Over a period of several months, a group of workers in a manufacturing plant brought a lengthy series of grievances to management, all of them involving wages, working conditions, and plant rules. The intensity with which these grievances were pursued, and their frequency, led the personnel manager to suspect that they were symptoms of a deeper problem. He finally succeeded in creating a situation in which these employees felt free to express their private feelings, and it turned out that his hunch was indeed correct. The real issue had nothing to do with the actual subject of the grievances, but with the fact that the behavior of their supervisor made them feel he regarded them as "stupid lunks" and "dirt under his feet." They recognized that they could not get anywhere by raising grievances over the largely intangible characteristics of his behavior, so they expressed their violent reaction by making issues over tangible but irrelevant matters.*

When the personnel manager discussed the whole question with the supervisor, he finally said, "I guess that's the way I do feel about them, but I can't imagine what I've done to show it. I knew it would

---

* This phenomenon has been well documented in the literature on dispute resolution. (See, for example, William Ury, Jeanne Brett, and Steve Goldberg, *Getting Disputes Resolved: Designing Systems to Cut the Costs of Conflict*, San Francisco: Jossey-Bass, 1988; Sandra Gleason (ed.), *Frontiers in Dispute Resolution in Labor Relations and Human Resources*, East Lansing: Michigan State University Press, 1997. On a personal basis, this is also documented in Joel Cutcher-Gershenfeld, "New Patterns in the Resolution of Shop Floor Disputes," in Cheryl Cutrona (ed.), *Bringing the Dispute Resolution Community Together*, 1985 Proceedings, 13th International Conference of the Society of Professionals in Dispute Resolution, Washington, D.C.: SPIDR, 1986.

make my job tougher, so I hid my feelings even when they were making trouble with all their grievances."

Consider now a manager with a contrasting set of attitudes. He has a relatively high opinion of the intelligence and capacity of the average human being. He may well be aware that he is endowed with substantial capacity, but he does not perceive himself as a member of a limited elite. He sees most human beings as having real capacity for growth and development, for the acceptance of responsibility, for creative accomplishment. He regards his subordinates as genuine assets in helping him fulfill his own responsibilities, and he is concerned with creating the conditions which enable him to realize these assets. He does not feel that people in general are stupid, lazy, irresponsible, dishonest, or antagonistic. He is aware that there are such individuals, but he expects to encounter them only rarely. In short, he holds to Theory Y.

The climate of the relationship created by such a manager will be vastly different. Among other things, he will probably practice effective delegation, thus providing his subordinates with opportunities to develop their own capabilities under his leadership. He will also utilize them as resources in helping him solve departmental problems. His use of participation will demonstrate his confidence in them.

Lawrence Appley, President of the American Management Association, once said that participation meant to him:

1. Analyzing a problem and arriving at the best solution he could find

2. Calling his subordinates together to discuss the problem

3. Leaving the meeting with a better solution than the one he began with

This comment indicates both the meaning of participation and the confidence in one's subordinates which is essential to its effective use.

Perhaps it is now clear that the all-important climate of the superior-subordinate relationship is determined not by policy and procedure, nor by the personal style of the superior, but by the subtle and frequently quite unconscious manifestations of his underlying conception of management and his assumptions about people in general. The most careful and well-conceived policies and procedures of personnel administration, the most elaborate training in the techniques of supervision, knowledge of all the tricks of winning friends and influencing people, will be interpreted by subordinates as manipulative and exploitative devices unless the climate is right. This is why the same policies and procedures yield different results in different organizations.

WHO DETERMINES THE CLIMATE?

The implication throughout this discussion has been that the superior in the interdependent superior-subordinate relationship is the one who really determines the quality of the relationship. It is reasonable to ask whether the subordinates' attitudes do not also have a great deal to do with the results. Of course they do. Personal attitudes, prejudices, and theoretical convictions about human beings aside, a superior cannot have confidence in a genuinely incompetent, or a dishonest, or a neurotically hostile subordinate. Moreover, some personalities are simply incompatible for reasons which neither party can do much about. Even with the best selection and placement procedures, managers sometimes face just such situations.

Under such conditions, it is nonsense to talk about creating positive expectations, mutual confidence, a healthy climate. The only real solution is to end the relationship, by transfer under some circumstances, or by termination of employment under others. If this is impossible, all that remains is to recognize that effective management in such a relationship is impossible, and to make the best of a bad situation.

Speaking generally of the superior-subordinate relationship, the dependence is greater upward than downward. This means that the superior exerts more control than the subordinate over the nature of the relationship. Sometimes situations which appear hopeless change when a new superior, because of his different attitudes, alters the psychological climate.

A few years ago I visited a large company where union-management relationships had been notoriously bad for a very long time until, about two years before my visit, they had changed dramatically for the better. The reason for my visit was that the company had been nominated by some officials of the international union and by citizens in the region as one deserving inclusion in a series of studies of constructive union-management relations.

McGregor's focus here is on improving union-management relations, but what about the overall productivity of the enterprise? In this respect, consider the following comments by Fred Stahl, a former executive with the Boeing Corporation who also served as the industry executive director of MIT's Lean Aerospace Initiative:

Integration of employee and employer goals sounds like an attractive remedy for Theory X, but I don't believe it is right. We know that industrial sociologists found no correlation between employee attitudes and productivity in twentieth-century factories. My own experience is that productivity follows when employee behavior is aligned with processes for wealth creation in enterprises. Consider the conceptual breakthrough by Dick Kleine, former general manager of John Deere's Harvester Works. Instead of the mindset that "a happy employee is a productive employee," he advanced the approach that "a productive employee is a happy employee." As a result, the focus shifted to ensuring a productive organization and management of social and physical systems. This goes significantly beyond Theory Y.

The story related by the management of this company was so simple that it would have been unbelievable except for the evidence of its correctness. The company had been plagued by a violently hostile union. The local union leaders, elected by a minority of the membership who took the trouble to vote in the elections, were the worst "troublemakers" in the company. Bargaining was a farce, grievances by the hundreds were pressed to the limit without regard for their merit, wildcat strikes were a regular phenomenon, restriction of production was widespread.

One influential member of top management persuaded his colleagues, after many heated discussions, to adopt a new approach. On the assumption that the bulk of the employees were decent human beings who would respond to reasonable treatment, the approach was to demonstrate in every possible way management's sincerity and integrity. The employee publications would no longer take a defensive position with respect to managerial practices. If a grievance hearing showed that management had been in the wrong, the error would be openly admitted and rectified immediately. Secrecy (motivated by fears of union misuse of information) would be replaced by complete openness and frankness. Extensive efforts would be made to help middle and lower management to understand and adopt this philosophy in their daily practice.

Within two years the whole relationship had become a different one as a result of this change in managerial strategy. Every one with whom I talked insisted there had been no other changed conditions which could explain what had happened. The former union leadership had been replaced by a group of highly respected, able individuals, grievances were down to a normal level, bargaining had been conducted in good faith and in an atmosphere of reasonableness, wildcat strikes had dropped to zero.

This management was still bemused and a little incredulous about what had happened. I could only think of Clinton Golden's sage comment that "By and large, and over the long run, management gets the kind of labor relations it deserves."

Underlying assumptions—theoretical considerations—influence

managerial behavior not only with respect to policies and procedures and techniques, but with respect to subtle aspects of everyday behavior which determine the "climate" of human relationships. These daily manifestations of theory and attitude in turn affect the expectations of subordinates concerning their ability to achieve their goals and satisfy their needs through membership in the organization. Formal policies, programs, and procedures will be administered, and in turn perceived in the light of the managerial climate. Its importance is primary—the "machinery" of administration is secondary.

REFERENCES

Kahn, Robert, and Daniel Katz, "Leadership Practices in Relation to Productivity and Morale," in D. Cartwright and A. Zander, *Group Dynamics: Research and Theory*. Evanston, Ill.: Row, Peterson & Company, 1953.

Kahn, Robert L., Floyd C. Mann, and Stanley Seashore, "Human Relations Research in Large Organizations," *Journal of Social Issues*, vol. 12, nos. 1 and 2, 1956.

Kline, Bennet E., and Norman H. Martin, "Freedom, Authority and Decentralization," *Harvard Business Review*, vol. 36, no. 3 (May–June), 1958.

Leavitt, Harold J., "Small Groups in Large Organizations," *The Journal of Business*, vol. 28, no. 1, 1955.

Likert, Rensis, "Developing Patterns of Management," American Management Association, General Management Series, no. 182, 1956.

Pelz, Donald C., "Influence: A Key to Effective Leadership in the First-line Supervisor," *Personnel*, vol. 29, no. 3, 1952.

Walker, Charles R., Robert H. Guest, and Arthur N. Turner, *The Foreman on the Assembly Line*. Cambridge, Mass.: Harvard University Press. 1956.

SELECTED REFERENCES TO THE ANNOTATED EDITION

Schein, Edgar, *Organizational Culture and Leadership,* San Francisco: Jossey-Bass, 1988.

DISCUSSION QUESTIONS FOR CHAPTER 10

1. Identify a managerial program, practice, or initiative and then list the many different kinds of patterns of interaction that will be essential to the success of that program, practice, or initiative.
2. If you are a new leader in a workplace with a managerial climate characterized by mistrust and disrespect, what would be key elements of a three-year plan to shift the climate toward one of trust and respect?
3. In addition to patterns of interaction, in what ways are organizational structure and strategy responsible for the managerial climate?

STAFF-LINE RELATIONSHIPS

Chapter 11 address staff-line relationships at a time when staff functions—human resources, accounting, sales, marketing, purchasing, quality control, logistics, maintenance, engineering, and others—were becoming increasingly professionalized. The Theory X emphasis on "unity of command" (every individual should have only one boss), McGregor notes, drives an unhealthy "struggle for power" between line and staff. He quotes a line manager as stating that "I keep away from the staff. They'd help me to death," and he notes the staff's common "jaundiced view" of the line managers as being "exclusively concerned with maintaining their authority and independence." In this context, McGregor warns of a particular trap for staff functions, which is when senior management uses functions "such as accounting, personnel, and engineering to develop and administer a system of managerial controls." In this case, senior management will have the pretence of participation and delegation, while the staff function will have the legitimacy of top management support. The cost of this arrangement, which McGregor terms "a travesty," is that the staff functions have abandoned their respective areas of expertise and have become tools for line management control. The emphasis in the training of staff professionals on "find[ing] 'the best answer'" exacerbates the dynamic. Such exclusively technical approaches are generally rejected by front-line managers, reinforcing the perception on the part of the staff that line managers are "stupid," while staff are seen as unconcerned about the welfare of the business as a whole." This further justifies the staff administering controls on behalf of top management. The bottom line is that the staff end up not performing their function and the climate of control is exacerbated.

Today, the principles of matrix organizations, project management, and systems engineering all take into account McGregor's observations on staff-line relationships. Yet, we still struggle with the core tensions that he identified. Consider, for example, the finding from the Space Shuttle *Columbia* Accident Investigation Board, which was that "the foam debris hit was not the single cause of the *Columbia* accident, just as the failure of the joint seal that permitted O-ring erosion was not the single cause of *Challenger*. Both *Columbia* and *Challenger* were lost also because of the failure of NASA's organizational system." Safety as a staff function had failed to maintain its ability to provide the necessary check-and-balance relationship with line operations.[1]

[1] Columbia Accident Investigation Board report (CAIB), August 2003, p. 195; see also Leveson, Nancy, Joel Cutcher-Gershenfeld, John S. Carroll, Betty Barrett, Alexander Brown, Nicolas Dulac, Lydia Fraila, and Karen Marais, "Systems Approaches to Safety: Socio-technical Systems, High Reliability Organizations, and Engineering Systems," in *Management Lessons from the Columbia Disaster,* Bill Starbuck and Moshe Farjoun, eds., New York: Blackwell, 2005.

CHAPTER 11

STAFF-LINE RELATIONSHIPS

The importance of the climate of the superior-subordinate relationship is fairly well recognized today, and a good deal of attention is given to its creation and maintenance. Another interdependent relationship, however, has been less extensively studied, and the significance of its climate to the welfare of the enterprise is not so well understood. This is the relationship between staff and line.

Conventional organization theory deals with the staff-line relationship in terms of the principle of authority, naturally. The central chain of command is that of operations; other functions provide services and advice to the line. They cannot be given authority (except within their own functions) because to do so would violate the principle of unity of command: that any individual must have only one boss. There can, of course, be more than one line function (sales, for example), so long as there is sufficient independence that the principle of unity of command is not violated.

A second relevant principle is that authority must equal responsibility. Since the line requires certain services in fulfilling its responsibilities, it must have authority over them.

These principles may be given formal recognition in organization charts and position descriptions, but one would never deduce them from study of the realities of organizational life! Every member of lower and middle line management is subject to influences from staff groups which are psychologically indistinguishable from the authority exercised by his line superiors.

Such influences are not limited to people above the manager in the hierarchy either. A clerk in accounting may disallow an expense item in the budget of a general manager; a proposed salary increase initiated by a plant superintendent may require approval by a clerk in the personnel department. The fact that these staff people are following procedures formally approved by the line does not alter the psychological nature of the influence involved or the reactions to it.

In the textbooks on organization one finds elaborate circumlocutions designed to reconcile such inconsistencies. However, euphemistic terms like "coordination," "the authority of knowledge," and "acting in the name of" do not hide the fact that the conventional staff-line distinction in terms of authority is an illusion. The industrial organization is an elaborate complex of interdependent relationships, and interdependence means that each party can affect the ability of the other to achieve his goals and satisfy his needs. So long as the basic managerial strategy is one of direction and control, authoritative forms of influence exercised by staff groups will creep into the relationship no matter what the logical principles require. The struggle for power in a setting where goal achievement is based on acquiring it will not be eliminated by recourse to logic.*

The climate of line-staff relationships in industry today does not often reflect the quality of mutual confidence described in Chapter 10. Quite typically, line managers regard staff groups as a "burden" rather than as a source of help. They see them as preoccupied with their narrow specialties to the point where they are unconcerned about the welfare of the business as a whole. They look on staff advice as generally impractical, usually hemmed in by overly standardized and bureaucratic procedures. As one line manager who was working out some difficult problems in union-management relations put it: "I keep away from the staff. They'd help me to death."†

---

* The principle of "checks and balances" is a particular form of interdependence that is not fully developed here. It is distinct from the principle of "unity of command" that McGregor criticizes, but it adds a power and control dimension that does go beyond interdependence among coequal functions.

† Unfortunately, these same tensions between line and staff functions can still be found in many of today's large corporations.

Staff groups, on the other hand, frequently have a jaundiced view of the line. They perceive line managers as exclusively concerned with maintaining their authority and independence, lacking in appreciation of the professional qualifications and accomplishments of staff groups, basically resistant to change and improvement.

These attitudes are often covered over by a quantity of humorous kidding, the hostility in which is barely concealed. There are exceptions, of course, but by and large staff-line relationships are far from ideal. In private conversation with either group, a casual comment about the other is often sufficient to start a torrent of deprecatory comment interspersed with "see if you can top this" illustrations. A term which frequently comes to minds is "scapegoating."

THE LINE UTILIZES THE STAFF

There are many causal factors behind this rather unsatisfactory state of affairs. One of the most important is related, I believe, to line management's growing appreciation of the inadequacy of authority as the exclusive means of managerial control. However, the appreciation is at the level of practice rather than theory, and this is the source of much difficulty.

Too much reliance on authority produces counterforces among subordinates. Even the manager who is committed to the assumptions of Theory X becomes aware of this. Among the alternatives which have been offered as solutions to this problem is that of delegation. This principle, as ordinarily presented, emphasizes such ideas as "putting decisions near the point of action," controlling subordinates "through policy," giving "general rather than detailed supervision," and allowing subordinates "the freedom to make mistakes."

The upper-level manager who holds to Theory X can usually accept the idea of delegation, but when he puts it into action he is faced with a loss of the control on which his whole conception of management is based. He is helpless before the possibility that poor decisions may be made; productivity may drop, things may get out of hand. Since he lacks genuine confidence in his subordinates, these fears are real.

Fortunately, as he usually discovers, there is a way out of the dilemma. He can delegate and yet keep control. He need not rely on authority in the direct sense *if he can assign to someone else* the responsibility (1) for making sure his subordinates stay within policy limits and (2) for collecting and providing him with data which will enable him to know what is happening in time to step in before serious trouble arises.

Accordingly, he begins to use staff groups such as accounting, personnel, and engineering to develop and administer a system of managerial controls. When he adopts a policy, he assigns to the appropriate staff the responsibility for working out the necessary procedures and making sure they are followed. (After all, he has made the essential decision; let the specialists work out the details. Moreover, he can't spend his time worrying about whether specific procedures are followed; his concerns are with policy and with results. Let the staff "coordinate" the implementation.)

As a manager it is his responsibility to know what goes on. He can't abdicate, even if he delegates. If he can get daily reports on certain crucial aspects of the operation, and weekly and monthly reports on other aspects, he will be able with very little expenditure of time (and without breathing down anybody's neck in the old authoritarian way) to delegate without losing his ability to direct and control.

As a further refinement, he discovers the principle of "management by exception." It is not necessary to study a lot of detailed reports of the activities of his subordinates. The staff can do this for him, and prepare reports which point up only those things which are out of line and therefore require his attention. He may even go one step further and assign to the staff the task of investigating the "variances" and correcting them—reporting to him only those they are unable to handle themselves.

Now things are in good shape. He no longer exercises close, direct authority over his subordinates. He has delegated to them. He directs by means of policy; the decisions are made at the point of action; his subordinates have the freedom to make mistakes. There is no risk involved because he has a group of staff specialists who keep a detailed eye on every important aspect of the operations. He can concern himself with major problems, with formulating policy, with the more important aspects of management, because things are "under control." If anything is not as it should be, either the staff will see that it is corrected or notify him so that he can take care of it before serious difficulties arise.*

A nice situation—or a travesty? It depends on your theoretical assumptions. There are textbooks, articles, and consulting firms which will provide help in setting up this kind of a managerial strategy, complete with control charts and colored signals. Of course, it will be necessary to reckon with some consequences. The staff have now become policemen, exercising by proxy the direct authority which was "relinquished" by the line. Countermeasures of a familiar kind will appear, but they will be directed toward the staff and, because the staff is neither particularly feared nor respected, the countermeasures may be even more effective than if they were directed at line management. There is a fair amount of research evidence indicating that middle and lower management groups tend to develop protective mechanisms which, although more elaborate and considerably more costly to the organization, are psychologically identical to those developed by workers to defeat the administration of individual incentive plans.

A large and successful manufacturing company discovered recently, after changing the management of a major division, what company top management described as "appalling" evidence of fudging of production and quality data, misreporting of costs, and ignoring of preventive maintenance which had been going on for years.

---

* Classic treatments of functional differentiation in organizations do not always attend to this sort of subtle co-opting of power. (See Paul Lawrence and Jay Lorsch, *Organization and Environment*, Cambridge, Mass.: Harvard University Press, 1967.)

The relevant headquarters staff groups, and even the division top staff people, were completely unaware of the situation until a new line management uncovered it.

The costs will not be trivial: subordinate managers will quickly develop their own independent data-gathering mechanisms (utilizing clerical time) to ensure that they will know at least as much as the staff about what is going on. Many man-hours will be consumed by the staff in tracking down variances which have already been discovered and corrected at the source. Ingenious methods for defeating staff control procedures will be developed, and the staff will be kept busy developing new ones to compensate for these. Antagonisms between line and staff will prevent the kind of collaboration that is essential for achieving organizational objectives. (Examples like those cited in Chapter 8 of the employees who "followed the blueprint" with glee when they knew that doing so would result in an unsatisfactory product will be multiplied many times over at various managerial levels.) Those controls which the superior indicates by his actions are important to him will be carefully watched by subordinates; others will be ignored.

If such costs as these are worth the gains, this form of "delegation and control" will work after a fashion. Human beings are surprisingly adaptable. Basically, however, there are few managerial practices which produce as many negative consequences for the organization as this one of assigning control responsibilities to the staff. Whether my analysis of the reasons for it is correct or not, the practice (in varying degrees and forms) is widespread.*

I believe these phenomena are responsible to a large degree for the "accordion effect" often noted in large companies. First, a big movement toward decentralization takes place. A few years later, after the

---

* McGregor asserts that the practice of assigning control responsibilities to staff was widespread at the time (based on his personal experience rather than on formal studies). Is this now so embedded in staff roles that we take it for granted? Or, is there reason to believe that this is less prevalent today?

consequences described above have taken their toll, top management decides that things have gotten out of hand, and there is a general tightening up in the direction of centralization. The inability to control a large, complex organization centrally leads after a while to a new attempt at decentralization. There are indications that this cycle has also occurred within Soviet industry, although the surface manifestations have been different.

The logic behind the strategy of control outlined above is so subtly persuasive that it is difficult to argue against it: Every manager is responsible for results within that portion of the organization which is under his supervision. He is held accountable by those above him. Obviously he cannot fulfill this responsibility unless (1) he knows what is going on within the unit, and (2) he is able to do something about things that go wrong.

This logic is unassailable if one accepts the assumptions of Theory X: that most people have to be made to do what is necessary for the success of the organization, that they will not voluntarily accept responsibility, that they are limited in capacity. Management by direction and control inevitably results in strategies similar to the one we have been examining.

The headquarters staff group in one large organization who are responsible for administering an elaborate control system throughout the company openly express the view that the only way to keep middle and lower management on their toes is to measure their performance constantly and in detail, and to "use the needle" unsparingly.

The assumptions of Theory Y, however, deny this conception of management and, therefore, the logic that flows from it. Human beings possess an internal "control mechanism" which can largely render ineffective any form of external control. This is true even of physical coercion under certain conditions. However, they will under appropriate conditions, exercise *self*-direction and *self*-control in the service of objectives to which they are committed. Every parent learns these truths as his children develop to adulthood. He will not be able to control their behavior once they are grown. Unless he begins at some point to rely on their capacity for self-direction and self-control, he will be helpless as they approach maturity. His task, therefore, is to help them discover socially acceptable objectives to which they can give their commitment, and to reduce gradually his own external control as they learn to exercise self-control. In this manner the great majority of children do become responsible adult members of society.

The industrial manager is dealing with adults who are only partially dependent. They can—and will—exercise remarkable ingenuity in defeating the purposes of external controls which they resent. However, they can—and do—learn to exercise self-direction and self-control under appropriate conditions. His task is to help them discover objectives consistent both with organizational requirements and with their own personal goals, and to do so in ways which will encourage genuine commitment to these objectives. Beyond this, his task is to *help* them achieve those objectives: to act as teacher, consultant, colleague, and only rarely as authoritative boss. He will not help them if he attempts to keep direction and control in his own hands; he will only hamper their growth and encourage them to develop countermeasures against him. Nor will he help them achieve organizational objectives if he establishes a police force, reporting to him, who will assume part or all of the task of control. This may divert the resentment, but it will intensify the negative consequences.

He can help them only if he is prepared to relinquish control in the conventional sense, only if he has enough confidence in their willingness and ability to achieve organizational objectives that he can risk some poor judgments and some mistakes as a natural cost of their growth.

In the retailing field, particularly during the past few years, some shifts in managerial attitude have yielded experiences which are instructive. A number of mail-order houses and department stores have abolished elaborate control procedures built around customer-purchase returns. It has been found that the great majority of customers are sufficiently honest that it is substantially cheaper to replace a returned purchase without question than it is to maintain elaborate policing and investigating procedures. To be sure, some people are dishonest. The question, however, is whether it is cheaper to set up procedures for dealing with the bulk of honest people or to build procedures for dealing with the dishonest few. In this field at least, the data are clear: the former strategy is economically superior.

Today, this approach is embodied in what some refer to as a "customer-for-life" approach. In "Impact of Practices and Policies on Performance" at www.chainlinkresearch.com, Bill McBeath comments that:

Customer-for-life retailers such as Nordstroms are legendary for giving their salespeople wide discretion in spending company resources (e.g. expedited freight, special gifts, etc.) to satisfy customers; Talbots offers substitute items for half price if a desired size/color is not in stock; SAKS can tell you instantly if an out-of-stock item is available at any other location and offers to have it shipped overnight to you at no extra cost; the Ritz Carlton empowers their employees to spend up to $2,000 on a customer to fix any problem.

Note that the first and last of these four examples clearly embody Theory Y assumptions, while the middle two are policies that could operate in either a Theory X or Theory Y context.

AND THE STAFF?

Line management's inept utilization of staff groups is but one of several causes of unsatisfactory staff-line relationships. Another, of perhaps equal importance, is the conception which staff specialists tend to have of their own role. In spite of the much greater emphasis on the social sciences in the undergraduate curriculum today, the engineer or the accountant or the personnel specialist typically enters industry with little understanding of the difficult role he will be required to take if he is to become an effective member of a staff group. The focus in his education has been upon the content of his specialty and upon its methods and techniques. The complex problems involved in an organization's effective utilization of his specialized knowledge and skills have seldom even been touched upon. He is usually completely naïve about his professional relationships and roles.

His training, as a matter of fact, tends to make him unusually vulnerable. He has been taught to find "the best answer." He has great confidence in the objectivity of his scientific techniques. His natural expectation is that the solutions resulting from his application of these techniques will be immediately and gratefully accepted by the organization. Management by direction and control seems perfectly reasonable, with the modification that "the authority of knowledge" is for him final. No reasonable human being would challenge it.

He soon finds, of course, that many of his fellow members of the organization are not reasonable human beings. Not only are they less than properly impressed with him as a person; they frequently reject the objective results of his scientific studies or refuse to use his latest-model techniques.

It does not take him long to conclude that a lot of line managers are stupid, relatively unconcerned about the welfare of the organization, preoccupied with maintaining their authority and independence.

In this setting he is more than happy to accept an assignment to develop a system of measurements for the control of line management operations. If he is an accountant or an engineer, he is likely to put great store by standardization and well-worked-out procedures and rules. The coordinative function is his meat. Here is a way to minimize the subjective, unpredictable elements in human behavior and obtain the kind of direction and control which will really improve the effectiveness of the enterprise. Now he can make use of his training and his talents. And, finally (and unconsciously), here is the way to get back at these so-and-so's who have no appreciation or understanding of the values of his specialized field.

This is certainly not the universal state of affairs, but it is common enough to create widespread difficulties in line-staff relations. Theory X is a congenial theory for a great many staff specialists. It explains the organizational world as they perceive it. Management by direction and control is a natural way of life, not only with respect to their subordinates in the staff function, but with respect to their relations with middle- and lower-level line management.

THE POWER OF THE STAFF

The final irony of this whole situation is that it is the staff and not the line which is beginning to represent the real power in the modern industrial corporation. Quite apart from their inheritance of the control function, staff groups are the ones who make it possible for management to solve the ever more intricate problems of today's world—in the financial, technical, scientific, legislative, economic, and human fields. Their knowledge and training in their specialties, their techniques for analyzing and solving problems are absolutely essential to the success of the modern enterprise.

Consequently, we have an odd reversal of conventional organization theory: The line—the central and fundamental authoritative chain of command—is becoming increasingly dependent upon a considerable number of specialized staff groups. Simultaneously the staff groups—the advisory and service groups who "cannot exercise authority" because of the logical necessity for unity of command—are becoming, both by virtue of the importance of their knowledge and skill and because of management's delegation to them of control and coordinative functions, the dominant, influential core of the organization. In one very large company, 70 per cent of the personnel above the second level of supervision are staff, and the proportion is growing.

Indirectly perhaps, but definitely and increasingly, *the industrial organization of today is being run by the staff.* Their knowledge and techniques have a profound influence on major decisions, they design and administer procedures, and their control functions provide much of the direction and control of the human resources of the enterprise.

Alice's Wonderland was not such a strange place after all.

REFERENCES

Argyris, Chris, "Human Problems with Budgets," *Harvard Business Review*, vol. 31, no. 1 (January–February), 1953.

Dalton, Melville, *Men Who Manage.* New York: John Wiley & Sons, Inc., 1959.

Glover, J. G., and C. L. Maze, *Managerial Control.* New York: The Ronald Press, 1937.

Myers, Charles A., and John G. Turnbull, "Line and Staff in Industrial Relations," *Harvard Business Review*, vol. 34, no. 4 (July–August), 1956.

DISCUSSION QUESTIONS FOR CHAPTER 11

1. What would be an example of a staff function that has been co-opted by operations? What would it take to reclaim its independent role?
2. What would be an example of line responsibilities that have been inappropriately assumed by a staff function? What would it take for the line operations to reclaim their appropriate role?
3. As a small entrepreneurial organization develops, at what point might you expect it to shift into a formal matrix structure (with different people in staff and line roles)—at 10 people, 25 people, 50 people, 100 people, 250 people? What are the advantages and disadvantages of formal differentiation happening earlier or later in the life cycle of an organization?

IMPROVING STAFF-LINE COLLABORATION

At the outset of Chapter 12, McGregor observes that many efforts by line and staff managers to influence one another "are like digging channels to get water to flow uphill." As he documented in Chapter 11, "even fruitful concepts like those of delegation and decentralization are warped completely out of shape" when Theory X assumptions dominate. McGregor rejects simple structural solutions. Using the example of the maintenance function, he notes that both highly constructive and friction-filled relationships can be observed when maintenance reports directly to front-line managers, as can a similar spectrum when a centralized maintenance function is established. To function effectively, McGregor urges that staff groups serve as professional resources for the entire organization in ways that scrupulously avoid their being co-opted into vehicles for control. Thus, he introduces what he acknowledges is a "radical conception," which is that data collected by expert staff (human resources, maintenance, engineering, etc.) should be reported to management only in aggregate form, so that the individual performance of separate people working under that manager can't be discerned. This is essential if staff are to be seen as trusted professionals by all members of the organization. It is of ever greater importance, McGregor notes, given the growing use by staff specialists of "an elaborate 'information technology.'" Even then, he noted that the "methods of measurement and data collection and analysis ... would have been inconceivable a quarter of a century ago." With a foundation of mutual respect,

McGregor calls for an interdependent "professional-client relationship" in which "neither typically exercises authority over the other although there is influence in both directions." This encompasses four key roles for staff functions:

1. Help in strategic planning.
2. Help in problem solving.
3. Help with respect to managerial controls (but focused on fostering self-control, not helping to impose controls).
4. Help in administering services.

Ultimately, he concludes that "it is probable that one day we shall begin to draw organization charts as a series of linked groups rather than as a hierarchical structure of individual 'reporting' relationships." In praise of the analysis in this chapter, one early reviewer commented, "The perspicacious examination of staff-line relationship in chapter 12 and the audacious contention that authority and responsibility do not have to be equal are alone worth the book."[1]

McGregor is highly critical of standardization in this chapter, as a "one-size-fits-all" approach that fails to take into account the individual needs and circumstances of different employees. On its face, this seems directly contrary to the important role of standardization as a foundation for continuous improvement in total quality, lean, Six Sigma, and related systems change initiatives. In fact, a close look at these initiatives reveals that the standardization is owned and driven by the front-line workforce in ways that are highly consistent with McGregor's views on

[1] Book review by Frank A. Heller, *The Human Side of Enterprise*, by Douglas McGregor. Reviewed by *Industrial and Labor Relations Review*, vol. 14, no. 3 (Apr. 1961), pp. 494–495.

participation and integration. Indeed, a key element of success in these cases is the opportunity for individual creativity within defined boundaries. It is comparable to the personal expression that is possible for a musician only after intensive, highly structured practice. This interplay between personal development and standardization is a promising area for further study.

Another important area for further study involves the growing trend of outsourcing staff functions. Does this better shield the staff operations from the sort of co-optation that McGregor highlights? Does this better enable line operations to value the independent expertise of staff functions? In some case, such as the outsourcing of logistics functions to companies that are highly regarded for their expertise, such as UPS, this may indeed be the case. For other areas, such as human resources or financial accounting, further study is clearly needed.

CHAPTER 12

IMPROVING STAFF-LINE COLLABORATION

The problem we face is that of creating a climate of mutual confidence around staff-line relationships which will encourage collaboration in the achievement of organizational objectives rather than guerilla warfare. The creation of that climate requires understanding by line and staff alike that many of their present attempts to influence behavior are like digging channels to get water to flow uphill. The needed changes simply cannot occur as long as the underlying assumptions are those of Theory X. As we have seen, even fruitful concepts like those of delegation and decentralization are warped completely out of shape when they are applied within this theoretical framework.

As far as the line is concerned, most of the changes in strategy implied by Theory Y and discussed elsewhere in this volume are relevant to relationships with staff. There are, however, two additional considerations which apply with special significance to this relationship. The first has to do with the traditional principle that authority must equal responsibility.

THE INEQUALITY OF AUTHORITY AND RESPONSIBILITY

Once more, the logic is impeccable: An individual cannot legitimately be held responsible for things he cannot control. However, as we have seen, the assumption that he *can* control them through the use of authority is fallacious. We have seen what happens when the manager fails to recognize the interdependence involved in his relationships with his subordinates. Similar consequences ensue when the interdependence between staff and line is ignored.

It is admittedly awkward and frustrating to be responsible for accomplishing objectives under conditions in which one cannot control the relevant factors in the situation. It would be much nicer if reality were different. However, given the complex interdependencies of modern society, we are often in such situations. Parents—responsible to society for bringing up their children to be effective citizens—face many influences on their children which they cannot control except in a very limited sense (the formal educational system provides an obvious illustration). The leaders of our Federal government—responsible for maintaining peace with other nations—are similarly limited.

Industrial management is responsible to the stockholders for the economic success of the enterprise. However, it cannot *control* consumers' preferences or their attitudes toward saving money or buying goods; the general economic health of the nation; legislation in municipal, state, or Federal bodies; labor unions; or a host of other phenomena, including the behavior of subordinates within the organization. It can *influence* many of these determining variables; it cannot control them—especially in the narrow sense of exerting authority over them.*

The realities of modern organizational life place the manager at any level of the organization in a position where he cannot control many things which affect the results for which he is responsible. It is foolish indeed to emphasize the logical idea that his authority must equal his responsibility. If he lacks confidence in his subordinates or in staff groups, if he expects indifference, antagonism, and lack of responsibility on their part, he is placed in a situation which is bound to create severe pressures on him. This unrealistic principle will encourage him to resort to the kinds of inappropriate methods of

* If anything, these and other interdependencies are even greater today, as some leading-edge organizations explore what are sometimes referred to as double or triple bottom lines—emphasizing outcomes not just for shareholders, but also for the workforce, the environment, communities, and other stakeholders.

control described in previous chapters. It will also encourage him to attempt to exercise authority over staff groups and thus to create other problems.

The friction which is common between lower levels of line production management and the maintenance function is at least to some extent created by the production manager's frustration with his inability to exercise authority over those who maintain the equipment for which he is responsible. Yet, in my experience, the existence of this friction is independent of whether maintenance is established as staff (in which case the production foreman theoretically possesses the necessary authority) or as part of a separate line engineering department (in which case the production foreman has no authority over those who maintain his equipment). The few instances I have encountered of genuinely effective collaboration between these groups have included examples of *both* types of formal relationship.

The requirement that authority must equal responsibility is not only impossible to fulfill; it is logically unnecessary *except within a system which makes authority the exclusive means of influence.* The first prerequisite for improving staff-line relationships is that we abandon this supposed requirement, and with it the corollary that the line exercises authority over the staff. The two groups are interdependent, and exclusive reliance on authority in this relationship is as inappropriate as it is in the superior-subordinate relationship.

Naturally, another casualty will be the practice on the part of any level of line management of assigning responsibilities to staff groups which entail their exercising authority (whether disguised by terms like "coordination" or "management by exception" or not) over lower levels of the organization. Let us see what this means in practice.

THE PRINCIPLE OF SELF-CONTROL

The manager's utilization of staff groups within the context of Theory Y will emphasize the principle of self-control. He will perceive the staff as a resource for the whole organization; consequently he will not seek help from staff groups in any way which simultaneously threatens his subordinates (as is the case if he uses them as policemen).

With respect to data and reports compiled by staff groups, the principle of self-control requires that they be provided to each member of management for controlling *his own*, not his subordinates' jobs. Delegation means that he will concern himself with the *results* of their activities and not with the details of their day-to-day performance. This requires a degree of confidence in them which enables him to accept certain risks. Unless he takes these risks there will be no delegation.

Every manager is entitled to all the detailed data he wishes for purposes of self-control. If, however, the data are broken down in a fashion which reveals the day-to-day performance of individual subordinates, they are no longer data for self-control. His use of such information vitiates the idea of delegation completely. (The same thing is true, of course, if he assigns to staff the responsibility of "controlling" his subordinates by this means.)*

This is a radical conception. It means, for example, that the manager of a division will have available to him data about the *division*, but not about the individual functions and departments within it. He may wish data about the division as a whole on a daily basis; he may wish a few general figures, or he may desire information on many aspects of divisional performance. His own preferences govern so long as he does not request details about the performance of individual subordinates. His subordinates in turn will operate in the same way, each reviewing whatever information he deems important to control his own, but not his subordinates', jobs.

If such summary data indicate to the manager that something is wrong within the organizational unit for which he is responsible, he

---

* This sort of detailed data is even more common with enterprise resource planning (ERP) software initiatives, yet relatively few such implementations integrate consideration of this human side of the enterprise.

will turn not to staff, but to his subordinates for help in analyzing the problem and correcting it. He will not assign staff "policemen" the task of locating the "culprit." If his subordinates have data for controlling their own jobs, the likelihood is that they will already have spotted and either corrected the difficulty themselves or sought help in doing so.

Procedures such as these will probably strike most managers as absurdly restrictive. They are stated this way in order to make perfectly clear the implications of the concept of self-control. Practically they may be accepted as ideals rather than formal requirements.

Self-control is a relative, not an absolute, concept. There may be more or less of it, depending upon a variety of circumstances. A subordinate who is new on the job is obviously not in a position to accept the responsibility for complete self-control. He and his superior might therefore agree to discuss the detailed data concerning his performance at frequent intervals. When some phase of organizational performance is temporarily given a critical importance, there may be the necessity for reducing the normal degree of self-control. A superior might, under such conditions, have an agreement with his subordinates that they would discuss with him immediately any important variances with respect to this variable.

The manager who understands the principle of self-control and is committed to it will adjust his tactics in many ways to meet the circumstances. Moreover, his subordinates will be fully aware of what he is doing and why. Knowing his commitment to the principle, they will accept the realistic necessities with little difficulty. In fact, when there is adequate understanding and commitment, it is of little consequence what data any manager receives. The problem is in the administrative misuse of such data by managers (line or staff) who either do not understand the implications of self-control or lack commitment to it. It takes but little observation to indicate how widespread these misuses are today. An important contributing factor is the almost complete lack of concern with the implications of self-control in the literature on managerial controls.

Managers frequently complain to me about the fact that subordinates "nowadays" won't take responsibility. They say, "I delegate, but they don't want the responsibility." I have been interested to note how often these same managers keep a constant surveillance over the day-to-day performance of subordinates, sometimes two or three levels below themselves.

The fundamental point, and the second prerequisite for improving staff-line relationships, is that management by integration and self-control involves the assumption that the subordinate can be helped to accept responsibility for his job and that he—not his superior or his superior's superior—should have the data he needs to control it.

One of the major fruits of industry's growing use of staff specialists during the past couple of decades has been the development of an elaborate "information technology."* We have today methods of measurement and data collection and analysis which would have been inconceivable a quarter of a century ago. These developments are tremendously powerful. Moreover, the future holds the promise of even more spectacular growth.

The tragedy is the way in which the power provided by this increase in knowledge is being misused. We are defeating the very purposes which it would enable us to achieve, primarily because of a failure to examine our underlying assumptions. "Control" seems superficially to be a straightforward and practical concept, when in fact it is an exceedingly complex one.

The strategy of control implied by Theory Y places the staff in a very different role than the one it now occupies. This changed role (which would involve different expectations on the part of line and

---

* McGregor is, of course, prescient here, including the further observation about the degree to which the IT function is dominated by unstated assumptions about human nature that are much closer to Theory X than to Theory Y.

staff alike) represents a crucial requirement for creating a climate of mutual confidence in which the two groups can collaborate effectively to achieve the objectives of enterprise.

THE APPROPRIATE ROLE OF STAFF

The appropriate role of any major staff group (excluding a few, like an economic forecasting department, whose relationships are relatively limited) is that of providing professional help *to all levels of management.* In some cases, such as engineering, the help is provided primarily to one or two functions, e.g., manufacturing and sales. In other cases, such as accounting and personnel, the help is provided to all other functions.

The hierarchical nature of the organization has tended to focus attention on help given to the level at which the staff group reports. Rewards and punishments for staff members come from there. Moreover, prestige and status are greater the higher the level of "attachment." In large companies, where there are both headquarters and field staff groups, it is particularly important that the headquarters groups recognize and accept their responsibilities for providing help to *all* levels of management.

The provision of professional help is a subtle and complex process. Perhaps the most critical point—and the one hardest to keep clearly in mind—is that help is always defined by the recipient. Taking an action with respect to someone because "it is best for him," or because "it is for the good of the organization," may be influencing him, but it is not providing help *unless he so perceives it.* Headquarters staff groups tend to rationalize the effects of many of their activities on the field organization in a paternalistic manner and, as a consequence, fail to see that they are relying on inappropriate methods of control. When the influence is unsuccessful, the usual reaction occurs: The recipients of the "help" are seen as resistant, stupid, indifferent to organizational needs, etc. The provision of help, like any other form of control or influence, requires selective adaptation to natural law. One important characteristic of "natural law" in this case is that help is defined by the recipient.

The concept of management by direction and control carries the implication that staff groups reporting to a given manager will do what he tells them to. If he assigns a responsibility to a staff group which provides help to him, but at the same time hampers the effective performance of lower levels of management, this is his prerogative. If he places a staff group in the untenable position of being both policemen and "helpers," this is his affair. The duty of the staff group is to follow his orders.

This presents a difficult problem. An independent professional—be he lawyer, doctor, or industrial consultant—faced with such demands would raise the point of conflicting obligations. His professional ethics will not permit him to undertake to help one client at the expense of another. Moreover, his clients usually recognize the potentiality of negative consequences for themselves and agree.

An internal professional staff specialist faces the necessity of persuading those to whom he reports that they will defeat their own purposes if they do not abstain from creating conflicting obligations. The problem is not an ethical one alone. As we saw in connection with the problem of managerial controls in the previous chapter, it is a problem of ineffective as opposed to effective methods of achieving objectives. In this respect, staff groups face the necessity of undertaking an educational role relative to their superiors—a somewhat unusual but not unheard of relationship! In fact, this role is a major one for staff in a number of respects.

Let us examine briefly four kinds of help which the typical staff group will find itself called upon to provide. With respect to all of them, a primary consideration is that help is defined by the recipient.

1. HELP IN STRATEGY PLANNING. The specialized knowledge and skill in the use of the techniques of problem analysis and research possessed by staff groups are increasingly utilized by management, particularly at upper levels, in planning. Often the research and knowledge of a staff group will be the major determinant of organization policy or of managerial strategy.

The role of the staff in providing such help may be compared to the role of an architect in helping a client plan a new home. (The analogy cannot be pressed too far because the architect's role during actual construction is typically *not* comparable to the staff role after a managerial strategy has been decided.) The client has ideas concerning the kind of house he wants, and lots of experience in living. The architect has professional knowledge which can help the client to end up with a house which will better serve his needs than one which he might design for himself. The problem faced by the architect is to bring about an integration of his own and his client's ideas which will satisfy the client and at the same time utilize his own professional competence.

The client's original idea of the house he wants may be quite naïve, perhaps impractical, sometimes unnecessarily expensive. However, if the architect takes a condescending, or an authoritarian, position with respect to the client's ideas, he may find himself out of a job (unless his prestige is so high that the client will accept him on any terms). On the other hand, if the architect simply accepts the client's initial ideas, regardless of their merit, he is not serving the purpose for which he was hired. Given a relationship of mutual confidence, and skill in the consultant role as well as professional knowledge on the part of the architect, the necessary integration may be achieved.

Staff groups helping management in strategy planning have a similar role to occupy. If they are not sensitive to management's needs—expressed and unexpressed—their professional knowledge will not be utilized. On the other hand, if they attempt slavishly to give management what it requests, without bringing to bear their own professional knowledge, they are not fulfilling their responsibilities either to management or to the organization as a whole.

A colleague in the personnel department of a manufacturing company was approached by several middle managers of a technical department who wanted a rapid reading course provided for their subordinates. Their diagnosis: The subordinates could not cope with the materials that piled up on their desks because they had insufficient reading skill. My colleague persuaded these managers to discuss the problem further with him. In the course of the discussion, they decided that it would be worth while to undertake a more detailed analysis of the situation, and they carried it out with his help. The findings: The heart of the problem lay, not in reading skill, but in job assignments, erroneous beliefs of the subordinates about what was expected of them, and other aspects of *the relationship between these managers and their subordinates.** Reading skill was a trivial factor.

The "clients" not only abandoned their original diagnosis and prescription; they involved my colleague as a helper in a rather complete reorganization of their department and a program focused on improving *their own* managerial competence.

While some staff groups—an economics department is a good example—devote their primary effort to strategy planning with upper-level management, others provide much less of this kind of professional help than they might. Many staff groups, for example, become so preoccupied with administering plans and programs and "putting out fires" that they do not fulfill this particular responsibility adequately. Others are unwilling to take the risks involved in attempting to persuade management that its diagnoses and prescriptions, in the absence of professional staff help, are often inadequate. Actually, much can be accomplished in top management education through competent professional help in strategy planning. Here the architect-client analogy is particularly relevant. Some of the recent

---

* Though this may seem patently simplistic, there continue to be a remarkable number of instances of complex organizational problems in which the attempt to address them is via relatively superficial skills training in communications and related capabilities.

talk, for example, about the "bankruptcy" of personnel administration may be significant in just this respect.

2. HELP IN PROBLEM SOLVING. This form of professional help is not unlike that involved in strategy planning except that (1) it is likely to be concerned with more immediate and specific problems, and (2) it is provided to all levels of the organization. Exactly the same role is called for.

The danger with respect to this kind of professional help (in contrast to strategy planning with top management) is that staff groups too easily forget in their dealings with middle and lower management that help is defined by the recipient. It is one of the favorite pastimes of headquarters groups to decide from within their professional ivory tower what help the field organization needs and to design and develop programs for meeting these "needs." Then it becomes necessary to get field management to accept the help provided, and a different role is taken by the staff: that of persuading middle and lower management to utilize the programs. The term "selling" is often used to describe this process, but the power of headquarters staff groups (by virtue of their direct access to top management) is such that field management usually perceives the process as one of "buy or else." Field visits of headquarters staff members are often devoted almost exclusively to such selling of headquarters-designed programs or to checking up to see whether the field is using them.

This kind of help is one reason why the term "burden" is so often applied to staff groups. It is why my young friend referred to earlier feared that the staff would help him to death. It is why many staff-conceived programs which are "bought" by top management achieve indifferent success in the field.

If the staff is genuinely concerned with providing professional help to all levels of management it will devote a great deal of time to exploring "client" needs directly, and to helping the client find solutions which satisfy him. Often the most effective strategy for this purpose is one in which the client develops his own solution with professional help. As indicated by the rapid reading example in the previous section, helping the client diagnose his problem may often be a critical step in this strategy.

Problem-solving help to all levels of management, competently and sensitively provided, is *the* way to develop line confidence in the staff. The needed skills and the understanding of what is involved in providing this kind of help are all too rare among staff specialists today. Professional education in some fields is beginning to include training along these lines, but the need appears not even to be recognized in most engineering schools or schools of business.

In providing this kind of help, the professional specialist will sometimes face the problem of conflicting interests.

A personnel staff member, for example, may be asked by management to give a judgment on the qualifications or performance of a "client" at some lower level of the organization. Or he may, in the course of his professional work, become persuaded that a particular manager is doing substantial harm to the organization through lack of qualifications for his job.

He will destroy the possibility of providing professional help to all levels of management if he permits himself to be used as a source of information or judgment in such situations as these. In the latter case, direct discussion with the individual himself may be called for. However, if the staff man fulfills his responsibility to the organization by revealing his judgments about members of management to their superiors, he will soon preclude the possibility of fulfilling his responsibility for providing help to all levels of management. He cannot help one member of management at the expense of another, nor can he occupy successfully both the role of judge and the role of professional vis-à-vis his "clients."

There probably are cases where the staff member must compromise with respect to such conflicting obligations, but these will be extremely rare. The problem today, all too often, is that no consideration is given to this crucial aspect of the helping role. The consequences for the climate of staff-line relations are readily observable.

3. **HELP WITH RESPECT TO MANAGERIAL CONTROLS.** This form of help has already been considered at some length, and it is perhaps now clear why conventional practice creates so many and such difficult problems. As indicated earlier, the principle of self-control requires that a staff group should never be asked to provide any manager with information to be used for the control of others. Granted that this is a theoretical requirement to which certain practical adjustments must be made, its significance should be very clearly understood by the staff. Otherwise, staff "help" will compound the problems discussed above.

The same principle—that staff provides help for self-control only—applies to what is usually called "coordination," but which means policing the organization with respect to policy and procedures. Help can consist in informing an individual that he is out of line, or that a contemplated action would be in violation of policy—*but with the full understanding by both parties that the staff member will not report his knowledge or opinion to anyone else.*

The helping role and the role of policeman are absolutely incompatible roles. To place an individual in the latter is to destroy the possibility of his occupying the former one successfully.

One further consideration with respect to the staff and controls deserves mention, and that is that maximum standardization is not necessarily accompanied by maximum efficiency. These two variables are less highly correlated than many professional specialists believe. In fact, there is a good deal to be said for establishing the goal of the *minimum* standardization* of human behavior consistent with the

---

* The goal of minimum standardization reveals an apparent contradiction. On the one hand, as McGregor makes clear, imposed standardization is counterproductive and inconsistent with Theory Y assumptions. On the other hand, standardization of processes and procedures is deemed essential for many types of continuous improvement initiatives. The resolution, as noted in Chapter 5, is that standardization represents an effective foundation for continuous improvement when it is led by the front-line workforce, rather than being imposed. (See Deming, *Out of Crisis*, Cambridge, Mass.: MIT Press, 1986.)

ability to operate the organization. This idea quickly runs afoul of the aims and practices of those working in the data processing field in particular. The essential point, however, is that the decision which achieves organizational objectives must be *both* (1) technically and scientifically sound and (2) carried out by people. If we lose sight of the second of these requirements, or if we assume naïvely that people can be made to carry out whatever decisions are technically sound, we run a genuine risk of decreasing rather than increasing the effectiveness of the organization.

Top management in a large, geographically decentralized company became concerned over the size of their permanent inventory of replacement parts. The dollar figure was staggering. Accordingly, a consulting firm was hired to design and install an efficient purchase and inventory control system. The desired objective was to cut the investment in parts inventory in half.

The system designed by this firm was a marvel of efficiency. It included several volumes of coded parts listings and procedures, and a sizable staff to administer the program. A year after it was installed, the inventory investment had been reduced to the desired figure.

During a series of discussions with middle- and lower-level field management about this time, I was simply overwhelmed by the vehement condemnation of this system and of the way it was being administered. Examples, literally by the dozens, were cited of sizable but unnecessary costs to the organization which were resulting. Gross inefficiencies of many kinds were made necessary by rules and procedures which took too little account of local conditions and which provided almost no opportunity for the exercise of managerial judgment.

Of course, many of these managers disliked the curtailment of their freedom and the tightening up of free and easy practices. But the kinds of examples that were cited made it clear that much more than this was involved. The attitude was frequently expressed that "if top management doesn't care any more about waste and inefficiency than this, why should we." Many competent, sincere men said, in one form or another, "We have been wasteful sometimes, but we sure had an interest in the company's welfare. We could have shown them many ways to reduce the parts inventory that would still have permitted us to operate efficiently. But now we are completely hemmed in, and we find we can't do anything to change these unworkable rules. The headquarters staff won't listen. So we live with the rules, and we find ways—sometimes costly—to get around them. *And we're beginning not to give a damn whether the company loses or gains.*"

When I reported these field reactions to top management, they were dismissed as "typical gripes of guys whose sloppy practices have been corrected." The system of control had been designed by a good company; it cost a lot of money to install; the results in terms of the inventory figure were just what had been desired. And that was that.

4. HELP IN ADMINISTERING SERVICES. A fourth activity of staff groups is essentially a line operating function. It consists of administering certain services: equipment maintenance, plant security, payroll administration, eating facilities, activities made necessary by legislation, data processing facilities, benefit plans, etc. Often these require more in the way of managerial than specialized professional skill, but they fall logically within the fields of competence of given staff groups, so they are left there to be administered.

This particular staff function is complicated today by the growing outsourcing of key staff services. Are contractors providing staff services more or less likely to co-opted by line management in the ways described by McGregor? In this context, consider the following comment by a student participating in a Spring 2002 MIT seminar on "Transforming Work, Organizations, and Society" and cited in the paper "Beyond McGregor's Theory Y: Human Capital and Knowledge-Based Work in the 21st Century Organization":

For many tasks and positions, a contracting arrangement does indeed provide a benefit to the government. After all, there is probably little difference with regard to maintenance workers, technicians, and other unskilled or low-skill support personnel as to whether they are government or private-sector employees. Tasks for these employees also tend to be better defined, and supervisory functions are limited to general personnel-related issues. My observation, however, is that when the jobs that are contracted out become more complex, requiring higher-level skills and increased experience, then the system breaks down and ceases to function properly. This leads to more waste, less productivity, and more frustration on the part of both the civil servants and the private-sector employees. I believe that this is due to several interrelated causes:

- *First, the structure of the contract is usually such that there is no incentive for the private contractor to hire the best-qualified candidate. Instead, the least-costly candidate that meets the minimum criteria as specified in the job description is the person that is hired. This is because if the contractor hired a more costly candidate, then he might exceed his proposed budget, which would count against him when profit is calculated or when the contract is up for renewal.*
- *Second, a weaker candidate that is available immediately is preferable over a stronger candidate who may be available in one or two months. The reason for this is that every month that the position goes unfilled will usually count against the contractor's performance or profit. So the private contractor has every reason to fill every position as fast as possible. Whether the candidate is the best or not does not really matter to the bottom line.*
- *Third, in positions requiring more experience or skills, supervisor, reporting, and chain-of-command-related issues become more common and more complex.*

> ➤ ***Fourth, one of the reasons that is often used to justify the on-site contractor structure is that it allows government programs to be more flexible in adjusting personnel levels, since the theory is that private contractors can lay off people more easily than the government. However, while this is true for many low-wage, low-skill positions, my observation is that most of these on-site contracts have significant job-protection guarantees built in. In one case, three-month notices are required before a layoff can occur. These policies, while socially laudable, diminish the value of the on-site contractor arrangement, making the need for such arrangements, especially with regard to higher-skilled jobs, questionable.***

There are no particular problems of staff-line relationships involved in this form of help except (1) poor administration when it occurs and (2) the problem just mentioned of the staff tendency to equate degree of standardization of practice with efficiency.

There is a danger, as previously indicated, that staff groups may become so preoccupied with these administrative responsibilities that they fail to provide the degree and kind of professional help that the organization requires. If the incumbents of staff jobs are former line managers, or technically but not professionally trained specialists, they are likely to find these activities highly congenial. If, however, staff departments include a preponderance of trained and sophisticated professional specialists, there is little danger that the administrative tasks will have priority over genuinely professional activities—unless line management establishes such a priority by its assignment of responsibilities to the staff.

SUMMARY

In order to create a climate of mutual confidence surrounding staff-line relationships within which collaboration in achieving organizational objectives will become possible, several requirements must be met:

1. The inadequacy of the conventional principles of unity of command and of equality of authority and responsibility must be recognized. Not only are these principles unrealistic in the modern industrial corporation, they are the source of many of the difficulties we are trying to correct. They are logically necessary within the context of Theory X, but flatly contradictory to Theory Y.

2. The primary task of any staff group is that of providing specialized help to *all levels* of management, not just to the level at which the group reports.

3. The proper role of the staff member is that of the professional vis-à-vis his clients. The genuinely competent professional recognizes (*a*) that help is always defined by the recipient and (*b*) that he can neither fulfill his responsibilities to the organization nor maintain proper ethical standards of conduct if he is placed in a position which involves conflicting obligations to his managerial "clients."

4. The central principle of managerial control is the principle of self-control. This principle severely limits *both* staff and line use of data and information collected for control purposes as well as the so-called coordinative activities of staff groups. If the principle of self-control is violated, the staff inevitably becomes involved in conflicting obligations, and in addition is required to occupy the incompatible roles of professional helper and policeman.

It may seem impractical to attempt to create a climate of staff-line relationships within the organization similar to that which characterizes effective professional-client relationships in private practice, yet this is essentially what is required. It becomes a possibility only within the context of Theory Y.

IN CONCLUSION

We are now in a position to consider a couple of interesting questions about the staff-line relationship. First, where is the issue of who exercises authority over whom?

With the approach suggested above, the traditional principles which define the role of staff evaporate. The professional-client relationship is an interdependent one in which neither typically exercises authority over the other although there is influence in both directions. The managerial client is dependent on the specialized knowledge and skill of the professional, but if he attempts to get the help he needs by authoritative methods he will defeat his purposes. It is not possible to obtain by command the imaginative, creative effort which distinguishes the competent professional from the glorified clerk. The manager who perceives staff members as flunkies to carry out his orders will never obtain *professional* staff help. On the other hand, the manager who perceives himself as a client utilizing the knowledge and skill of professional specialists will not attempt to achieve this purpose by relying on his authority over them.

The professional, in turn, is dependent upon his clients. Unless they accept and use his help, he has no value to the organization and therefore there is no reason for employing him. If, however, he attempts to impose "help" authoritatively (whether directly or by accepting assignments of control and coordinative responsibilities from his superiors), he places himself in the role of policeman, which is completely incompatible with the professional role.

There is, in fact, no solution to the problem of staff-line relationships in authoritative terms which will achieve organizational objectives adequately. Waste of human resources, friction and antagonism, elaborate and costly protective mechanisms, and lowered commitment to organizational objectives are the inescapable consequences of the traditional conception of the relationship.

Second, what has happened to the distinction between line and staff? It has become evident as a result of our examination of line management's task in the preceding chapters of this volume that the most appropriate roles of the manager vis-à-vis his subordinates are those of teacher, professional helper, colleague, consultant. Only to a limited degree will he assume the role of authoritative boss. The line manager who seeks to operate within the context of Theory Y will establish relationships with his subordinates, his superiors, and his colleagues which are much like those of the professional vis-à-vis his clients. He will become more like a professional staff member (although in general rather than specialized ways) and less like a traditional line manager.

The various functions within the organization differ in many ways (in the number of other functions with which they are related, for example), but not particularly in terms of the traditional line-staff distinction. All managers, whether line or staff, have responsibilities for collaborating with other members of the organization in achieving organizational objectives. Each is concerned with (1) making his own resources of knowledge, skill, and experience available to others; (2) obtaining help from others in fulfilling his own responsibilities; and (3) controlling his own job. Each has *both* line and staff responsibilities.

One consequence of this approach is the greater significance which the managerial *team* acquires at each level of organization. Much of the manager's work—be he line or staff—requires his collaboration with other managers in a relationship where personal authority and power must be subordinated to the requirements of the *task* if the organizational objectives are to be achieved. Effective collaboration of this kind is hindered, not helped, by the traditional distinctions between line and staff. The goal is to utilize the contributions of all the available human resources in reaching the best decisions or problem solutions or action strategies.

The modern industrial organization is a vast complex of interdependent relationships, up, down, across, and even "diagonally." In fact, the interdependence is so great that only collaborative team efforts can make the system work effectively. It is probable that one day we shall begin to draw organization charts as a series of linked groups rather than as a hierarchical structure of individual "reporting" relationships. These points will be considered further in Chapter 16.

REFERENCES

Baumgartel, Howard, "Leadership, Motivations, and Attitudes in Research Laboratories," *Journal of Social Issues*, vol. 12, no. 2, 1956.

Bursk, Edward C., *The Management Team*. Cambridge, Mass.: Harvard University Press, 1954.

Leavitt, Harold J., and Thomas L. Whisler, "Management in the 1980's," *Harvard Business Review*, vol. 36, no. 6 (November–December), 1958.

Lippitt, Ronald, Jeanne Watson, and Bruce Westley, *Dynamics of Planned Change*. New York: Harcourt, Brace and Company, Inc., 1958.

McGregor, Douglas, "The Staff Function in Human Relations," *Journal of Social Issues*, vol. 4, no. 3, 1948.

Pelz, Donald C., "Motivation of the Engineering and Research Specialist," American Management Association, General Management Series, no. 186, 1957.

Sampson, Robert C., *The Staff Role in Management*. New York: Harper & Brothers, 1955.

Shepard, Herbert A., "Supervisors and Subordinates in Research," *The Journal of Business*, vol. 29, no. 4, 1956.

SELECTED REFERENCES TO THE ANNOTATED EDITION

Deming, W. Edwards, *Out of Crisis*, Cambridge, Mass.: MIT Press, 1986.

Imai, Maasaki, *Kaizen: The Key to Japan's Competitive Success*, New York: McGraw-Hill, 1986.

Kochan, Thomas, et al., "Beyond McGregor's Theory Y: Human Capital and Knowledge-Based Work in the 21st-Century Organization," in Thomas Kochan and Richard Schmalensee (eds.), *Management: Inventing and Delivering Its Future*, Cambridge, Mass.: MIT Press, 2003.

DISCUSSION QUESTIONS FOR CHAPTER 12

1. Reflect on the line and staff functions in an organization with which you are familiar. What would a typical "week in the life" look like if the line and staff were to operate as more of a "team" in the ways that McGregor recommends?
2. Does the current trend toward outsourcing staff functions help or hinder the line-staff collaboration that McGregor advocates? What are the implications?
3. Select a staff function in a given organization—HR, finance, information systems, sales, marketing, purchasing, maintenance, safety, logistics, etc.—and assess the percentage of time that is currently devoted to each of the four functional roles identified by McGregor, with the total being 100 percent of available staff time. This "current state" is:
   - Help in strategic planning __________%
   - Help in problem solving __________%
   - Help with respect to managerial controls __________%
   - Help in administering services __________%

Now, do the same allocation for how things ***should be in three to five years***, which would be the following "desired state":

- Help in strategic planning __________%
- Help in problem solving __________%
- Help with respect to managerial controls __________%
- Help in administering services __________%

100%

What are the implications?[1]

[1] This exercise is adapted from a conceptual framework and exercise developed by Russ Eisenstat and further adapted by Jan Klein. In the framework, three functional roles are identified: (1) oversight/audit, (2) service/administration, and (3) transformation/change agent. This framework is also reflected in Jan Klein, "The Evolution of HR Professionals from Traditional Managers to Change Agents in Strategic Partnership for High Performance," Work in America Institute, 1995.

PART THREE

THE DEVELOPMENT OF MANAGERIAL TALENT

INTRODUCTION TO CHAPTER 13

AN ANALYSIS OF LEADERSHIP

In Chapter 13, McGregor rejects the classic debate over whether leaders are born or made, as well as any detailed listing of the attributes of leaders. Instead, he urges us to understand leadership as the product of four interacting variables, which are

1. The characteristics of the leader
2. The attitudes, needs, and other personal characteristics of the followers
3. Characteristics of the organization, such as its purpose, its structure, the nature of the tasks to be performed
4. The social, economic, and political milieu

In other words, "it is more fruitful to consider leadership as a relationship between the leader and the situation than as a universal pattern of characteristics possessed by certain people." Given that these circumstances are sure to change over time, McGregor concludes that it will be impossible to select today the individuals who will be needed in the future as leaders. Instead, he concludes that one of management's major tasks is "*to provide a heterogeneous supply of human resources from which individuals can be selected to fill a variety of specific but unpredictable needs.*" Further, he concludes that management development programs "should involve many people within the organization rather than a select few." The development should also emphasize "the unique capacities and potentialities of each individual rather than common objectives for all participants." Finally, McGregor observes that promotion policies "should be administered that these heterogeneous resources are actually considered when openings occur." Ultimately, McGregor concludes that "outstanding leadership *at any level* [is] a precious thing."

A classic resource for leaders developing in the ways outlined by McGregor is Warren Bennis's 1989 book, *On Becoming a Leader.*[1] In 2002, Warren Bennis was joined by Robert Thomas, and the two provide a unique demonstration of the way values and patterns of interaction shape leaders across different eras in their book *Geeks and Geezers.*[2] Although the substantive leadership challenges facing different generations may vary, they document enduring crucibles of leadership that build on the very elements highlighted by McGregor.

Although McGregor called for a more diverse and broadly distributed approach to leadership, it still reflected a primary orientation toward executive and managerial positions. Taken to the extreme, this has led to what Rakesh Khurana called the cult of the charismatic CEO.[3] Contrast this approach with the needs of modern networked and knowledge-based organizations, combined with the underlying principles of Theory Y management (with its emphasis on participation, integration, and mutual influence in line-staff relations). It is in this spirit that faculty members at MIT developed and adopted "distributed leadership" as the model guiding the teaching of this subject. The basic

---

[1] Warren G. Bennis, *On Becoming a Leader*, Reading, Mass.: Addison-Wesley, 1989.

[2] Warren G. Bennis and Robert J. Thomas, *Geeks and Geezers: How Era, Values, and Defining Moments Shape Leaders*, Boston: Harvard Business School Press, 2002.

[3] Rakesh Khurana, *Searching for a Corporate Savior: The Irrational Quest for Charismatic CEOs*, Princeton, N.J.: Princeton University Press, 2004.

assumption underlying this approach is that leadership is a process that can and should be exercised by people at all levels of an organization as they take independent actions and work together in teams and networks.[4]

[4] This view sees leadership as being closely tied to managing organizational change successfully and argues that leadership development is a lifelong process shaped by one's personal values and requiring an ability to learn from one's successes and failures throughout life. See Deborah Ancona, "Leadership in the Age of Uncertainty," in Deboran Ancona, Thomas Kochan, Maureen Scully, Eleanor Westney, and John VanMaanen, *Managing for the Future: Organizational Behavior and Processes*, 3d ed., Cincinnati: South-Western College Publishing, 2004.

CHAPTER 13

AN ANALYSIS OF LEADERSHIP

Are successful managers born or "made"? Does success as a manager rest on the possession of a certain core of abilities and traits, or are there many combinations of characteristics which can result in successful industrial leadership? Is managerial leadership—or its potential—a property of the individual, or is it a term for describing a relationship between people? Will the managerial job twenty years from now require the same basic abilities and personality traits as it does today?

The previous chapters of this volume suggest tentative answers to these questions. Knowledge gained from research in the social sciences sheds additional light on these and other questions relevant to leadership in industry. It does not provide final, definitive answers. There is much yet to be learned. But the accumulated evidence points with high probability toward certain ones among a number of possible assumptions.

Prior to the 1930s it was widely believed that leadership was a property of the individual, that a limited number of people were uniquely endowed with abilities and traits which made it possible for them to become leaders. Moreover, these abilities and traits were believed to be inherited rather than acquired.

As a consequence of these beliefs, research studies in this field were directed toward the identification of the universal characteristics of leadership so that potential leaders might be more readily identified. A large number of studies were published—many based on armchair theorizing, but some utilizing biographical or other empirical data.

Examination of this literature reveals an imposing number of supposedly essential characteristics of the successful leader—over a hundred, in fact, even after elimination of obvious duplication and overlap of terms. The search still continues in some quarters. Every few months a new list appears based on the latest analysis. And each new list differs in some respects from the earlier ones.

However, social science research in this field since the 1930s has taken new directions. Some social scientists have become interested in studying the behavior as well as the personal characteristics of leaders. As a result, some quite different ideas about the nature of leadership have emerged.

The research in this field in the last twenty years has been prolific. A recent summary cites 111 references, of which six were published prior to 1930. As a result of such work, a number of generalizations about leadership may be stated with reasonable certainty. Among these, the following are particularly significant for management.

GENERALIZATIONS FROM RECENT RESEARCH

It is quite unlikely that there is a single basic pattern of abilities and personality traits characteristic of all leaders. The personality characteristics of the leader are not unimportant, but those which are essential differ considerably depending upon the circumstances. The requirements for successful political leadership are different from those for industrial management or military or educational leadership. Failure is as frequent as success in transfers of leaders from one type of social institution to another.* The reasons are perhaps evident in the light of the discussion in earlier chapters of this volume.

---

* Research on what came to be termed "situational leadership" builds on the approach outlined here. (See Kenneth Blanchard, P. Zigarmi, and D. Zigarmi, *Leadership and the One Minute Manager: Increasing Effectiveness through Situational Leadership*, New York: William Morrow, 1985; Robert R. Blake, Robert Mouton, and Jane S. Mouton, *The Managerial Grid III: The Key to Leadership Excellence*, Houston: Gulf Publishing Co., 1985; Paul Hershey and Kenneth Blanchard, *Management of Organizational Behavior: Utilizing Human Resources*, 5th ed., Englewood Cliffs, N.J.: Prentice-Hall, 1988.)

Even within a single institution such as industry, different circumstances require different leadership characteristics. Comparisons of successful industrial leaders in different historical periods, in different cultures, in different industries, or even in different companies have made this fairly obvious. The leadership requirements of a young, struggling company, for example, are quite different from those of a large, well-established firm.

Within the individual company different functions (sales, finance, production) demand rather different abilities and skills of leadership. Managers who are successful in one function are sometimes, but by no means always, successful in another. The same is true of leadership at different organizational levels. Every successful foreman would not make a successful president (or vice versa!). Yet each may be an effective leader.

On the other hand, leaders who differ notably in abilities and traits are sometimes equally successful when they succeed each other in a given situation. Within rather wide limits, weaknesses in certain characteristics can be compensated by strength in others. This is particularly evident in partnerships and executive teams in which leadership functions are, in fact, *shared*. The very idea of the team implies different and supplementary patterns of abilities among the members.

Many characteristics which have been alleged to be essential to the leader turn out not to differentiate the successful leader from unsuccessful ones. In fact, some of these—integrity, ambition, judgment, for example—are to be found not merely in the leader, but in any successful member of an organization.

Finally, among the characteristics essential for leadership are skills and attitudes which can be acquired or modified extensively through learning. These include competence in planning and initiating action, in problem solving, in keeping communication channels open and functioning effectively, in accepting responsibility, and in the skills of social interaction. Such skills are not inherited, nor is their acquisition dependent on the possession of any unique pattern of inborn characteristics.

It is, of course, true that the few outstanding leaders in any field have been unusually gifted people, but these preeminent leaders differ widely among themselves in their strengths and weaknesses. They do not possess a pattern of leadership characteristics in common. The evidence to date does not prove conclusively that there is no basic universal core of personal qualifications for leadership. However, few of the social scientists who have worked extensively during recent years in this field would regard this as a promising possibility for further work. On the contrary, the research during the past two decades has shown that we must look beyond the personal qualifications of the leader if we wish to understand what leadership is.

LEADERSHIP IS A RELATIONSHIP

There are at least four major variables now known to be involved in leadership: (1) the characteristics of the leader; (2) the attitudes, needs, and other personal characteristics of the followers; (3) characteristics of the organization, such as its purpose, its structure, the nature of the tasks to be performed; and (4) the social, economic, and political milieu.* The personal characteristics required for effective performance as a leader vary, depending on the other factors.

This is an important research finding. *It means that leadership is not a property of the individual, but a complex relationship among these variables.* The old argument over whether the leader makes history or history makes the leader is resolved by this conception. Both assertions are true within limits.

The relationship between the leader and the situation is essentially circular. Organization structure and policy, for example, are established by top management. Once established, they set limits on

---

* McGregor has been criticized for primarily focusing on patterns of interaction within the organization, but here is one of the few instances where he formally includes the "social, economic, and political milieu."

the leadership patterns which will be acceptable within the company. However, influences from above (a change in top management with an accompanying change in philosophy), from below (following recognition of a union and adjustment to collective bargaining, for example), or from outside (social legislation, changes in the market, etc.) bring about changes in these organizational characteristics. Some of these may lead to a redefinition of acceptable leadership patterns. The changes which occurred in the leadership of the Ford Motor Company after Henry Ford I retired provide a dramatic illustration.

The same thing is true of the influence of the broader milieu. The social values, the economic and political conditions, the general standard of living, the level of education of the population, and other factors characteristic of the late 1800s had much to do with the kinds of people who were successful as industrial leaders during that era. Those men in turn helped to shape the nature of the industrial environment. Their influence affected the character of our society profoundly.

Today, industry requires a very different type of industrial leader than it did in 1900. Similarly, today's leaders are helping to shape industrial organizations which tomorrow will require people quite different from themselves in key positions.

An important point with respect to these situational influences on leadership is that they operate selectively—in subtle and unnoticed as well as in obvious ways—to reward conformity with acceptable patterns of behavior and to punish deviance from these. The differing situations from company to company, and from unit to unit within a company, each have their selective consequences. The observable managerial "types" in certain companies are illustrative of this phenomenon. One consequence of this selectively is the tendency to "weed out" deviant individuals, some of whom might nevertheless become effective, perhaps outstanding, leaders.

Even if there is no single universal pattern of characteristics of the leader, it is conceivable at least that there might be certain universal characteristics *of the relationship* between the leader and the other situational factors which are essential for optimum organized human effort in all situations. This is doubtful. Consider, for example, the relationship of an industrial manager with a group of native employees in an underdeveloped country on the one hand, and with a group of United States workmen who are members of a well-established international union on the other.* Moreover, even if research finally indicates that there are such universal requirements of the relationship, there will still be more than one way of achieving them. For example, if "mutual confidence" between the leader and the led is a universal requirement, it is obvious that there are many ways of developing and maintaining this confidence.

We have already considered some of the significant conditions for the success of certain relationships involving interdependence in industrial organizations today. To achieve these conditions, the supervisor requires skills and attitudes, *but these can be acquired by people who differ widely in their inborn traits and abilities*. In fact, one of the important lessons from research and experience in this field is that the attempt to train supervisors to adopt a single leadership "style" yields poorer results than encouraging them to create the essential conditions *in their individual ways* and with due regard for their own particular situations. Note also in this connection how organization structure and management philosophy may either encourage or inhibit the supervisor in establishing these conditions.

It does not follow from these considerations that *any* individual can become a successful leader in a given situation. It *does* follow that successful leadership is not dependent on the possession of a single universal pattern of inborn traits and abilities. It seems likely that leadership potential (considering the tremendous variety of situations for which leadership is required) is broadly rather than narrowly distributed in the population.

---

* The contrast is, of course, no longer obvious.

Research findings to date suggest, then, that it is more fruitful to consider leadership as a relationship between the leader and the situation than as a universal pattern of characteristics possessed by certain people.* The differences in requirements for successful leadership in different situations are more striking than the similarities. Moreover, research studies emphasize the importance of leadership skills and attitudes which can be acquired and are, therefore, not inborn characteristics of the individual.

It has often happened in the physical sciences that what was once believed to be an inherent property of objects—gravity, for example, or electrical "magnetism," or mass—has turned out to be a complex relationship between internal and external factors. The same thing happens in the social sciences, and leadership is but one example.

IMPLICATIONS FOR MANAGEMENT

What is the practical relevance for management of these findings of social science research in the field of leadership? First, if we accept the point of view that leadership consists of a relationship between the leader, his followers, the organization, and the social milieu, and if we recognize that these situational factors are subject to substantial changes with time, we must recognize that we cannot predict the personal characteristics of the managerial resources that an organization will require a decade or two hence. Even if we can list the positions to be filled, we cannot define very adequately the essential characteristics of the people who will be needed in those situations at that time. *One of management's major tasks, therefore, is to provide a heterogeneous supply of human resources from which individuals can be selected to fill a variety of specific but unpredictable needs.*†

---

* This is a potential forerunner for the term *situational leadership*.

† This strong implication of McGregor's analysis contrasts with the underlying assumptions in many leadership development programs, which are rarely oriented around supplying a heterogeneous mix of new leaders.

This is a blow to those who have hoped that the outcome of research would be to provide them with methods by which they could select today the top management of tomorrow. It is a boon to those who have feared the consequences of the "crown prince" approach to management development. It carries other practical implications of some importance.

With the modern emphasis on career employment and promotion from within, management must pay more than casual attention to its recruitment practices. It would seem logical that this process should tap a variety of sources: liberal arts as well as technical graduates, small colleges as well as big universities, institutions in different geographic regions, etc. It may be necessary, moreover, to look carefully at the criteria for selection of college recruits if heterogeneity is a goal. The college senior who graduates in the top 10 per cent of his class may come from a narrow segment of the range of potential leaders for industry. What of the student who has, perhaps for reasons unrelated to intellectual capacity, graduated in the middle of his class because he got A's in some subjects and C's and D's in others? What of the student whose academic achievement was only average because the education system never really challenged him?

As a matter of fact there is not much evidence that high academic achievement represents a necessary characteristic for industrial leadership. There may be a positive correlation, but it is not large enough to provide a basis for a recruitment policy. In fact, the current President of the United States would have been passed over at graduation by any management recruiter who relied on this correlation! It may be, on the contrary, that the *intellectual* capacity required for effective leadership in many industrial management positions is no greater than that required for graduation from a good college. Of course, there are positions requiring high intellectual capacity, but it does not follow that there is a one-to-one correlation between this characteristic and success as an industrial leader. (This question of intellectual capacity is, of course, only one reason why industry seeks the bulk of its potential managerial resources among college graduates today. There are other factors involved: confidence and social poise, skill acquired through participation in extracurricular activities, personal ambition and drive, etc. These, however, are relatively independent of class standing.)

It may be argued that intellectual *achievement*, as measured by consistently high grades in all subjects, is evidence of motivation and willingness to work. Perhaps it is—in the academic setting—but it is also evidence of willingness to conform to the quite arbitrary demands of the educational system. There is little reason for assuming that high motivation and hard work *in school* are the best predictors of motivation and effort in later life. There are a good many examples to the contrary.

A second implication from research findings about leadership is that a management development program should involve many people within the organization rather than a select few.* The fact that some companies have been reasonably successful in developing a selected small group of managerial trainees may well be an artifact—an example of the operation of the "self-fulfilling prophecy." If these companies had been equally concerned to develop managerial talent within a much broader sample, they might have accomplished this purpose with no greater percentage of failures. And, if the generalizations above are sound, they would have had a richer, more valuable pool of leadership resources to draw on as a result.

Third, management should have as a goal the development of the unique capacities and potentialities of each individual rather than common objectives for all participants. This is a purpose which is honored on paper much more than in practice. It is difficult to achieve, particularly in the big company, but if we want heteroge-

---

* This focus on distributed leadership has been incorporated into the "Sloan Leadership Model," which is a core part of the curriculum for the MBA and related professional practice degrees at MIT's Sloan School of Management. (See Deborah Ancona, Thomas Kochan, Maureen Scully, Eleanor Westney, and John VanMaanen, *Managing for the Future: Organizational Behavior and Processes*, 3d ed., Cincinnati: South-Western College Publishing, 2004.)

neous leadership resources to meet the unpredictable needs of the future we certainly won't get them by subjecting all our managerial trainees to the same treatment.

Moreover, this process of developing heterogeneous resources must be continuous; it is never completed. Few human beings ever realize all of their potentialities for growth, even though some may reach a practical limit with respect to certain capacities. Each individual is unique, and it is this uniqueness we will constantly encourage and nourish if we are truly concerned to develop leaders for the industry of tomorrow.

Fourth, the promotion policies of the company should be so administered that these heterogeneous resources are actually considered when openings occur. There is little value in developing a wide range of talent if only a small and possibly limited segment of it constitutes the field of candidates when a particular position is being filled.

In view of the selective operation of situational variables referred to above, there may be legitimate questions concerning the value of an *exclusive* policy of "promotion from within." It is conceivable that in a large and reasonably decentralized company sufficient heterogeneity can be maintained by transfers of managerial talent between divisions, but it is probable that fairly strenuous efforts will be required to offset the normal tendency to create and maintain a "type," a homogeneous pattern of leadership within a given organization. Without such efforts competent individuals who don't "fit the pattern" are likely to be passed over or to leave because their talents are not rewarded. Many industrial organizations, for example, would not easily tolerate the strong individualism of a young Charles Kettering today.

Finally, if leadership is a function—a complex relation between leader and situation—we ought to be clear that every promising recruit is *not* a potential member of top management. Some people in some companies will become outstanding leaders as foremen, or as plant superintendents, or as professional specialists. Many of these would not be effective leaders in top management positions, at least under the circumstances prevailing in the company.

If we take seriously the implications of the research findings in this field, we will place high value on such people. We will seek to enable them to develop to the fullest their potentialities in the role they can fill best. And we will find ways to reward them which will persuade them that we consider outstanding leadership *at any level* to be a precious thing.

REFERENCES

Bennis, Warren G., "Leadership Theory and Administrative Behavior," *Administrative Science Quarterly*, vol. 4, no. 3, 1959.

Fortune Editors, *The Executive Life*. New York: Doubleday & Company, Inc., 1956.

Gibb, Cecil A., "Leadership," in Gardner Lindzey (ed.), *Handbook of Social Psychology*. Reading, Mass.: Addison-Wesley Publishing Company, 1954, vol. II.

Ginzberg, Eli, *What Makes an Executive*. New York: Columbia University Press, 1955.

Knickerbocker, Irving, "Leadership: A Conception and Some Implications," *Journal of Social Issues*, vol. 4, no. 3, 1948.

Selznick, Philip, *Leadership in Administration*. Evanston, III.: Row, Peterson & Company, 1957.

SELECTED REFERENCES TO THE ANNOTATED EDITION

Ancona, Deborah, "Leadership in the Age of Uncertainty," in Deborah Ancona, Thomas Kochan, Maureen Scully, Eleanor Westney, and John VanMaanen, *Managing for the Future: Organizational Behavior and Processes*, 3rd ed., Cincinnati: South-Western College Publishing, 2004

Bennis, Warren G., *On Becoming a Leader*, Reading, MA: Addison-Wesley, 1989.

Bennis, Warren G., and Robert J. Thomas, *Geeks & Geezers: How Era, Values, and Defining Moments Shape Leaders*, Boston: Harvard Business School Press, 2002.

Blake, Robert R., Robert Mouton, and Jane S. Mouton, *The Managerial Grid III: The Key to Leadership Excellence,* Houston: Gulf Publishing Co., 1985.

Hershey, Paul, and Kenneth Blanchard, *Management of Organizational Behavior: Utilizing Human Resources,* 5th ed., Englewood Cliffs, NJ: Prentice Hall 1988.

DISCUSSION QUESTIONS FOR CHAPTER 13

1. McGregor calls for broad involvement in management development by leaders at all levels. To what degree has that become a reality today?

2. What would be key features of a leadership development process that is oriented around developing the unique capabilities of each individual, as McGregor recommends?

3. What are examples of leadership selection processes that are designed to produce a diverse set of next-generation leaders, as McGregor recommends, rather than selecting leaders that just fit within a relatively narrow range?

MANAGEMENT DEVELOPMENT PROGRAMS

Two approaches to management development are highlighted in Chapter 14—the manufacturing approach and the agricultural approach. Under the manufacturing approach, "people have been assigned the *engineering* task of *designing* a program and *building* the necessary *machinery*, toward the end of *producing* the needed *supply* of managerial talent." This is contrasted with an agricultural view that "the individual will grow into what he is capable of becoming, provided we can create the proper conditions for that growth." Of course the climate, soil, and cultivation methods of concern to McGregor are "(1) economic and technological characteristics of the industry and the firm, (2) policies and practices of the company, and (3) the behavior of the immediate superior." The link between the micro process of management development and the larger macro context is flagged by McGregor, but remains a promising domain for analysis. His focus on policies and practices highlights a common disconnect in the managerial learning that takes place.[1] "Top management wants its subordinates to be concerned with the business as a whole; but the actual rewards and punishments

[1] This form of "oppositional learning" is identified as one of six distinct modes of organizational learning in Chapter 6 of Joel Cutcher-Gershenfeld and J. Kevin Ford, *Valuable Disconnects in Organizational Learning Systems: Integrating Bold Visions and Harsh Realities*, New York: Oxford University Press, 2004.

(from the type of structure, from performance criteria, from policies and control systems, and from the behavior and attitudes of his boss and his peers) may well have the opposite effect. Learning will occur, but not growth in the desired direction."

Too often the terms *knowledge worker* and *the knowledge economy* are equated with the elite professional, managerial, and technical workforce. Yet we know that front-line workers likewise can, and indeed must, be mobilized to contribute their knowledge and skills to the modern workplace. In this sense, management development is just one part of development for the full workforce. As former president of South Korea and Nobel Peace Prize recipient Kim Dae Jung observed:

> *In the age of the knowledge-based economy, every citizen must become a new intellectual. Everyone should acquire the skill to make the most of their minds to create new value for society and generate income for themselves.*[2]

A larger question arises concerning a deeply embedded assumption in McGregor's writing, which is that the choice to emphasize a Theory Y approach rests with management leadership. Consider the alternatives that are brought up in the following comment by MIT Professor Thomas Kochan:

> *Maybe management is too important to be left to managers. Indeed, the rise of business schools and MBA programs since 1960 fueled this idea. Perhaps we need to ask what broader societal institutions should shape managerial behavior so that organizations reflect societal values. If we want a better*

[2] From a World Bank Conference in Seoul, South Korea, 2001; cited in Thomas Kochan, "Restoring Trust in the Human Resource Management Profession," *Asia Pacific Journal of Human Resources*, vol. 42, no. 2, 2004, p. 138.

balance between Theory X and Y in organizations, then we might need laws and institutions that constrain Theory X and promote Theory Y. That is, the more we allow low-cost, low-wage competitive strategies to survive, the more we encourage command and control models of management. So public policies and institutions that limit the viability of these low-road strategies would encourage development and diffusion of more Theory Y assumptions and behaviors. Business school curricula and business school cases would need to be framed quite differently than they are now—less the manager as the autonomous leader and more attention to distributed leadership and distributed influence and organizational processes.

CHAPTER 14

MANAGEMENT DEVELOPMENT PROGRAMS

There was a time when it was widely believed that management development was an automatic process requiring little attention. It was felt that the normal operation of the industrial organization would permit the cream to rise to the top, where it would become visible and could be skimmed off as needed. It will become apparent as we examine the subject that there is more than a little to be said in favor of this theory *provided conditions are created which permit the cream to rise.* However, most managements of large companies have discarded this theory and proceeded along other lines. Particularly since World War II we have seen an unprecedented growth in management development programs and activities throughout the whole Western World. It is rare to find a large or even medium-sized company today which does not have a formal program and a staff to administer it.

If we grant that management development cannot be left entirely to chance, there are several alternatives open. Many companies have followed one of these which might be characterized as the "manufacturing" approach. Management has not phrased its philosophy this way, but it has looked on the problem essentially as a production problem. People have been assigned the *engineering* task of *designing* a program and *building* the necessary *machinery*, toward the end of *producing* the needed *supply* of managerial talent. The evidence of this philosophy is to be seen on every hand. We have management inventories, replacement charts with elaborate codes and colors, formal machinery for recruiting and selecting potential managerial talent, special indoctrination programs for the new recruits, appraisal programs, job rotation, and a welter of training activities. The production of managerial talent is itself a big business.*

This manufacturing philosophy of management development is a natural concomitant of management by direction and control. The requirements of the organization are paramount. Individuals are selected, oriented, appraised, rotated, promoted, sent to school—all within an administrative framework which leaves them relatively little voice in their own career development. The concept of integration is not so much ignored as assumed to be automatic: Of course, people "with potential" want to get ahead, acquire status, obtain economic rewards, be developed. They should welcome, therefore, these many activities and programs which provide for their needs.

Most people do want the things that management development programs provide. However, each individual is unique in terms of his capacities, his interests and goals, his talents. The manufacturing approach to management development does many things *to* him and *for* him, but generally with the tacit assumption that what is good for the organization is good for him. The specific, uniquely individual, mutually adaptive characteristics† of the integrative process tend to be missed by this approach.

In the last analysis the individual must develop himself, and he will do so optimally only in terms of what *he* sees as meaningful and valuable. If he becomes an active party to the decisions that are made about his development, he is likely to make the most of the opportunities that are presented. If, on the other hand, he is simply a passive agent being rotated or sent to school, or promoted, or otherwise manipulated, he is less likely to be motivated to develop himself.

It would be a mistake to dismiss the accomplishments in this field as insignificant. Management's concern with the problem has been

---

* Needless to say, this "manufacturing" language and approach continue to characterize many formal management development programs in industry.

† The concept of a mutually adaptive management development program is particularly compelling.

real, and its efforts have by no means been unsuccessful. One cannot escape the impression, however, that the individual frequently "gets lost in the machinery," and that this is not merely a consequence of company size or of the complexity of the problem. It is to a considerably greater extent a consequence of management's conception that the task is one of manufacturing talent from available raw materials.

An alternative approach to management development is somewhat analogous to that of agriculture. It is concerned with "growing" talent rather than manufacturing it. The fundamental idea behind such an approach is that the individual will grow into what he is capable of becoming, provided we can create the proper conditions for that growth. Such an approach involves less emphasis on manufacturing techniques and more on controlling the climate and the fertility of the soil, and on methods of cultivation.

Taking this point of view, let us consider some of the important environmental conditions which affect the growth of managers. We will look at three groups of factors: (1) economic and technological characteristics of the industry and the firm, (2) policies and practices of the company, and (3) the behavior of the immediate superior.

ECONOMIC AND TECHNOLOGICAL CHARACTERISTICS OF THE FIRM

Obviously, a rapidly growing industry, characterized by substantial and continuous technological innovation, represents a different environment for managerial growth than a static or contracting industry facing severe economic difficulties, and in which there is little technological innovation.* There may be differences of opinion concerning the degree to which top management can control these broad environmental characteristics, but there is no question that they do influence the nature and the rate of managerial development.

---

* This focus on the economic and technological characteristics of the firm and the way they shape management development is one of the few instances in this book where the larger organizational context is taken into account.

The difference was brought home sharply to me recently when I spent a couple of days in each of two companies. The first was a division of a large company which was developing one of the new intercontinental ballistic missiles. The people who make up this organization are young; they are tremendously excited over the challenge represented by their task. The technology of the industry is growing so fast that it is almost impossible to keep up with it. Changes and innovations—some of them revolutionary—take place almost daily. Growth is rapid, and opportunities for advancement and new experience occur faster than people can quite meet them. Almost no one seemed to feel that he was genuinely "on top of his job," and yet it was clear that the organization was doing an effective job, that morale was high, and that people were growing.

I went directly from this company to the headquarters of a major railroad. The contrast in atmosphere left me bemused for days. The managers with whom I talked there showed almost none of the excitement and challenge which had been so vividly demonstrated in the other organization. They expressed generally cynical views about the opportunities for growth and development; they talked about the rigidities of the organization and about the lack of challenge in their work. While there was a fundamental enthusiasm among them for railroading, I got the impression that it was focused on the romantic past rather than on the future. Promotions and new job opportunities were seen as depending primarily upon openings created by death or retirement. The climate for managerial growth under these conditions is certainly not optimum, even though this particular company is one that is making sincere and reasonably effective efforts to overcome its economic difficulties and to improve the caliber of its management generally.

These aspects of the organizational environment are perhaps relatively uncontrollable, at least in short-run terms. They are like the differences between the conditions faced by the vegetable grower in the San Joaquin Valley of California and the New Hampshire farmer. Nevertheless, within a given environment, the nature and the quality of the processes of growth can be influenced by managerial philosophy and practice. Successful crops *are* grown in New Hampshire.

THE EFFECTS OF COMPANY STRUCTURE, POLICY, AND PRACTICE

Growth and development of the human being—changes in attitudes, perceptions, and behavior—are processes which involve learning. Learning, in turn, is a function of rewards and punishments. These may be external and tangible (a salary increase, praise from the boss, increased status, etc.) or internal and intangible (the satisfaction of solving a tough problem, of acquiring new knowledge or new skill, or the frustration of being blocked in pursuing one's goals). The development of the individual is materially influenced by the kinds of rewards and satisfactions on the one hand, or punishments and frustrations on the other, which are characteristic of his company. Organization structure and management philosophy as represented in policies and their associated practices involve a variety of rewards and punishments and thus affect his growth.*

For example, a centralized organization structure, with rigid lines between departments and functions and many hierarchical levels, restricts the opportunities for the individual manager to assume responsibility, to try out new ideas, to exercise judgment. Such a structure limits growth. This is one of the major arguments for decentralization and for a wide span of control such as is inherent in flat organizations. A decentralized organization provides an environment in which the individual, through taking greater responsibility for his own behavior, obtains intrinsic rewards in the form of ego and self-actualization satisfactions, which in turn encourage him to take still more responsibility and thus to grow.

---

* This focus on structure, policy, and practice anticipates the work by Miles and Snow in *Organizational Strategy, Structure and Process*, New York: McGraw-Hill, 1978.

This orientation toward adapting training and development to match the context is signaled by the American Society for Training and Development (ASTD) in its learning manifesto, which states,

The focus on our profession on developing people, in the light of the knowledge economy, is the key to competitive advantage. There is a new world of learning emerging—one that links people, learning, and performance—and a new community growing around it.

The control over behavior exerted by managerial procedures also affects growth. As we have already seen, tight systems of control negate the positive advantages of decentralization. If his superiors keep him under constant surveillance by means of detailed reports on his behavior, he has no real freedom of action.

Is the company operated in such a way that the individual manager is rewarded for narrow departmental loyalties and for efforts devoted exclusively to improving the operation of his particular function, or is he rewarded for behavior which contributes to the objectives of the organization as a whole? Obviously, top management wants its subordinates to be concerned with the business as a whole; but the actual rewards and punishments (from the type of structure, from performance criteria, from policies and control systems, and from the behavior and attitudes of his boss and his peers) may well have the opposite effect. Learning will occur, but not growth in the desired direction.

What are the rewards for the individual who elects to pursue a staff career, or for the brilliant researcher who is not motivated to enter research administration? Is the salary structure one which offers comparable rewards for staff and line at any given level? Does it, for example, put a ceiling on the salary of the researcher unless he becomes a manager? And, beyond salary, what are the prevailing attitudes in the company toward jobs other than those in line management? Are they considered to be a "burden," second-class forms of "busywork"? The organization needs people who will grow in the direction of specialized professional competence as well as those who will become high-level line managers. Do the rewards and punishments—both formal and informal—encourage both these forms of growth?

What about the way in which promotions are administered? Is promotion considered to be the only real measure of success for the individual? In some companies, the environment of attitude and practice is such that the individual who is not promotable is considered to be a failure. It is said of him that he "lacks potential," or that he "has reached his ceiling." Not only is this attitude in itself punishing, but the rewards for further growth—salary, status, recognition, etc.—are lacking (the formal machinery cannot encompass such exceptions). This, despite the probability that he could, if adequate rewards were available, continue to grow and to increase his contribution to the organization at his present level. Can the individual who for personal reasons does not want to climb higher on the organizational ladder, but instead wishes to make his contribution to the enterprise an outstanding one at his present level, remain there without being punished in a variety of subtle ways for having made this choice?

In an organization where promotion is the sole measure of success, most people are oriented to the job to which they hope to move next. Naturally, they want to be promoted in order to prove their value, so their performance on the present job is geared exclusively to those things which will get them out of it! This, too, is learning resulting from rewards and punishments, but is it growth in the direction management desires?

Is there what Larry Appley has so appropriately termed "the timely elimination of the incompetent"? This form of punishment has substantial effects not only on those who may be asked to leave the organization, but on others who remain. It indicates something about management's standards of performance, about what kind of behavior will be rewarded.

Universities are often criticized by industrial management for their permanent tenure system under which a faculty member achieves job security under certain conditions and after a probationary period of several years' duration. They see this as encouraging mediocre performance because the individual with tenure is not subject to the threat of being fired, except under rare and extreme conditions. However, most industrial organizations have an informal tenure system which is equivalent in its operation to the formal policies of the university. It is relatively rare after eight or ten years for an individual to be fired for incompetence; after fifteen or twenty years it is almost unheard of. The difficulty is that in industry the individual slips into the status of permanent tenure without a definite decision as to whether he merits it. He acquires tenure by default.

The advantage of the university tenure system is that it provides a formal decision point. At a stated time, a careful evaluation is made of the individual and of the probability of his long-run contribution to the institution. Up to this time, any reasonable benefit of doubt with respect to his performance is resolved in favor of the individual; he is given another chance. At this point, however, the benefit of doubt shifts and is resolved in favor of the institution. If there are doubts concerning his long-term contribution, the refusal of permanent tenure results, and the individual leaves. Properly administered, this formal tenure policy can lead to the timely elimination of the incompetent. Far from being a handicap, it is a genuine asset which has considerable impact on the growth of all members of the university faculty.

Another policy which, with its associated practices, materially affects growth is that of job rotation to give the individual a wider range of experience and to test out his abilities. Companies differ greatly in the way they apply this principle, and the differences in administration yield quite different rewards and punishments.

In one company managers are moved so rapidly from job to job throughout a large geographic area that the common label for rotation among them is "suitcase supervision." The consequence of this kind of rotation is not the growth that management desires. The individual moves into a job knowing that he is likely to be there for a very short time. He does not take full responsibility; his concern is simply to keep things on an even keel until he is relieved. He does not innovate, he does not take risks, he does not, in fact, operate as a manager, but as though he were an assistant "acting" during the temporary absence of the boss.*

There is some question as to whether the learning that takes place under such conditions is really as great as it would be if the individual merely *observed* the regular manager in action for an equivalent period. Keeping the chair warm is not conducive to growth.

Toward the other extreme are companies who utilize the rotational principle only in a very limited sense. Rotation is confined to moves within a given department or function, at least until the individual has climbed a good way up the ladder. When he does get an opportunity to move into a different function he may be past forty and in a rather substantial job. Unless he is to be demoted, a move will put him in a key spot in another department or function. This is often risky. The pressures on him will be severe. But what is more important is that he is unlikely to give the leadership and the guidance in the new job that the organization under him requires. He has to be carried along by his subordinates. If by any chance he is unwilling to accept this form of help and attempts an autocratic kind of leadership, he is likely to make serious mistakes. Meanwhile, the organization under him suffers, particularly if the rotation into this spot is frequent.

A critical factor affecting the growth of the individual on a rotational job is the behavior of the superior to whom he now reports.

---

* The point at which job rotation becomes churning rather than cross-learning is highlighted here and is a pressing issue in many organizations today.

The new boss can make the rotation a genuine learning experience for the incumbent, but only if he devotes considerable time and thought to doing so. This he is unlikely to do unless *his* superiors in turn recognize his efforts and reward him for it. We will consider a little later what this means. At the moment, it is enough to ask whether those who administer programs of job rotation take this important growth factor into account.

Rotation serves to minimize the dangers of personal prejudice in assessments of the individual's performance and potential. We noted earlier in examining appraisal methods that such judgments may be as much a function of the superior's attitude and methods of managing as of the subordinate's behavior. However, if the individual spends a reasonable amount of time under a succession of managers, the effects of these factors are likely to be reduced.

Clearly, job rotation can be an effective means of affording opportunities for the growth of managers. Whether it is will depend on when the individual is moved, into what positions, for how long, under what kind of supervision, and upon the degree to which his own career goals are taken into account. All of these aspects of the administration of rotational programs involve important rewards and punishments. To conceive of rotation *in itself* as significant, leaving these related factors to chance, is to utilize a machinery in a way which is likely to hamper rather than to facilitate growth.

THE BEHAVIOR OF THE IMMEDIATE SUPERIOR

Within the broader context of the climate created by company policy and practice, organization structure, and general philosophy, there is the climate created by the individual manager's immediate superior. As we saw in Chapter 10, the climate of this relationship is critical. It is probably the most important influence affecting managerial development.

Every encounter between a superior and subordinate involves learning of some kind for the subordinate. (It should involve learning for the superior, too, but that is another matter.) When the boss gives an order, asks for a job to be done, reprimands, praises, conducts an appraisal interview, deals with a mistake, holds a staff meeting, works with his subordinates in solving a problem, gives a salary increase, discusses a possible promotion, or takes any other action with subordinates, he is teaching them something. The attitudes, the habits, the expectations of the subordinate will be either reinforced or modified to some degree as a result of every encounter with the boss.* This is why "on-the-job training" is such a significant process. It is why the results of classroom supervisory training are often discouraging. The day-by-day experience on the job is so much more powerful that it tends to overshadow what the individual may learn in other settings.

Whether the manager is aware of his powerful influence for better or worse upon his subordinates' growth, and whether he considers this responsibility a significant one to which he will devote extensive thought, time, and energy, will depend on the environment in which *he* operates. It is typical to say that each manager is responsible for the growth and development of subordinates, but the reward and punishment system of the company is not always consistent with this statement. An example from the academic field may serve to make the point.

Most universities stress as part of their promotion policy two major responsibilities of the faculty member: teaching and scholarly research. While it is recognized that individuals will not always be equally competent in both of these, the formal policy usually indicates that promotions will go to those who are outstanding in one and at least satisfactory in the other.

This is policy; practice is usually something else. It is commonly

* There is a growing trend today in coaching and mentoring to emphasize the reciprocal nature of the process—the coach or mentor stands to learn as much from the interaction as the individual being coached or mentored—just as McGregor suggests here.

believed, and there is at least some evidence for the belief, that promotions are in practice based primarily on scholarship as indicated by quantity of publication and by colleague judgments of research competence. Promotions go with considerable frequency to faculty members who are competent and productive scholars, but who are poor and ineffective teachers. The reward and punishment system operates in such a way that there is little encouragement for the average faculty member in the big university to devote time and energy to improving his teaching skills. In fact, he may be defeating his own career goals if he emphasizes his teaching at the expense of his research and publication.

In industry, rewards in the form of promotions, salary increases, and recognition generally go to those who demonstrate competence in activities other than the development of their subordinates. In querying management representatives of a number of companies whose activities with respect to management development are extensive, I have discovered only a couple of cases in which it is felt that achievement in the development of subordinates is given genuine recognition. However, unless the manager is made truly accountable for creating a climate conducive to growth, and unless rewards and punishments for him are clearly related to his performance along these lines, we can expect that it will be given scant attention.

Some managers, aware of their dependence downward, do give a great deal of attention to the development of their subordinates, even though their efforts may not be recognized and rewarded "upstairs." They recognize that their own ability to manage depends to an important extent on the performance of those below them. Others, who do not recognize this downward dependence (and these are in the majority), are more concerned with their own performance and their own rewards and punishments than with the growth of their subordinates. In fact, they are fearful of having subordinates who are too competent—they worry about having their own weaknesses shown up. This self-protective orientation creates a climate which hampers rather than facilitates growth.

Perhaps it is now apparent why the "manufacturing" approach to management development is less effective than one might wish: It focuses management's attention on the wrong things. The formal programs may even have negative effects if the environment is not itself conducive to growth. The research findings that supervisory training courses are ineffective unless the things they teach are reinforced by the daily environment on the job is but one example. The same thing is true concerning the results obtained from every form of management development "machinery." If we want growth of managerial talent, we must give attention to the conditions which affect it.* Some of these are subtle and difficult to influence, others are obvious and subject to modification once we pause to examine them.

THE ROLE OF THE MANAGEMENT DEVELOPMENT STAFF

If there is a staff department concerned with management development along the lines suggested by Theory Y, it is obvious that one of its major activities will be a professional one: strategy planning with top management. Such a staff will be concerned with the organizational environment, broadly as well as narrowly. It will study company policies and practices and endeavor to help management to understand their significance for growth so that organization structure, company policy, and day-to-day managerial behavior will aid the development of managerial talent.

Such a staff will have as its second function that of providing competent counsel and help to managers who are attempting to fulfill their responsibilities for the development of their subordinates. This help cannot be forced on the organization or "sold" to it. A compe-

---

* There are many in the management community who are now emphasizing the importance of this learning in context. (See Julian Birkinshaw and Gita Piramal (eds.), *Sumantra Ghoshal on Management: A Force for Good*, New York: Prentice-Hall, 2005; Henry Mintzberg, "Teaching Leadership in Context," *Fast Company*, Feb. 1, 2001.)

tent staff will, under proper conditions, find itself sought for this purpose. The help it will be prepared to give will seldom take the form of detailed formal procedures or canned training courses. It will be help to managers—individually or collectively—in finding and utilizing whatever means will best meet *their* needs. The analogy of the architect vis-à-vis his clients suggested in Chapter 12 is particularly relevant in this connection.

As a third and distinctly minor aspect of the function, such a staff will be concerned with problems of administration. Certain data for purposes of replacement planning and management inventory will be required. However, a staff group concerned with problems of growth will not be trapped into reliance on mechanically coded color charts and statistical analyses as a substitute for concern with the conditions influencing growth. Records and statistics are not methods for developing managerial talent; they are means of keeping track of the process.

A staff group in a large company made a concentrated attempt several years ago to follow the "manufacturing" approach to management development by creating an elaborate formal program and attempting to sell it to management. After some time, this group became aware that the desired purposes were not being achieved. The program was not operating well; most managers were not using the procedures or the forms, and there was rather generally a passive resistance to the whole field of management development.

Instead of concluding (as some management development staff groups have under these familiar circumstances) that the remedy was more "selling," or a training program to teach management how to use the formal machinery, this group decided to start again using an entirely different approach. This involved just one activity: annual meetings of the president of the company with each of his immediate subordinates, individually, in which the subordinate reported in detail to the president on his activities and accomplishments in creating an environment conducive to the growth of his subordinates.

Each individual reporting to him, and each individual at the second level below him, were discussed with the president in detail. The emphasis was on what the manager was doing to make it possible for his subordinates to further their own self-development. The president made it clear—not only in words, but also in action—that he held his own subordinates accountable for this managerial function, and that how well they fulfilled the responsibilities in these respects would make a substantial difference in their own rewards and punishments.

After a couple of years, the effects of this single activity were substantial. The management development staff were being asked for help by some of the same managers who, two or three years before, were resistant and antagonistic toward the whole function. The managers reporting to the president found that they could not fulfill this responsibility without encouraging a similar process among those reporting to them, and so the general emphasis upon accountability for management development began to move down in the organization. The managers themselves learned a good deal as they attempted to fulfill this new responsibility.

This approach involved little formal machinery. Each manager was encouraged to develop his own methods for presenting his analysis to the president and his own ways of working with his subordinates to further their growth. The management development staff were ready and willing to provide professional help to those who sought it.

The experience of this company adds one more bit of evidence to a generalization which my observation of the field of management development has tended to support: There is almost no relationship between the amount of formal programming and machinery of management development and the actual achievement of the organization in this respect. I sometimes think the correlation may be negative! Programs and procedures do not *cause* management development, because it is not possible to "produce" managers the way we produce products. We can only hope to "grow" them, and growth depends less on the tools we use than on the environment which is created. If it is conducive to growth, the main job may be keeping the soil in good tilth and keeping the weeds down.

There is probably no single activity which will do more to create an environment conducive to managerial growth than the "target-setting" approach described in Chapter 5. However, as we saw in considering this subject, what is involved is a theory of management, not a formula or a mechanical procedure. The concept of management by integration and self-control cannot be successfully developed as a packaged program and sold to management, but a competent professional staff can help management discover its value. In doing so they will not face the difficult task of persuading management to add to its already heavy load. On the contrary, they will be helping management to manage in a way which accomplishes organizational objectives better *and at the same time* encourages the growth of subordinates. If a climate and soil conditions conducive to growth are created by the way management manages, the cream *will* rise to the top, in the sense that individual managers throughout the whole organization will be involved in a process of self-development leading to the realization of their potentialities. In this way, effective management of the enterprise and the development of managerial talent become a single integrated activity, and managers no longer face a conflict between these two responsibilities.

REFERENCES

Acton Society Trust, *Management Succession*. London: 1956.

American Management Association, *Organization Planning and Management Development*, Personnel Series, no. 141, 1951.

Dooher, Joseph M., and Vivienne Marquis (eds.), *The Development of Executive Talent: A Handbook of Management Development Techniques and Case Studies*. New York: American Management Association, 1952.

Mace, Myles L., *The Growth and Development of Executives.* Boston: Division of Research, Graduate School of Business Administration, Harvard University, 1950.

Martin, Norman H., and Anselm L. Strauss, "Patterns of Mobility within Industrial Organization," *The Journal of Business*, vol. 29, no. 2, 1956.

National Industrial Conference Board, Inc., "Management Development: A Ten-year Case Study," Studies in Personnel Policy, no. 140, 1953.

SELECTED REFERENCES TO THE ANNOTATED EDITION

Miles, Raymond E., and Charles C. Snow, *Organizational Strategy, Structure and Process*, New York: McGraw-Hill, 1978.

DISCUSSION QUESTIONS FOR CHAPTER 14

1. When McGregor urges us to attend to the climate, soil, and cultivation methods for management development, what is he referring to? Why does he favor this "agricultural" model over a "manufacturing" model for management development?
2. What are examples of company structures, policies, and practices that enable the sort of individualized management development that McGregor recommends? What are examples of structures, policies, and practices that undercut this sort of management development?
3. If management development staff were fully engaged in strategic planning with top management, as McGregor recommends, what threats and opportunities would be a particular focus of their efforts?

ACQUIRING MANAGERIAL SKILLS IN THE CLASSROOM

McGregor begins Chapter 15 by stating that the job environment, far more than any classroom learning, is "the most important variable" affecting the development of managers. He cites a colleague stating that "the chief purpose of formal education for the manager is to increase his ability to learn from experience," to which he adds a second purpose, to "help his subordinates learn from experience." Motivation to learn is a key concern for McGregor. If the individual wants new knowledge, he observes, "the acquisition of knowledge is a fairly straightforward process." "However," he adds, "if he doesn't want the knowledge or if he doesn't know he needs it, we will have considerable difficulty." This motivation comes, he points out, through a participative process in which learning objectives are identified on a collaborative basis, not imposed. It is a process of "integration," McGregor notes, "between the individual manager's needs, readiness for learning, and past experience on the one hand and organizational requirements on the other." Further, it is a process that depends on practice and feedback.

McGregor is skeptical about the impact of standard courses in communications, supervisory methods, leadership, counseling, brainstorming, group dynamics, the use of staff, and other topics, since such training has to overcome deeply embedded "ego investment[s] in what we now know." He does see promise in what were then early experiments at the National Training Labs (NTL)[1] with what were termed "T groups." The "T" stood for "training" and involved the open-ended exploration of the impact of our behavior on others.

Although the title of this chapter suggests classroom learning in educational institutions, which he does discuss, McGregor is just as focused on the many forms of formal and informal learning that take place in organizations and in other settings. In this regard, he anticipates the vast literature that has emerged on workplace training, continuous learning, and organizational learning.[2] This even includes current work highlighting the learning associated with constructive and unconstructive approaches to mistakes or what we might now call learning from disconnects.[3] McGregor states:

> *If... "post mortems" comprise no more than a search for a culprit in order to place the blame, they will provide learning of one kind. If, on the other hand, it is recognized that mistakes are an inevitable occurrence in the trial-and-error process of acquiring problem solving skills, they can be the source of other and more valuable learning.*

---

[1] The NTL, McGregor notes on page 300, was then a division of the National Educational Association (NEA), which may be an unexpected institutional connection for many readers.

[2] See, for example, Anthony P. Carnevale, Leila J. Gainer, and Janice Villet, *Training in America: The Organization and Strategic Role of Training*, San Francisco: Jossey-Bass, 1990; and Peter Senge, *The Fifth Discipline: The Art and Practice of the Learning Organization*, New York: Doubleday, 1990.

[3] See, for example, Peter Senge, Art Kleiner, Charlotte Roberts, Richard Ross, George Roth, and Bryan Smith, *The Dance of Change: The Challenges to Sustaining Momentum in Learning Organizations*, New York: Doubleday, 1999; and Joel Cutcher-Gershenfeld and J. Kevin Ford, *Valuable Disconnects in Organizational Learning Systems: Integrating Bold Visions and Harsh Realities*, New York: Oxford University Press, 2004.

There is today a growing chorus of observers suggesting that leadership can't just be taught in the classroom,[4] and a growing number of management degree programs feature field internships and other ways of placing students in the business context as an integral part of the learning process.

---

[4] As noted in the previous chapter, see Julian Birkinshaw and Gita Piramal (eds.), *Sumantra Ghoshal on Management: A Force for Good*, New York: Prentice-Hall, 2005; Henry Mintzberg, "Teaching Leadership in Context," *Fast Company*, Feb. 1, 2001.

CHAPTER 15

ACQUIRING MANAGERIAL SKILLS IN THE CLASSROOM

The job environment of the individual is the most important variable affecting his development. Unless that environment is conducive to his growth, none of the other things we do to him or for him will be effective. This is why the "agricultural" approach to management development is preferable to the "manufacturing" approach. The latter leads, among other things, to the unrealistic expectation that we can create and develop managers in the classroom.

A colleague once said that the chief purpose of formal education for the manager is to increase his ability to learn from experience. To this I would add a second purpose: to increase his ability to help his subordinates learn from experience, i.e., to enable him to learn how to create an environment conducive to their growth.

The principle of leaders serving as teachers cuts across many successful transformation initiatives. For example, in the 1980s, the "Leadership Through Quality" (LTQ) initiative at Xerox was centered on each successive level of management learning key quality principles and then teaching those principles to the next level. Similarly, in the 1990s, the "Business Leadership Initiative" (BLI) at the Ford Motor Company was centered on managers understanding key business data and then teaching this to their direct reports. These are just two of many such examples. Yet most management education fails to teach leaders how to be effective teachers.

In considering classroom learning for managers (in the plant or in the academic institution), it is necessary to make some distinctions. There are various kinds of learning, and the methods which are appropriate vary with the kind of learning which is sought.

ACQUIRING INTELLECTUAL KNOWLEDGE

An electrical engineer may need more knowledge than he now possesses about circuit design. A new employee may require knowledge about company policies and work rules. A plant manager may need an awareness of the potentialities of linear programing. A foreman may require information about the new provisions in the labor agreement.

The acquisition of knowledge is a fairly straightforward process *provided the individual wants the new knowledge.* It can be made available to him in several ways. However, if he doesn't want the knowledge or if he doesn't know he needs it, we will have considerable difficulty getting him to learn it. Many of the methods we utilize in this kind of education are designed to influence his motivation to learn. In school, the formal grade is a major device for this purpose, although the method of presentation of the material may also be important. In industry the attempts to create a "felt need" for the new knowledge are many: implied or promised rewards, such as more chance for promotion, making the job easier, pleasing the boss, keeping out of trouble, and implied or promised punishments which are mostly the obverse of such rewards.

The problems involved in this kind of managerial education arise primarily from neglect of the principle of integration. The individual may recognize his need for knowledge in some area, or his superior may show him how it would be valuable. If there are courses available in nearby academic institutions or in a company-operated program, he is likely to acquire the necessary knowledge with no more ado. Partial tuition refunds, or time off from work, may provide an incentive, but if the individual is persuaded of his need such rewards will make little difference.

It is the elaboration, and particularly the standardization, of this process for large numbers of people which lessens its value. It is all too easy for higher-level management or staff groups to decide for others what they need in the way of additional knowledge. Courses and programs are then prepared and offered. If these are genuine "offerings," and the individuals can really choose whether to accept them, few problems will arise except that some such programs will be less patronized than may have been expected.

What tends to happen is that upper management becomes convinced that a given program is a Good Thing for subordinates. (A British colleague refers to supervisory training as "the aspirin of higher management"!) The "offering" then becomes a scheduled assignment for whole categories of people (sometimes all of management, but more often lower levels only). The need for the new knowledge is now not the individual's "felt" need, but a need which others think he ought to have. The integrative principle is abandoned in favor of a form of control which can be used only where dependence is high (for example, in the elementary public school), and which is not very effective even then. "Giving" courses in this manner is generally not an appropriate method of influence. The learning is limited because the motivation is low. Moreover, this strategy soon generates negative attitudes toward training in general and thus hampers the creation of an organizational climate conducive to growth.

There may be courses which do, in fact, meet widespread "felt" needs, or which are so well presented that they arouse such needs. These are bound to be few, because individual situations vary so greatly even within a single category such as first-line supervision. Admittedly, it is difficult to create a climate such that individuals can exercise freedom of choice with respect to courses or programs which their superiors believe to be a Good Thing. Yet the failure to do so is one of the major reasons why much classroom education of managers is relatively ineffective. It is asking too much to expect the trainer to create the necessary motivation for learning under such circumstances, regardless of his skills or the methods he uses.

Even where the circumstances dictate the desirability of a course for a large group of managers, there can be some adjustment to the individual. Certainly not all first-line supervisors, for example, are equally ready at one time to benefit from any given course. Certainly some do not perceive that they need it at all (and are, therefore, likely to benefit but little from it). It is possible to create a climate within which such courses are taken on a truly voluntary basis. The word "truly" is important. The voluntary character is distinctly altered if people perceive that they are expected to "volunteer," and that they may face the disapproval of the boss if they don't.

If there are needs which can be met by a given kind of training, some at least of those "in need" are likely to be aware of it. An initial step can often be planned *with them.* If the resulting activity meets their needs, they will be the ones who create a demand among others for it. This is what happened, for example, in one plant a few years ago.

A few of the younger and more ambitious foremen came to the personnel director to discuss their concern that they were not increasing their managerial competence at a rate sufficient to meet the requirements of the situation. They felt that their future careers in the company would be adversely affected unless they acquired more skill as managers. The initial work done to try to help these men flowered eventually into a variety of training activities that were actively sought by most of the supervisory force.

It may be worth noting that the first of these activities was not a training course, but a series of meetings having as an objective a clearer understanding of the foremen's responsibilities. During the course of these discussions many beyond the original group became involved. The outcome was a statement concerning the foremen's responsibilities which was accepted almost without change by the top management of the company. There was considerable learning for all concerned in this activity, although no one—including the personnel director—thought of it as "training." The same thing was true of several other projects undertaken subsequently by these supervisors with the help of the personnel staff.

The acquisition of knowledge or information requires the motivation of the learner. He can, of course, be motivated by threats of punishment. The risks involved in this method of control (even when the threat is the unspoken implication that he will be regarded less highly by his superiors if he doesn't attend the course) are the usual countermeasures correlated with management by direction and control.

Above all, it is necessary to recognize that knowledge cannot be pumped into human beings the way grease is forced into a fitting on a machine. The individual may learn; he is not taught. Effective education is always a process of influence by integration and self-control.

Up to this point the emphasis has been on the acquisition of knowledge in the specific sense. What about the "broadening" of the manager through a more general educational experience which includes a wide range of intellectual fare? These experiences are usually provided through university programs of several months' duration. A few companies, partly because of their size, but more often because of their unique needs as they perceive them, have established academic facilities within the organization to provide this form of education.

It is an obvious and important fact that the managerial task is becoming increasingly complex today. The effective manager must be clearly aware of social, political, and economic trends in society. He needs a general intellectual knowledge of a number of specialized fields so that he can grasp the scope of his own responsibilities, understand the role of his company in the economy and in the political milieu, and know when he needs professional help.

This form of education for the manager is important not only as a stimulus to innovation but as a requirement for adjustment to a rapidly changing world. The education of the manager should be a continuing process, and it can be aided periodically by his participation in these formal academic programs. Moreover, after he has been out of school for a while and faced up to some of the realities of organizational life, he often is in a position to learn much more than would have been possible earlier. It is common experience among those of us who teach in these programs that experienced managers understand and grasp our subject matter more readily than college students who have not yet had much exposure to the industrial world.

The university is the proper place for education like this. University faculty members can provide a perspective which is difficult to acquire within the industrial organization. By and large, the best teaching talent for these purposes is to be found in the university setting and is unlikely to be attracted into full-time industrial positions. In the university setting it is acceptable to be critical of the *status quo*; there are few sacred cows that must be respected. Ideas can be followed where they lead, rather than being tempered by sensitivity to the prejudices of a boss. Finally, it is the function of the university to provide leadership in intellectual fields, and it is, therefore, to the academic world that industry should look for the best, the most up-to-date, and the most critical thinking on the broad matters which affect the managerial task.*

There is another important value for the industrial manager in the university program: the opportunity, through the exchange of

---

* A growing number of universities are expanding their focus to emphasize lifelong learning along the very lines suggested by McGregor. While McGregor is correct to highlight the free exchange of ideas that is valued in the university context, it should also be noted that the decades of progressive specialization into disciplines and subdisciplines does serve as a barrier to the integrative, cross-disciplinary perspective that most lifelong learners bring to the classroom.

experience and ideas with other managers, to discover something about the similarities as well as the differences between industries and companies. Many participants in these programs see this as the primary value of the whole experience. It is important to recognize, however, that this interchange occurs within the context of problems and theoretical issues that are raised by the university faculty. An ordinary bull session of the same group of managers outside of the university context would usually have less value because it would lack this structure.

Finally, it is important to recognize that activities other than the classroom lecture form a significant part of many of these university programs. For one thing, the requirement that the manager must do a considerable amount of reading of a kind to which he has probably been unaccustomed since his college days is of some importance. Many participants in these programs report that the experience has rekindled their interest in intellectual ideas, and that after their return home they have done more of this kind of reading than they had for a number of years previously. Then there are activities like, for example, the trip that the Sloan Fellows make to Washington during the course of their year at MIT. While there they have opportunities for discussion with key members of the executive, legislative, and judicial departments of our government. As a result they gain a perspective and an insight into industry-government relationships which would be difficult to achieve through classroom experience alone. In another of the MIT executive programs the group has several opportunities to meet with top research faculty in some of the major technical and scientific fields to explore with them the frontiers of knowledge and research, and to see through their eyes some of the most probable future developments which may affect management. This, too, is outside the formal classroom setting and is an experience which is difficult to arrange except on the university campus.

Many companies have spent a substantial amount of money in sending managers to university programs, and they have recently begun to ask pointed questions about the worth of such experiences. The "evaluation" of the impact of such education on the manager has been a subject of considerable concern in the last few years. There is a real danger that the pressure for evaluation may lead us to try to measure the wrong things and, therefore, to miss entirely the true value of experiences of this kind. The purpose of most of these generalized university courses is not, and should not be, direct practical application of the learning to the job. Their purpose is not to provide answers to problems, formulas, or tricks of the trade. It is to broaden the manager's understanding of his job, to challenge some of his preconceptions, to make him better able to learn from experience when he gets back home because he will have acquired a more realistic understanding of the causes and effects with which he must deal. To the extent that this kind of education is successful, it will not reveal itself in immediate or obvious changes in his behavior back home. The learning which takes place will more probably be reflected in fairly subtle ways of which he himself may often be unaware. Nevertheless, these changes in perception do affect behavior, sometimes profoundly. It is certainly reasonable that management should want to evaluate the achievements of university programs in management development, but it is important that we understand the purposes of these programs so that we evaluate the right things.

We come now to some questions of who should go to such programs and when. In this connection we can profitably concern ourselves with the matter of integration between the individual manager's needs, readiness for learning, and past experience on the one hand and organizational requirements on the other. We do not need to approach the problem on a mass basis or treat the individual as a pawn on a chessboard.

It is often ironic that management's purpose in sending a man to one of these programs is entirely different than the man's perception. It is not uncommon for managers to worry all through such programs about why they have been *sent*. What have they done wrong? Where have they failed? What weaknesses were they supposed to correct?

Many participants in university programs ask themselves questions like these because their assignment to the programs has been handled poorly. When a manager is "sent" to school because his boss has decided he needs it, there is a threatening character to the assignment and there is likely to be less learning as a result.

Another fairly common practice in some companies is to send some men to university programs as a reward for faithful service, and not with the expectation that it will make any substantial difference in their subsequent behavior. This may be nice for the men, although it is likely to raise some anxieties. The important point, however, is the effect of scattering a number of such people in a group of managers who are strongly motivated to learn and who regard the opportunity as a challenge rather than a reward. Management would be well advised to consider carefully whether this practice of using university programs as rewards for conscientious service, or as a device to avoid the appearance of discrimination, is really a wise one.

In the context of joint target setting, the needs of the individual manager for further education are quite likely to appear. Moreover, he will often be the one to perceive his needs and to raise questions about how they might be met. These needs will not alone be for the correction of weaknesses, but for purposes of self-realization and the utilization of strengths. If, in this setting, the decision is reached that a university program would be helpful, the question of his anxieties and his motivation are likely to be resolved in directions which will benefit both him and the organization.

ACQUIRING MANUAL SKILLS

The manager does not require many ordinary manual skills in the performance of his job. Examples of such skills in other contexts are learning to drive a car, operate a lathe, play golf, play a musical instrument, type. The science student acquires certain skills in applying scientific method through his laboratory courses.

A brief glance at learning of this kind will be helpful later when we examine the learning of the skills of social interaction, which are of great importance to the manager. The two kinds of learning have many things in common, although manual skills are by far the more easily acquired.

The acquisition of a manual skill requires practice, or experience accompanied by feedback. Pure trial-and-error learning can be appreciably speeded up by guidance, but the individual cannot learn unless he performs and unless he receives cues which tell him about the success of his efforts. In most motor learning the cues are fairly direct and immediate; for example, the golf ball slices into the woods, or "ht" instead of "th" appears on the sheet of paper in the typewriter. The smooth, effortless performance of the expert represents, of course, a level of learning in which the cues are responded to without conscious awareness, and in which many originally discrete acts have blended into wholes.

It is more obvious in acquiring motor skills than in acquiring intellectual knowledge—but no more true—that learning is an active process rather than a passive one. The necessary effort will be expended only if there is a "felt" need on the part of the learner.

ACQUIRING PROBLEM-SOLVING SKILLS

Much of a manager's work is solving problems. These include organizing his own and his subordinates' activities, planning (for either anticipated or unanticipated circumstances), choosing his own managerial strategies, and a wide range of other decision-making activities. There are skills involved in diagnosing problems, acquiring and interpreting relevant data, assessing and testing alternative solutions, and getting feedback concerning the effectiveness of both the solution and the process used in arriving at it. These skills can be improved, and classroom education is one method utilized for this purpose.

As with any skill, practice (experience) and feedback are essential for learning. The most widely used classroom method for improving problem-solving skills is the case method. In the hands of a skillful teacher, it can be highly effective. There is some scattered evidence that—when used alone—diagnostic skills may be improved without materially affecting the quality of solutions. Perhaps this is because traditionally there has been relatively little emphasis on theory in the exclusive use of the case method. It is recognized that there is seldom a single "best answer" to complex problems such as are represented by the cases. However, if underlying theoretical assumptions are not consciously and critically examined, they are likely to determine the answer unwittingly despite the care given to the analysis of the problem.

When the manager is on the job, practice in problem solving is, of course, inevitable. However, an important source of feedback for improving skills is frequently overlooked. This is the critical examination of mistakes that have occurred in order to understand what happened and why.* If such "post mortems" comprise no more than a search for the culprit in order to place the blame, they will provide learning of one kind. If, on the other hand, it is recognized that mistakes are an inevitable occurrence in the trial-and-error process of acquiring problem-solving skills, they can be the source of other and more valuable learning.

One unpublished study in a large company carried a strong implication that the way in which a manager dealt with his subordinates' mistakes was the most important factor in determining whether his

---

* As noted earlier, the field of organizational learning is increasingly highlighting the important ways in which "mistakes" represent key learning opportunities. (See, for example, Peter Senge, Art Kleiner, Charlotte Roberts, Richard Ross, George Roth, and Bryan Smith, *The Dance of Change: The Challenges to Sustaining Momentum in Learning Organizations*, New York: Doubleday, 1999; Joel Cutcher-Gershenfeld and J. Kevin Ford, *Valuable Disconnects in Organizational Learning Systems: Integrating Bold Visions and Harsh Realities*, New York: Oxford University Press, 2005.)

delegation to them was effective, i.e., whether they learned to take responsibility for their own performance.

It is obvious that the analysis of successful problem-solving efforts can also provide effective feedback for learning.

This kind of education can be carried into the classroom through the use of role playing. The behavior of the participants in the problem-solving exercise is directly observed and becomes the object of critical examination afterward. While it is true that role playing is not real life, it is surprising how real it becomes under proper circumstances. Moreover, it is conducive to learning because it is a "safe" situation (the only consequences occur in the classroom) in which the individual can practice forms of behavior which he might not be willing to use in real life. In addition, the situation can be replayed to test alternative approaches, thus providing opportunities for feedback which are seldom available on the job.

Another method which yields increased insight and understanding, if not directly improved skill in problem solving, is exposure under certain conditions to the thinking of others who face similar problems to one's own. As already noted, managers from different companies and different industries who are thrown together for several weeks in university programs learn a lot from discussions with each other outside the classroom. The subjects discussed in class stimulate outside arguments and exchanges of experience from which any but the individual who already knows all the answers can learn.

In one such program these experiences are augmented still further by exposing the group of middle management students to a series of top-level executives from different companies. At each such off-the-record meeting, the guest is quizzed by the group about his most serious managerial problems and his way of dealing with them. It is interesting to observe the increase in critical sophistication of the students (reflecting increased insight and understanding) as the series proceeds.

Another method which has proved effective for learning of this kind is a "clinic" in which a closely related group of managers (a department head and his subordinates, for example) meet with a "trainer" to consider together the actual problems they are currently trying to solve on the job. This affords an opportunity for the trainer to help them look critically not only at the problems but at the methods they are using to solve them, and thus to acquire understanding of their "processes" of problem solving and to increase their skills with respect to them.

Typically, this method reveals an important aspect of managerial problem-solving activities beyond the purely intellectual: the interactions among people which are often crucial in determining success or failure. Some managerial problem solving is carried out individually, but ordinarily it occurs in a group of at least two people. In groups a complex set of factors come into play which reveal the need for skills of social interaction.

ACQUIRING SKILLS OF SOCIAL INTERACTION

Recognition of the crucial importance of these skills for effective managerial problem solving has led to a welter of educational efforts: courses in communications, supervisory methods, leadership, counseling, brainstorming, group dynamics, the use of staff, etc. The relatively small amount of research evidence available indicates two things: (1) effective learning in this field requires the solution of some exceedingly complex problems, and (2) lasting changes in behavior as a result of conventional classroom methods are quite unlikely.* The reasons are not far to seek.

Every adult human being has an elaborate history of past experience in this field, and additional learning is profoundly influenced

---

* Chris Argyris has argued that a second learning loop is needed to produce lasting behavioral change. Note that he was a contemporary of Douglas McGregor, teaching at Yale at the time that *The Human Side of Enterprise* was published. He continues to extend this discussion in Chris Argyris, "Teaching Smart People How to Learn," *Harvard Business Review*, vol. 69 (May–June, 1991), pp. 99–109.

by that history. From infancy on, his ability to achieve his goals and satisfy his needs—his "social survival"—has been a function of his skills in influencing others. Deep emotional currents—unconscious needs such as those related to dependency and counterdependency—are involved. He has a large "ego investment" in his knowledge and skill in this area, and the defenses he has built to protect that investment are strong and psychologically complex.

It may be said of most of us that in organizational situations involving our superiors or subordinates we *react* (unconsciously, of course) to internal needs and fears and hopes to a greater extent than we *act* with respect to the situation itself. We attempt to exercise power or to gain acceptance, to lead or to take a minor role, to fight or to withdraw, to demonstrate our talents or hide our foibles—not so much because the situation requires it as because our own internal adjustment does.

Learning new skills of social interaction in the context of these factors is a difficult matter indeed. Inspirational lectures, or discussion of the principles of supervision, or conferences on human relations can provide us with new words, perhaps new insights into the behavior of others, but seldom more than new rationalizations with which to defend our own present behavior. The intensity of our own ego investment in what we now know and do is great enough to warp our perceptions to fit our needs.

But what is even more important, we normally get little feedback of real value concerning the impact of our behavior on others. If they don't behave as we desire, it is easy to blame *their* stupidity, *their* adjustment, *their* peculiarities. Only under rather extreme conditions do our subordinates even attempt to tell us how our behavior affects them. When our superiors sometimes make the attempt, we find it difficult to understand what they are driving at, and mostly we disagree with their perceptions of us. Above all, it isn't considered good taste to give this kind of feedback in most social settings. Instead, it is discussed by our colleagues when we are not present to learn from it.

Finally, with the ego investment we all have in our present skills of social interaction, and with the defenses we have erected to protect our belief in their adequacy, we are seldom strongly motivated to change. Unconsciously, we fear inevitable failure if we "try on" ways of behaving that differ materially from those we have learned with such difficulty over so long a period. A new gimmick or minor technique certainly, but not a major shift in strategy involving the acquisition of new and strange skills.

None of the educational methods discussed above brings about real changes in the skills of social interaction. An occasional individual may have encountered failure and difficulty so often that he is prepared to learn new skills. Individuals whose skills are already similar to those being taught may improve them somewhat. But these are not the results that are hoped for.

There are two educational methods in current use which appear to bring about significant improvements in the skills of social interaction. Only modest claims can be made for either of them, but they are becoming more effective as knowledge accumulates. The first of these is psychotherapy. Unfortunately, this form of education has only limited usefulness for management development today. It is widely perceived as relevant only when individuals are in serious trouble. It lends itself only to individual, or at best small group, applications. Finally, it is very time-consuming.

Nevertheless, as social standards change so that mental illness is no longer seen as the only reason for psychotherapy, this form of education is becoming more widely used. Groups of social scientists, like those at the Menninger Clinic, are pioneering applications of psychotherapy to managerial problems. Individual managers who find themselves in need of help are persuaded with less difficulty than in the past to seek it through psychological counseling and therapy. It is likely that we will see major developments in this field during the next decade or two.

The other method is a form of "laboratory" training developed during the last dozen years by a number of social scientists affiliated with the National Training Laboratory for Group Development in Washington. This organization, a division of the National Education Association, carries on its activities through a series of annual programs in various parts of the country. The programs are staffed by social scientists, some of whom are faculty members in academic institutions; some are professionals engaged in private practice; and some are employees of industrial, social service, and government organizations. All these individuals have participated actively with NTL in the development of its methods or in research in the field.

University of California, Berkeley Professor (emeritus) George Straus was a student of McGregor at MIT in the 1940s. He recalls that:

Nondirective listening, first introduced in Hawthorne, was another major interest in the 1930–1940s. Doug saw it as key to problem resolution. As students we spent much class time role playing the handling of boss-subordinate and steward-foreman relations. Many problems resulted from misunderstanding, he believed. Good listening was a first step toward solving them. Even when misunderstanding was not the problem, a well-trained listener could help people resolve problems by themselves.

The core of this educational method for improving the skills of social interaction is called the "T" (for training) Group. It consists of ten to fifteen individuals and a trainer who meet for a number of successive periods. A rather common pattern involves a two-week program during which the T Group meets daily for two hours. The T Group supplies its own content for learning in the form of the behavior of its members during its meetings. This behavior includes social interactions of all kinds which are utilized by the individuals to increase their understanding (1) of the impact of their own behavior on others, (2) of their reactions to the behavior of others, (3) of the phenomena of group activity and their significance. Since participation in the T Group involves practice and feedback of a unique nature, the opportunity is present for improving the skills of social interaction.

The feedback in a T Group is of special importance because it differs sharply from that which occurs normally in group situations. Some of its comes from the trainer, but most of it is provided by the members to each other. The "ground rules" which the group establishes for feedback are important. With the help of the trainer, the group usually comes to see the differences between providing help and attempting to control or punish a member, between analyzing and interpreting a member's adjustment (which is taboo) and informing him of the impact it has on others. It is frequently amazing to observe the high degree of sensitivity and skill which develops in such groups as the members help each other to learn.

Naturally, the T Group is designed to facilitate kinds of behavior which can be most useful for learning about social interaction. Typically, certain features of everyday group activity are blurred or removed. The trainer, for example, does not provide the leadership which a group of "students" would normally expect. This produces a kind of "power vacuum" and a great deal of behavior which, in time, becomes the basis for learning. There is no agenda, except as the group provides it. There are no norms of group operation (such as *Robert's Rules of Order*) except as the group decides to adopt them.

The T Group is for some time a confusing, tension-laden, frustrating experience for most participants. But these conditions have been found to be conductive to learning in this field. Naturally, some individuals learn a great deal, while others resist the whole process. It is rare, however, for an individual to end a two-week experience in a T Group feeling that he has learned nothing.

An early effort to apply McGregor's ideas to the U.S. Department of State during the Kennedy administration is documented by Professor Scott Highhouse, Bowling Green State University, in a history of organizational development that he has written. He describes a 1967 report by Chris Argyris on a series of T-Group sessions in which a State Department participant comments on the recommended shift to an open, Theory Y approach:

> ***If I were to be very honest, I think that one reason I have succeeded is that I have learned not to be open; not to be candid. Do the powers that be realize what you fellows (turning to the staff) are implying—that we should strive to be more open? That's like asking us to commit organizational suicide.***

This initiative involved training and structural change, such as eliminating six layers in the organizational hierarchy. In the end, however, it was judged too rapid and too difficult a change to incorporate into the organization.

Surrounding the T Group in programs of this kind are theoretical lectures, "skill-practice" sessions, demonstrations, sessions devoted to providing individuals with consultation in analyzing their "back-home" problems, and sessions designed to improve the skills required in helping others. All of these activities are designed in advance by the staff to provide a patterned whole, rather than a scrap basket of unrelated experiences. Each program is different in some ways from past ones as staff learning and research findings accumulate and as innovations are conceived.

Finally, such programs are conducted in locations which are psychologically if not geographically remote from everyday life. Bethel, Maine, Columbia's Arden House, and such locations make it possible to create a "cultural island" in which the significance of the whole experience is intensified. This, too, appears to aid learning, partly because the unreality creates an environment in which individuals are more flexible in trying on new behaviors to see how they fit.

One of the very real problems connected with this highly unconventional approach to education in the skills of social interaction is the difficulty which participants have in communicating meaningfully about their experience after it is over. They often succeed only in making the program sound highly mysterious and esoteric. This is not surprising. The most profound and significant insights into one's own behavior are often distressingly simple. An individual, for example, may seriously interfere with his effectiveness because he talks too much. For reasons which are psychologically complex, he cannot even hear—let alone understand—ordinary feedback on this matter. Nor does he perceive how his "snowing" others under with words not only interferes with their effectiveness, but defeats his own purposes.

If, as might happen, the T Group experience revealed to him what he was doing to others and to himself, he might, as a result, improve his skill in social interaction substantially. However, he would feel silly telling his colleagues on his return that he had learned the consequences of talking too much. If the insight had led to a real understanding of the intricate significance of this behavior in his adjustment, he would be even more at a loss in talking about it.

There is nothing mysterious about this form of education. It is manipulative only in the sense that it is designed to create conditions under which people may—if they desire—improve their understanding of themselves and of others, and their skills of social interaction. It does tend to demonstrate dramatically what a complex and difficult thing it is to learn even basically simple things in this field. Thus, in describing it, the participant may not communicate very well. That its consequences are of genuine significance, however, is being demonstrated by the growing demand for opportunities to obtain this education.

Incidentally, the criticisms that these programs are examples of "group-think," that they create subservience and conformity to social pressures, undermine individualism, and stifle creativity are based on complete ignorance of the educational methods involved. Almost anyone who has participated in an NTL activity will offer evidence to the contrary. One learns how powerful group pressure can be, but one learns simultaneously how valuable the resources of a group may be in achieving one's own goals. Moreover, one learns something about counteracting the former and utilizing the latter characteristics of group behavior.

As is the case with psychotherapy, these methods of laboratory training in the skills of social interaction will be elaborated and improved greatly in the years ahead. However, they have amply demonstrated their value already.

IN SUMMARY

Managerial competence is created on the job, not in the classroom. However, classroom education can be used as a powerful aid to the process of management development, providing there is sufficient understanding of the different kinds of learning which are involved and of the different methods and strategies that are appropriate to these. Only disillusionment can result from the naive attitude that education is a Good Thing regardless of the need to be met. A few general conclusions seem worthy of reiteration:

1. Classroom learning is effective only within an organizational climate conducive to growth. A negative environment will wipe out the gains from classroom education in a relatively short time.

2. The motivations of the individual—his "felt needs" for new knowledge or increased skill—are absolutely critical factors in any learning. The principle of integration is, therefore, impor-

tant in the administration of all activities relating to managerial education.

3. Learning is an active process. The "grease gun" conception of education is useless.
4. Practice (experience) and effective feedback are essential aspects of any learning which involves behavior change. Where skills are involved, educational methods which fail to provide for these requirements are valueless.
5. The skills of social interaction are, at the same time, among the most essential for the manager and the most difficult to improve in the classroom. Ordinary methods of education appear to be relatively ineffective in producing learning in this area. However, laboratory methods providing special conditions for experience and feedback have demonstrated their value.
6. In view of the complexities and difficulties involved in improving managerial competence through classroom learning, our expectations should be modest. This is not to undervalue the contributions of classroom education, but to suggest that managers (like parents vis-à-vis the public school system) sometimes expect formal education to relieve them of responsibility for the growth *on the job* of their subordinates. Attempts to evaluate classroom training programs which ignore the effects of the job climate will inevitably yield misleading results.

REFERENCES

Andrews, Kenneth R., "Is Management Training Effective?" *Harvard Business Review*, vol. 35, nos. 1 and 2 (January–February and March–April), 1957.

Hoy, George A., Jr., "A Brand-new Breakthrough in Management Development," *Factory*, July, 1959.

Johnson, Howard W., "A Framework for Reviewing the Contribution of University Executive Development Programs," Cambridge:

Massachusetts Institute of Technology, School of Industrial Management Reprint 27, 1956.

Maier, Norman R. F., Alden R. Solem, and Ayesha A. Maier, *Supervisory and Executive Development: A Manual for Role Playing.* New York: John Wiley & Sons, Inc., 1957.

National Industrial Conference Board, Inc., "Company Programs in Executive Development," Studies in Personnel Policy, no. 107, 1950.

SELECTED REFERENCES TO THE ANNOTATED EDITION

Argyris, Chris, "Teaching Smart People How to Learn," ***Harvard Business Review*****, 69, May-June 1991, pp. 99–109.**

Mintzberg, Henry, "Teaching Leadership in Context," ***Fast Company Magazine*****, February 1, 2001.**

Senge, Peter, Art Kleiner, Charlotte Roberts, Richard Ross, George Roth, and Bryan Smith, ***The Dance of Change: The Challenges to Sustaining Momentum in Learning Organizations*****, New York: Doubleday, 1999.**

DISCUSSION QUESTIONS FOR CHAPTER 15

1. **If, as McGregor suggests, managerial competence is created on the job, what is the role of classroom learning?**

2. **How can classroom learning be designed to ensure that each student is motivated by his or her "felt needs" for new learning rather than using a "one size fits all" approach?**

3. **McGregor praises the personal self-awareness that commonly emerged from "T-group" experiences. To what degree is this sort of intense, interpersonal feedback and shared learning relevant in today's organizations?**

THE MANAGERIAL TEAM

In contrast to a predominant focus on individuals and bilateral relationships in organizations, McGregor devotes this final chapter to teams and groups. He cites a contemporary writer who disparages groups as having a "downward leveling effect," stifling "individualism" and "nullif[ying] creativ[ity]." He notes that "in general we are remarkably inept in accomplishing objectives through group effort," but also adds: "This is not inevitable." Research led by Kurt Lewin and others on "group dynamics," he notes, has encountered the same sort of resistance that first confronted Darwin's theories of evolution and Freud's concept of psychoanalysis.

What makes for a successful group or team? McGregor anticipates the vast literature that has emerged on teams and group as he points to an "informal, comfortable, relaxed" atmosphere, broad participation in discussions, tasks or objectives that are well understood, constructive disagreement, decisions mostly reached by consensus, lack of domination by the chair, the group frequently stopping "to examine how well it is doing," and, he notes, "members listen[ing] to each other!" McGregor is always attuned to relationships, so it is perhaps not surprising that he rejects what he calls "the mistaken idea that the effectiveness of the group depends solely upon the leader." "As a matter of fact," he goes on to state, "the research evidence indicates quite clearly that *skillful and sensitive membership behavior is the real clue to effective group operation.*"

Of course, McGregor is careful to "distinguish between the

team concept of management as a gimmick ... applied ... [through] direction and control and the team concept as a natural correlate of management by integration and self-control." McGregor is not optimistic about our making a rapid transition from "our conception of an organization as a pattern of individual relationships to one of a pattern of relationships among groups." Yet, he points out, "we cannot hope much longer to operate the complex, interdependent, collaborative enterprise which is the modern industrial company on the completely unrealistic premise that it consists of individual relationships." McGregor concludes, "When a few managements begin to discover the economic as well as the psychological advantages of really effective team operation, their competitive advantage will provide all the stimulus necessary to accelerate this transition."

CHAPTER 16

THE MANAGERIAL TEAM

A few years ago, two of MITs Sloan Fellows undertook a joint master's thesis on the subject of staff-line relationships. One of them concentrated on the accounting function, the other on personnel. They studied several companies and found the usual kinds of difficulties and frictions. The quality of the relationships appeared to have little correlation with the degree of conformity to textbook principles such as unity of command and equality of responsibility and authority.

One division of a large company provided a puzzle. The managers in this organization—line and staff alike—completely ignored the usual distinction between the two types of functions. The researchers found staff people exercising authority quite directly and line people giving advice. *Yet they found little evidence of friction or antagonism between the two groups.* Moreover, the division was regarded as one of the best managed and most economically successful in the company.

The one clue which helped to explain this anomalous situation was the relationship between the general manager and the several managers of both line and staff functions who reported to him. He had been in his job for about two years, and he had created a remarkable spirit of teamwork within this group. They worked together a great deal, and they demonstrated both a high commitment to the objectives they had jointly evolved and a high degree of informal collaboration in achieving them. The formal boundaries between their responsibilities seemed of little consequence to them. Their interest was in getting a job done by whatever means seemed to make sense. The rest of the divisional organization reflected their attitudes.

The conclusion of the researchers was that this group was characterized by a genuine "unity of purpose" which largely obviated the necessity for such formal arrangements as unity of command, equality of authority and responsibility, and staff-line distinctions.*

In 1965 Abraham Maslow explicitly extended Theory Y with a series of studies of high-performing teams and other organizational processes. He reported on a key individual in a high-performing team as cited in Peter Senge's *The Fifth Discipline*:

The task was no longer separate from the self... but rather he identified with this task so strongly that you couldn't define his real self without including that task.

[Peter Drucker commented on Maslow's *Euspychian Management* in 1995: "He wrote it to bring McGregor and me down to earth" (www.maslow.org/sub/eup.php)].

The significance of unity of purpose within a managerial team is given some lip service by most managers, but it is not always recognized that this objective can only be achieved by a closely knit *group*. Most so-called managerial teams are not teams at all, but collections of individual relationships with the boss in which each individual is vying with every other for power, prestige, recognition, and personal autonomy. Under such conditions unity of purpose is a myth.

One research study of top management groups found that 85 per cent of the communications within the group took place between individual subordinates and the superior (up *and* down), and only

* There is extensive research on groups that certainly confirms the importance of what McGregor terms "unity of purpose." The larger challenge is in mixed-motive situations where a leadership team includes diverse stakeholders who have both common and conflicting interests or goals.

15 per cent laterally between the subordinates. Many executives who talk about their "teams" of subordinates would be appalled to discover how low the actual level of collaboration is among them, and how high is the mutual suspicion and antagonism. Yet these same executives generally create the very conditions which would appall them if recognized. They do so by managing individuals rather than helping to create a genuine group.

THE INDIVIDUAL OR THE GROUP?

The subject of groups within management tends to generate a good deal of feeling. There are those who have no use for group effort at all and who appear to believe that an organization can operate effectively on the basis of relationships between pairs of individuals. In many companies, for example, committees are held in low esteem. The definition of a camel as a horse put together by a committee reflects a common attitude.

William H. Whyte of *Fortune* magazine, in his *Organization Man*, takes an even stronger position. He argues that group activity has a downward leveling effect on the individual, forces conformity and denies the expression of individualism, nullifies creative activity, and is in general a hampering and limiting form of human activity.

These views deny the realities of organizational life. Many activities simply cannot be carried on and many problems cannot be solved on an individual basis or in two-person relationships. The problem of the group versus the individual is not an either-or problem at all. There are kinds of activities which are appropriate to the individual, others that are appropriate to the pair, and others that are appropriate to larger groups. Under the right conditions, there are positive advantages to be achieved from group effort. In addition, there are severe negative consequences when we ignore the necessity for group action and attempt to solve certain problems in terms of pair relationships.

In general we are remarkably inept in accomplishing objectives through group effort. This is not inevitable. It is a result of inadequate understanding and skill with respect to the unique aspects of group operation.* We accept the fact that we have to learn how to operate successfully in our individual relationships with subordinates. If we gave no more time and attention to this phase of managerial activity than we do to group operations, we would experience the same low level of effectiveness in both.

Whyte's thesis that we have given undue emphasis to group phenomena, and in the process lost track of individuals, misses the point altogether. The real problem is that we have given so little attention to group behavior that management does not know enough about how to create the conditions for individual growth and integrity in the group situation. The problem is one of ignorance based on underemphasis, not overemphasis.

Research on group behavior was relatively slow in getting started. For many years, almost the only question that interested psychologists in this field was whether more work got done when people operated together or separately. The tasks selected for study—for example, the performance of mathematical computations—were often not group tasks at all. The researchers failed to differentiate between activities appropriate to the individual and activities appropriate to the group. As a result, the research findings led nowhere.

During the last couple of decades, there has been a concentrated effort to carry on productive research on group behavior, and it is beginning to pay off handsomely. Kurt Lewin and his students initiated this work in the 1930s by asking themselves some meaningful scientific questions: What behavior occurs in face-to-face task-oriented groups, and how does this behavior differ (if it does) from behavior in other situations? Are there variables of forces operating

---

* Today, of course, team-based work systems are more the norm than the exception in most medium- and and large-sized organizations.

in the group situations which are unique to it? If there are, what are their consequences?*

From these beginnings, there has emerged a major field of research endeavor that has produced an impressive body of knowledge. Lewin called this field "group dynamics" because he recognized what has subsequently been verified—that there are important aspects of group behavior which can be best understood by study of the group as a field of forces. He saw this subject as analogous to the physicist's "dynamics."

It often happens that a new field of study, as it turns up findings which challenge long-established and emotionally based convictions, encounters considerable hostility. The intensity of feeling generated by Darwin's study of evolution has died down today, and we regard this field as a legitimate and scientifically respectable one. It is somewhat difficult for the younger generation to appreciate the intensity of feeling that was generated a half century ago over the issues which Darwin raised. Some of us, however, remember the Scopes trial in Tennessee which literally filled the newspapers for some time. Freud's psychoanalysis generated hostilities which have not completely disappeared even today. The field of group dynamics has encountered similar difficulties.

It was natural, as the earlier researchers discovered that there were characteristics of group effort which differentiated this form of human activity from others, to apply their growing insights to practical situations. They began to ask what people could do to be more

---

* Kurt Lewin's work on group dynamics highlighted what he called "interdependence of fate" and "task interdependence"—both of which would bind groups together. He then probed matters of conflict, decision making, and other aspects of group dynamics. (See, for example, Kurt Lewin, *Resolving Social Conflicts: Selected Papers on Group Dynamics*, ed. Gertrude W. Lewin, New York: Harper & Brothers, 1948; and Kurt Lewin, *Field Theory in Social Science: Selected Theoretical Papers*, ed. D. Cartwright, New York: Harper & Brothers, 1951.)

effective in groups. As this field of application grew, there were of course those who oversold it, and there were others who jumped on the bandwagon to exploit the findings for their own economic ends. Finally, there were the strong feelings of those who feared that emphasis on group behavior would undermine their power. Group dynamics acquired a bad name.

EFFECTIVE AND INEFFECTIVE GROUPS

If we take a balanced and reasonably objective view of the large body of research evidence on group behavior, certain things are clear. First, there are no mysterious and secret skills which will enable the "expert" to manipulate groups toward his own ends. Knowledge in this field, like knowledge in any scientific field, can be misused, but the dangers of its misuse are substantially less than, for example, in the field of atomic physics. In fact, one of the major contributions of research on group behavior has been to show how such manipulative misuse tends to be self-defeating.

Second, despite the rantings of a few "converts," the field is not a cult. It has its own jargon, but consider in comparison the vocabulary that has grown up within the missile field in the past decade!

Third, groups can be effective decision-making and problem-solving entities.* All the arguments to the effect that "only the individual" can be responsible, make decisions, innovate, are shibboleths. The fact that many, or even most, groups do not do these things well proves nothing but our lack of knowledge about group behavior and our lack of skill in operating within groups.

The basic questions which the serious researchers in this field are pursuing quite independently of the lunatic fringe are: What forces are uniquely operative in the face-to-face group situations? How do

* The literature on group decision making has expanded in many directions, spanning decision science, work design, team interactions, group boundary, spanning, and other domains.

they operate and how can knowledge of them be applied to improve the functioning of groups? This is a worth-while endeavor.

Let us attempt to lay aside for a moment our prejudice, pro or con, with respect to group activity and consider in everyday common-sense terms some of the things that are characteristic of a well-functioning, efficient group. Occasionally, one does encounter a really good top management team or series of staff meetings or committee. What distinguishes such groups from other less effective ones?

1. The "atmosphere," which can be sensed in a few minutes of observation, tends to be informal, comfortable, relaxed. There are no obvious tensions. It is a working atmosphere in which people are involved and interested. There are no signs of boredom.

2. There is a lot of discussion in which virtually everyone participates, but it remains pertinent to the task of the group. If the discussion gets off the subject, someone will bring it back in short order.

3. The task or the objective of the group is well understood and accepted by the members. There will have been free discussion of the objective at some point until it was formulated in such a way that the members of the group could commit themselves to it.

4. The members listen to each other! The discussion does not have the quality of jumping from one idea to another unrelated one. Every idea is given a hearing. People do not appear to be afraid of being foolish by putting forth a creative thought even if it seems fairly extreme.

5. There is disagreement. The group is comfortable with this and shows no signs of having to avoid conflict or to keep everything on a plane of sweetness and light. Disagreements are not suppressed or overridden by premature group action. The reasons are carefully examined, and the group seeks to resolve them rather than to dominate the dissenter.

On the other hand, there is no "tyranny of the minority." Individuals who disagree do not appear to be trying to dominate the group or to express hostility. Their disagreement is an expression of a genuine difference of opinion, and they expect a hearing in order that a solution may be found.

Sometimes there are basic disagreements which cannot be resolved. The group finds it possible to live with them, accepting them but not permitting them to block its efforts. Under some conditions, action will be deferred to permit further study of an issue between the members. On other occasions, where the disagreement cannot be resolved and action is necessary, it will be taken but with open caution and recognition that the action may be subject to later reconsideration.

6. Most decisions are reached by a kind of consensus in which it is clear that everybody is in general agreement and willing to go along. However, there is little tendency for individuals who oppose the action to keep their opposition private and thus let an apparent consensus mask real disagreement. Formal voting is at a minimum; the group does not accept a simple majority as a proper basis for action.

7. Criticism is frequent, frank, and relatively comfortable. There is little evidence of personal attack, either openly or in a hidden fashion. The criticism has a constructive flavor in that it is oriented toward removing an obstacle that faces the group and prevents it from getting the job done.

8. People are free in expressing their feelings as well as their ideas both on the problem and on the group's operation. There is little pussyfooting, there are few "hidden agendas." Everybody appears to know quite well how everybody else feels about any matter under discussion.

9. When action is taken, clear assignments are made and accepted.

10. The chairman of the group does not dominate it, nor on the contrary, does the group defer unduly to him. In fact, as one observes the activity, it is clear that the leadership shifts from time to time, depending on the circumstances. Different members, because of their knowledge or experience, are in a position at various times to act as "resources" for the group. The members utilize them in this fashion and they occupy leadership roles while they are thus being used.

    There is little evidence of a struggle for power as the group operates. The issue is not who controls but how to get the job done.

11. The group is self-conscious about its own operations. Frequently, it will stop to examine how well it is doing or what may be interfering with its operation. The problem may be a matter of procedure, or it may be an individual whose behavior is interfering with the accomplishment of the group's objectives. Whatever it is, it gets open discussion until a solution is found.

These and other observable characteristics are generally found in the effective task group. Every one of them represents important ways of dealing with forces which are present in every group. A substantial amount of sensitivity, understanding, and skill is required of all the members—not of the leader alone—to create such a setting as this.

It has been my privilege to be a member of a staff of six or eight individuals comprising the faculty of an NTL-sponsored training program on a number of occasions. Each time I am impressed anew by the demonstration of effective group action given by these colleagues as they come together to design the program.

Normally a day is set aside for the purpose. The task is clear, but there is always the expectation that this program will contain innovations—perhaps major ones—which will make it not merely different, but better than anything that has been done before. No one knows what these will be, or how they will evolve, but the group confidently expects to use the resources of its members to do a genuinely creative job. This confidence is rarely mistaken.

In addition to designing the program there are dozens of decisions to be made, many necessary assignments of specific tasks and responsibilities, a variety of individual interests and desires to be integrated with the requirements of the program. Conflicts arise and are argued out, sometimes with a lot of heat. These colleagues are individualists, and no one of them is prepared to have his individuality submerged. Nevertheless, there is the kind of commitment to the common purpose that yields genuine self-control.

The task is accomplished with amazing efficiency, yet there is plenty of kidding and good humor. Group "maintenance functions" are performed as the need arises. There is a chairman, but the leadership moves around the group as the situation dictates. Everyone participates actively, yet no one dominates the group. I have never known a vote to be taken except as a joke. Every decision is unanimous.

And, most significant of all, each such group has a different composition. Some individuals may have worked together before, but there are always several new members. Within minutes of the start of the meeting they are as much a part of the group as if they had been members for years.

It is truly an exhilarating experience to participate in such an activity. I usually come away wishing some of my good friends in management who have a jaundiced view of groups could have observed the meeting.

Now let us look at the other end of the range. Consider a poor group—one that is relatively ineffective in accomplishing its purposes. What are some of the observable characteristics of its operation?

1. The "atmosphere" is likely to reflect either indifference and boredom (people whispering to each other or carrying on side con-

versations, individuals who are obviously not involved, etc.) or tension (undercurrents of hostility and antagonism, stiffness and undue formality, etc.). The group is clearly not challenged by its task or genuinely involved in it.

2. A few people tend to dominate the discussion. Often their contributions are way off the point. Little is done by anyone to keep the group clearly on the track.

3. From the things which are said, it is difficult to understand what the group task is or what its objectives are. These may have been stated by the chairman initially, but there is no evidence that the group either understands or accepts a common objective. On the contrary, it is usually evident that different people have different, private, and personal objectives which they are attempting to achieve in the group, and that these are often in conflict with each other and with the group's task.

4. People do not really listen to each other. Ideas are ignored and overridden. The discussion jumps around with little coherence and no sense of movement along a track. One gets the impression that there is much talking for effect—people make speeches which are obviously intended to impress someone else rather than being relevant to the task at hand.

   Conversation with members after the meeting will reveal that they have failed to express ideas or feelings which they may have had for fear they would be criticized or regarded as silly. Some members feel that the leader or the other members are constantly making judgments of them in terms of evaluations of the contributions they make, and so they are extremely careful about what they say.

5. Disagreements are generally not dealt with effectively by the group. They may be completely suppressed by a leader who fears conflict. On the other hand, they may result in open warfare, the

consequence of which is domination by one subgroup over another. They may be "resolved" by a vote in which a very small majority wins the day, and a large minority remains completely unconvinced.

There may be a "tyranny of the minority" in which an individual or a small subgroup is so aggressive that the majority accedes to their wishes in order to preserve the peace or to get on with the task. In general only the more aggressive members get their ideas considered because the less aggressive people tend either to keep quiet altogether or to give up after short, ineffectual attempts to be heard.

6. Actions are often taken prematurely before the real issues are either examined or resolved. There will be much grousing after the meeting by people who disliked the decision but failed to speak up about it in the meeting itself. A simple majority is considered sufficient for action, and the minority is expected to go along. Most of the time, however, the minority remains resentful and uncommitted to the decision.

7. Action decisions tend to be unclear—no one really knows who is going to do what. Even when assignments of responsibility are made, there is often considerable doubt as to whether they will be carried out.

8. The leadership remains clearly with the committee chairman. He may be weak or strong, but he sits always "at the head of the table."

9. Criticism may be present, but it is embarrassing and tension-producing. It often appears to involve personal hostility, and the members are uncomfortable with this and unable to cope with it. Criticism of ideas tends to be destructive. Sometimes every idea proposed will be "clobbered" by someone else. Then, no one is willing to stick his neck out.

10. Personal feelings are hidden rather than being out in the open. The general attitude of the group is that these are inappropriate for discussion and would be too explosive if brought out on the table.

11. The group tends to avoid any discussion of its own "maintenance." There is often much discussion after the meeting of what was wrong and why, but these matters are seldom brought up and considered within the meeting itself where they might be resolved.

Why is it that so many groups seem to resemble this example rather than the first one? There are a number of reasons. In the first place, most of us have rather low expectations of group accomplishment. Our experience with really effective groups has been so limited that we do not have clear standards of what could be. In the second place, most of us have relatively little knowledge of what is important to good group functioning. We are not aware of current research findings concerning the significant requirements for effective group operations, and therefore the things we attempt to do to improve a given group are not always relevant.

One of the most important reasons for poor group functioning is the general fear of conflict and hostility which leads us to behave in ways that hamper rather than help. Hostilities, hidden agendas, and other personal factors inimical to group functioning are very commonly present, particularly with a newly constituted group. To ignore these or to suppress them is to let them determine the level of effectiveness of the group. Yet, our fear of personal feuding and conflict is such that that is exactly what normally happens.

Another significant factor resulting in poor group activity is the mistaken idea that the effectiveness of the group depends solely upon the leader. As a matter of fact, the research evidence indicates quite clearly that *skillful and sensitive membership behavior is the real clue to effective group operation*. In a really competent and skilled group, the members can in fact carry on highly effective operation with no designated leader whatever.*

Finally, along with our fears of conflict and hostility, is a lack of recognition of the necessity for paying attention to the maintenance of the group itself. Like any complex organization, a group requires attention to its functioning. If it is to operate at peak efficiency, it will require constant maintenance. Most groups deal with maintenance problems only in the post mortems outside the meetings, and these seldom result in action within the group.

Behind all these specifics, frequently, is a deeper attitude associated with Theory X: Management by direction and control is jeopardized by effective group functioning. The principle of "divide and rule" is eminently sound if one wishes to exercise personal power over subordinates. It is the best way to control them.

If, however, the superior recognizes the existence of the intricate interdependence characteristic of modern industry, and if he is less interested in personal power than in creating conditions such that the human resources available to him will be utilized to achieve organizational purposes, he will seek to build a strong group. He will recognize that the highest commitment to organizational objectives, and the most successful collaboration in achieving them, *require unique kinds of interaction which can only occur in a highly effective group setting*. He will in fact discourage discussion or decision making on many matters which affect his organization except in the group setting. He will give the idea of "the team" full expression, with all the connotations it carries on the football field.

THE POTENTIALITIES OF TEAMWORK

The face-to-face group is as significant a unit of organization as the individual. The two are not antithetical. In a genuinely effective group the individual finds some of his deepest satisfactions. Through

* This focus on membership behavior, not just leadership behavior, is a key insight that has taken many years to get appropriate attention.

teamwork and group activity many of the difficult organizational problems of coordination and control can be solved. However, these values can be realized only if certain requirements are met.

First, we will have to abandon the idea that individual and group values are necessarily opposed, that the latter can only be realized at the expense of the former. If we would look to the family, we might recognize the possibilities inherent in the opposite point of view.

Second, we will have to give serious attention to the matter of acquiring understanding of the factors which determine the effectiveness of group action and to the acquisition of skill in utilizing them. This means much more than offering courses in conference leadership. It means, above all, acquiring skills in group *membership*. The laboratory method of training developed by the National Training Laboratory (discussed in Chapter 15) is a particularly effective one for acquiring these skills.

Third, we will need to learn to distinguish between those activities which are appropriate for groups and those that are not.

Finally, we will need to distinguish between the team concept of management as a gimmick to be applied within the strategy of management by direction and control and the team concept as a natural correlate of management by integration and self-control. The one has nothing in common with the other.

To the extent that these requirements are met, we will make some significant discoveries. For example:

1. Group target setting offers advantages that cannot be achieved by individual target setting alone. The two are supplementary, not mutually exclusive.

2. An effective managerial group provides the best possible environment for individual development. It is the natural place to broaden the manager's understanding of functions other than his own and to create a genuine appreciation of the need for collaboration. It is the best possible training ground for skill in problem solving and in social interaction.

3. Many significant objectives and measures of performance can be developed for the group which cannot be applied to the individual. The members of cohesive groups will work at least as hard to achieve group objectives as they will to achieve individual ones.
4. In an effective managerial team the aspects of "dog-eat-dog" competition, which are actually inimical to organizational accomplishment, can be minimized by the development of "unity of purpose" without reducing individual motivation.

It seems to me unlikely that the transition will be rapid from our conception of an organization as a pattern of individual relationships to one of a pattern of relationships among groups. We have too much to learn, and too many prejudices to overcome. I do believe, however, that such a transition is inevitable in the long run. We cannot hope much longer to operate the complex, interdependent, collaborative enterprise which is the modern industrial company on the completely unrealistic premise that it consists of individual relationships. The costs of doing so—although they are mostly hidden and unrecognized—are completely unjustifiable. When a few managements begin to discover the economic as well as the psychological advantages of really effective team operation, their competitive advantage will provide all the stimulus necessary to accelerate this transition.

Fads will come and go. The fundamental fact of man's capacity to collaborate with his fellows in the face-to-face group will survive the fads and one day be recognized. Then, and only then, will management discover how seriously it has underestimated the true potential of its human resources.

REFERENCES

Bennis, Warren G., and Herbert A. Shepard, "A Theory of Group Development," *Human Relations*, vol. 9, 1956.

Cartwright, Dorwin, and Alvin Zander, *Group Dynamics, Research and Theory*. Evanston, Ill.: Row, Peterson & Company, 1953.

Coser, Lewis A., "The Functions of Small Group Research," *Social Problems*, vol. 3, no. 1, 1955.

Fiedler, Fred E., *Leader Attitudes and Group Effectiveness*. Urbana, Ill.: University of Illinois Press, 1958.

Gordon, Thomas, *Group Centered Leadership*. Boston: Houghton Mifflin Company, 1955.

Hare, A. Paul, Edgar F. Borgatta, and Robert F. Bales, *Small Groups*. New York: Alfred A. Knopf, Inc., 1955.

National Training Laboratory in Group Development, *Explorations in Human Relations Training: An Assessment of Experience, 1947–1953*. Washington, D.C.: 1953.

Olmsted, Michael S., *The Small Group*. New York: Random House, Inc., 1959. (Paperback SS 16.)

Thelen, Herbert, *Dynamics of Groups at Work*. Chicago: University of Chicago Press, 1954.

SELECTED REFERENCES TO THE ANNOTATED EDITION

Ancona, Deborah, and D. Caldwell, "Bridging the Boundary, External Activity and Performance of Organizational Teams," *Administrative Science Quarterly*, vol. 37, 1992.

Allison, Grahm T., *Essence of Decision: Explaining the Cuban Missile Crisis*, Boston: Little, Brown, 1971.

Donnellon, Ann, *Team Talk: The Power of Language in Team Dynamics*, Boston: Harvard Business School Press, 1996.

Hackman, J., et al., *Work Redesign*, Reading, Mass.: Addison-Wesley, 1980.

Raifa, Howard, *Decision Analysis: Introductory Lecture on Choices under Uncertainty*, New York: McGraw-Hill, 1997.

Senge, Peter, *The Fifth, Discipline: The Art and Practice of the Learning Organization*, New York: Doubleday, 1990.

Tversky, Amos, and D. Kahnemann, "The Framing of Decisions and the Psychology of Choice," *Science*, vol. 211, 1981.

DISCUSSION QUESTIONS FOR CHAPTER 16

1. McGregor points to group members, more than group leaders, as the key to group or team effectiveness. Do you agree or disagree?
2. In 1960, McGregor stated that "management does not know enough about how to create the conditions for individual growth and integrity in the group situation." To what degree have theory and practice advanced since then?
3. McGregor anticipated an inevitable transition from conceiving of organizations as "a pattern of individual relationships" to conceiving of them as "a pattern of relationships among groups." Is there a logical next step to conceiving of an interconnected pattern of relationships among organizations?

CONCLUSION

Developments in physical science theory during the first half of the twentieth century have led to the creation of a new world. If anyone had been able to predict in 1900 what life in the United States would be like in 1960, he would have been regarded as a complete fool. Passenger travel 6 to 8 miles above the earth at 600 miles per hour, space vehicles circling the moon, radar, a nuclear-powered submarine traveling under the icecap at the North Pole, air conditioning, television, frozen foods, stereophonic reproduction of the music of world-renowned musicians in the home—these things and hundreds more were almost inconceivable sixty years ago. They would still be inconceivable were it not for developments in scientific theory and man's inventive genius in exploiting them.

Although the parallel may seem unreasonable to some, we are today in a period when the development of theory within the social sciences will permit innovations which are at present inconceivable. Among these will be dramatic changes in the organization and management of economic enterprise. The capacities of the average human being for creativity, for growth, for collaboration, for productivity (in the full sense of the term) are far greater than we yet have recognized. If we don't destroy life on this planet before we discover how to make it possible for man to utilize his abilities to create a world in which he can live in peace, it is possible that the next half century will bring the most dramatic social changes in human history.

Former World Bank economist David Ellerman highlights Douglas McGregor's work as one of eight foundational scholars in his book *Helping People Help Themselves: From the World Bank to an Alternative Philosophy of Development Assistance* (Ann Arbor: University of Michigan Press, 2005). In separate correspondence, Ellerman writes:

> In economic development and in management, one party, the helper or manager, tries to get another party, the doer, to

> undertake a set of actions that are relatively subtle, going far beyond just a physical effect. There is always a conundrum: For the actions to be done well, they need to grow out of some type of intrinsic motivation which cannot be supplied externally by the helper or manager. McGregor understood well this basic conundrum from his early paper on the staff-line relationship to the development of the distinction between Theory X and Theory Y. With Theory Y, McGregor delves into the subtle and indirect process of managing in ways that structure the work process to align the doer's intrinsic motivation with organizational ends. The general features of the Theory Y approach are applicable to development assistance as well as a broad range of human relationships where people are trying to get others to undertake actions that are best performed and are only sustainable when they come out of intrinsic motivation.

I believe that the industrial enterprise is a microcosm within which some of the most basic of these social changes will be invented and tested and refined. As Peter Drucker has pointed out, the modern, large, industrial enterprise is itself a social invention of great historical importance. Unfortunately, it is already obsolete. In its present form it is simply not an adequate means for meeting the future economic requirements of society. The fundamental difficulty is that we have not yet learned enough about organizing and managing the human resources of enterprise. Fortunately, an increasing number of managers recognize the inadequacy of present methods. In this recognition lies the hope of the future. Industrial management has again and again demonstrated an amazing ability to innovate once it is persuaded of the opportunity to do so.

Management is severely hampered today in its attempts to innovate with respect to the human side of enterprise by the inadequacy of conventional organization theory. Based on invalid and limiting assumptions about human behavior, this theory blinds us to many possibilities for invention, just as the physical science theory of a half century ago prevented even the perception of the possibility of radar or space travel.

It is not important that management accept the assumptions of Theory Y. These are one man's interpretations of current social science knowledge, and they will be modified—possibly supplanted—by new knowledge within a short time. It *is* important that management abandon limiting assumptions like those of Theory X, so that future inventions with respect to the human side of enterprise will be more than minor changes in already obsolescent conceptions of organized human effort.*

Theoretical assumptions such as those of Theory Y imply some conditions which are unrealizable in practice (like the perfect vacuum implied by physical theory). This is not a handicap; it is the stimulus to invention and discovery. Assumptions like those of Theory X provide us with no standard except present accomplishment and thus encourage us, as Joe Scanlon was fond of saying, to "face the past and back into the future."

The ideas with respect to changed managerial strategies consistent with Theory Y which have been discussed in this volume—target setting, the Scanlon Plan, participation, the professional role of staff, the "agricultural" approach to management development—are no more than beginning steps toward management by integration and self-control. Once management becomes truly persuaded that it is seriously underestimating the potential represented by its human resources—once it accepts assumptions about human behavior more consistent with current social science knowledge than those of Theory X—it will invest the time, money, and effort not only to develop

---

* McGregor and MIT colleague Richard Beckhard are credited with coining the term "organization development" to describe the application of behavioral science to major organizational change—the core challenge identified by McGregor in this conclusion (Bowling Green professor Scott Highhouse, citing Weisbord, M.R., *Productive Workplaces*, San Francisco, CA: Jossey-Bass Publishers, 1987).

improved applications of such ideas as have been discussed in these pages, but to invent more effective ones. As always, however, invention will go hand in hand with new theory.

The purpose of this volume is not to entice management to choose sides over Theory X or Theory Y. It is, rather, to encourage the realization that theory is important, to urge management to examine its assumptions and make them explicit. In doing so it will open a door to the future. The possible result could be developments during the next few decades with respect to the human side of enterprise comparable to those that have occurred in technology during the past half century.

And, if we can learn how to realize the potential for collaboration inherent in the human resources of industry, we will provide a model for governments and nations which mankind sorely needs.

CONCLUSION TO THE ANNOTATED EDITION

JOEL CUTCHER-GERSHENFELD

Douglas McGregor's legacy is twofold. He helps us to see the importance of critical thinking about deep, underlying assumptions and he places a spotlight on one particular set of assumptions—Theory Y—that are uniquely important in facing future organizational and societal challenges. His conclusion is brief and to the point. "It is not important," he notes, "that management accept the assumptions of Theory Y. These are one man's interpretations of current social science knowledge.... It *is* important that management abandon limiting assumptions like those of Theory X." In order to deeply understand the limits of established Theory X assumptions, McGregor quotes Joe Scanlon, who stated that with these assumptions, we would "face the past and back into the future." At the same time, McGregor cautions against the unthinking rejection of Theory X or an unthinking embrace of Theory Y: "The purpose of this volume is not to entice management to choose sides over Theory X or Theory Y. It is, rather, to encourage the realization that theory is important, to urge management to examine its assumptions and make them explicit."

Ultimately, however, McGregor believed that "once management becomes truly persuaded that it is seriously underestimating the potential represented by its human resources ... it will invest the time, money, and effort not only to develop improved applications of such ideas as have been discussed in these pages, but to invent more effective ones." Further, McGregor concludes, in realizing "the potential for collaboration inherent in the human resources of industry, we will provide a model for governments and nations which mankind sorely needs." Even though this book was published 45 years ago, it marks the beginning of serious consideration of the assumptions, values, and research orientation that would ultimately guide us into the twenty-first century. The book is both prescient and foundational.

APPENDIX

ARCHIVED MATERIAL

ON LEADERSHIP

Douglas McGregor

From Antioch Notes, *vol. 31, no. 9, May 1, 1954*

In a few weeks I shall preside over the commencement exercise of Antioch's 101st year. Then, with mixed feelings, I shall become an ex-president of one of the most exciting educational institutions in America.

On the one hand, I am eager to renew direct acquaintance with students in the classroom and to rejoin my colleagues in the planning and execution of research on the problems of human relations in industry. On the other hand, I am reluctant to leave the wonderful people of Antioch who have provided me with such a rich experience during the past six years. They have taught me a new conception of education and a new appreciation of the potentialities of young people.

It will require time to think back over the many events that have been crowded into these few years and to draw a proper meaning from them. However, two related convictions have developed slowly but steadily out of this experience. Perhaps they are worth brief elaboration.

THE BOSS MUST BOSS

The first is a conviction which has been derived from my personal struggle with the role of college president. Before coming to Antioch I had observed and worked with top executives as an adviser in a number of organizations. I thought I knew how they felt about their responsibilities and what led them to behave as they did. I even thought that I could create a role for myself which would enable me to avoid some of the difficulties they encountered.

I was wrong! It took the direct experience of becoming a line executive and meeting personally the problems involved to teach me what no amount of observation of other people could have taught.

I believed, for example, that a leader could operate successfully as a kind of adviser to his organization. I thought I could avoid being a "boss." Unconsciously, I suspect, I hoped to duck the unpleasant necessity of making difficult decisions, of taking the responsibility for one course of action among many uncertain alternatives, of making mistakes and taking the consequences. I thought that maybe I could operate so that everyone would like me—that "good human relations" would eliminate all discord and disagreement.

I couldn't have been more wrong. it took a couple of years, but I finally began to realize that a leader cannot avoid the exercise of authority any more than he can avoid responsibility for what happens to his organization. In fact, it is the major function of the top executive to take on his own shoulders the responsibility for resolving the uncertainties that are always involved in important decisions. Moreover, since no important decision ever pleases everyone in the organization, he must also absorb the displeasure, and sometimes severe hostility, of those who would have taken a different course.

A colleague recently summed up what my experience has taught me in these words: "A good leader must be tough enough to win a fight, but not tough enough to kick a man when he is down." This notion is not in the least inconsistent with humane, democratic leadership. Good human relations develop out of strength, not of weakness.

I'm still trying to understand and practice what is implied in my colleague's statement.

THE FIGHT AGAINST BIGOTRY

The second conviction relates to institutional rather than personal leadership. It emerged from direct experience with the anti-intellectual attitudes, the suspicion, the fear, the damning accusations, which characterize our life today. National and international tensions make us wary of nonconformity everywhere. It is an easy, popular pastime to link nonconformity with "Communist tendencies."

Our colleges and universities, Antioch among them, are frequently attacked by those who cannot countenance any views but their own. Because such attacks are persistent and melodramatic, a great many sensible people erroneously conclude that "where there is smoke, there must be fire." As a result, irreparable damage is often done to individuals and to organizations.

Antioch is a small college. It has a teaching faculty of about seventy-five people. After six years, I can say with some assurance that I know my faculty. I am convinced that there are no communists, or near Communists, among them.

There is no educational institution in America more intimately interwoven with free-enterprise ideals. Our work-study plan is based on belief in our American economic system. Our college government is completely patterned on the American principles of representative government. The College has been a seed bed for many successful private enterprises. It is currently engaged in a major "risk capital" venture: the operation of a multimillion dollar shopping center in Florida. These things are evidence of our faith in the American way.

But there are other facts, less well understood, about Antioch. For sound educational reasons, we try to recruit a student body which is representative of various geographic regions, various national and ethnic groups. And on our campus we do not differentiate among people because of the color of their skin or their religious affiliation. This is regarded by many as a radical policy, and probably Communist inspired.

We value the individual at Antioch. We think that he should have the freedom to grow intellectually according to his own abilities. We do not challenge his right to disagree, or to act on the basis of his beliefs, provided only that he acts openly in accord with the principles of democracy, and with honesty and integrity.

But these values, absolutely essential to any educational program worthy of the name, are widely distrusted today. If a college permits, let alone encourages, the right of disagreement, it is quickly accused of being under Communist influence.

I am no longer willing to take a defensive position with respect to these things. I am on the offensive. Antioch's philosophy, like that of colleges and universities throughout the country, is in accord with the fundamental principles of Christian ethics and of the Constitution of the United States. Its policies and procedures are openly developed through a system of representative government. It is doing a fine job of maintaining our American traditions and at the same time guarding against subversive infiltration. There is no basis whatever for Antioch to apologize to anyone for its personnel, its policies, or its practices.

It was, therefore, a source of great satisfaction to me when the Antioch trustees this month gave unanimous expression to the following statement:

> As members of the Board of Trustees of Antioch College, we are aware of the unnatural pressures that are brought against institutions of learning today. We wish to reaffirm our confidence in the administration, faculty, and student body of Antioch College. As loyal Americans, we believe that freedom of inquiry and belief by responsible scholars is essential to the moral health and spiritual progress of the nation. We commend Antioch College for the reasonableness with which it is preserving decent traditions of human relations. We urge the administration, faculty, and students to maintain intact their devotion to democratic principles against that golden day when Americans will no longer fear or distrust each other.

My second conviction thus relates also to leadership, but in an institutional rather than a personal sense: It is the business of colleges and universities to create a climate within which freedom of responsible inquiry and belief can flourish. These institutions must be tough enough to win the fight against whatever forces seek to destroy this freedom.

The college must lead, or the ideals of our founding fathers, and of thoughtful people everywhere, will wither away.

Douglas McGregor

Dr. McGregor leaves the presidency of Antioch College at the end of June to join the faculty of the School of Industrial Management, Massachusetts Institute of Technology.

THE HUMAN SIDE OF ENTERPRISE

Professor Douglas M. McGregor
School of Industrial Management,
Massachusetts Institute of Technology

It has become trite to say that the most significant developments of the next quarter century will take place not in the physical but in the social sciences, that industry—the economic organ of society—has the fundamental know-how to utilize physical science and technology for the material benefit of mankind, and that we must now learn how to utilize the social sciences to make our human organizations truly effective.

Many people agree in principle with such statements; but so far they represent a pious hope—and little else. Consider with me, if you will, something of what may be involved when we attempt to transform the hope into reality.

Reprinted from *Adventure in Thought and Action*, Proceedings of the Fifth Anniversary Convocation of the School of Industrial Management, Massachusetts Institute of Technology, Cambridge, April 9, 1957. Published by the School, 50 Memorial Drive, Cambridge, Massachusetts 02139, June 1957. The reprint included this introductory note: Management's effort to improve its use of human resources has commanded increasing attention in the past decade. But no management has as yet solved to its full satisfaction the sensitive and delicate problem of the effective organization of human effort. Douglas Murray McGregor, who left his post as President of Antioch College in 1954 to return to M.I.T., has earned a national reputation in social psychology and its application to personnel and industrial administration. Dr. McGregor's scholarship is combined with an extensive experience in industry. He now heads the School's work in industrial human relations.

I.

Let me begin with an analogy. A quarter century ago basic conceptions of the nature of matter and energy had changed profoundly from what they had been since Newton's time. The physical scientists were persuaded that under proper conditions new and hitherto unimagined sources of energy could be made available to mankind.

We know what has happened since then. First came the bomb. Then, during the past decade, have come many other attempts to exploit these scientific discoveries—some successful, some not.

The point of my analogy, however, is that the application of theory in this field is a slow and costly matter. We expect it always to be thus. No one is impatient with the scientist because he cannot tell industry how to build a simple, cheap, all-purpose source of atomic energy today. That it will take at least another decade and the investment of billions of dollars to achieve results which are economically competitive with present sources of power is understood and accepted.

It is transparently pretentious to suggest any *direct* similarity between the developments in the physical sciences leading to the harnessing of atomic energy and potential developments in the social sciences. Nevertheless, the analogy is not as absurd as it might appear to be at first glance.

To a lesser degree, and in a much more tentative fashion, we are in a position in the social sciences today like that of the physical sciences with respect to atomic energy in the thirties. We know that past conceptions of the nature of man are inadequate and in many ways incorrect. We are becoming quite certain that, under proper conditions, unimagined resources of creative human energy could become available within the organizational setting.

We cannot tell industrial management how to apply this new knowledge in simple, economic ways. We know it will require years of exploration, much costly development research, and a substantial amount of creative imagination on the part of management to discover how to apply this growing knowledge to the organization of human effort in industry.

May I ask that you keep this analogy in mind—overdrawn and pretentious though it may be—as a framework for what I have to say this morning.

Management's Task: Conventional View

The conventional conception of management's task in harnessing human energy to organizational requirements can be stated broadly in terms of three propositions. In order to avoid the complications introduced by a label, I shall call this set of propositions "Theory X":

1. Management is responsible for organizing the elements of productive enterprise—money, materials, equipment, people—in the interest of economic ends.

2. With respect to people, this is a process of directing their efforts, motivating them, controlling their actions, modifying their behavior to fit the needs of the organization.

3. Without this active intervention by management, people would be passive—even resistant—to organizational needs. They must therefore be persuaded, rewarded, punished, controlled—their activities must be directed. This is management's task—in managing subordinate managers or workers. We often sum it up by saying that management consists of getting things done through other people.

   Behind this conventional theory there are several additional beliefs—less explicit, but widespread:

4. The average man is by nature indolent—he works as little as possible.

5. He lacks ambition, dislikes responsibility, prefers to be led.

6. He is inherently self-centered, indifferent to organizational needs.

7. He is by nature resistant to change.

8. He is gullible, not very bright, the ready dupe of the charlatan and the demagogue.

The human side of economic enterprise today is fashioned from propositions and beliefs such as these. Conventional organization structures, managerial policies, practices, and programs reflect these assumptions.

In accomplishing its task—with these assumptions as guides—management has conceived of a range of possibilities between two extremes.

The Hard or the Soft Approach?

At one extreme, management can be "hard" or "strong." The methods for directing behavior involve coercion and threat (usually disguised), close supervision, tight controls over behavior. At the other extreme, management can be "soft" or "weak." The methods for directing behavior involve being permissive, satisfying people's demands, achieving harmony. Then they will be tractable, accept direction.

This range has been fairly completely explored during the past half century, and management has learned some things from the exploration. There are difficulties in the "hard" approach. Force breeds counterforces: restriction of output, antagonism, militant unionism, subtle but effective sabotage of management objectives. This approach is especially difficult during times of full employment.

There are also difficulties in the "soft" approach. It leads frequently to the abdication of management—to harmony, perhaps, but to indifferent performance. People take advantage of the soft approach. They continually expect more, but they give less and less.

Currently, the popular theme is "firm but fair." This is an attempt to gain the advantages of both the hard and the soft approaches. It is reminiscent of Teddy Roosevelt's "speak softly and carry a big stick."

Is the Conventional View Correct?

The findings which are beginning to emerge from the social sciences challenge this whole set of beliefs about man and human nature and about the task of management. The evidence is far from conclusive, certainly, but it is suggestive. It comes from the laboratory, the clinic, the schoolroom, the home, and even to a limited extent from industry itself.

The social scientist does not deny that human behavior in industrial organization today is approximately what management perceives it to be. He has, in fact, observed it and studied it fairly extensively. But he is pretty sure that this behavior is *not* a consequence of man's inherent nature. It is a consequence rather of the nature of industrial organizations, of management philosophy, policy, and practice. The conventional approach of Theory X is based on mistaken notions of what is cause and what is effect.

"Well," you ask, "what then is the *true* nature of man? What evidence leads the social scientist to deny what is obvious?" And, if I am not mistaken, you are also thinking, "Tell me—simply, and without a lot of scientific verbiage—what you think you know that is so unusual. Give me—without a lot of intellectual claptrap and theoretical nonsense—some practical ideas which will enable me to improve the situation in my organization. And remember, I'm faced with increasing costs and narrowing profit margins. I want proof that such ideas won't result simply in new and costly human relations frills. I want practical results, and I want them now."

If these are your wishes, you are going to be disappointed. Such requests can no more be met by the social scientist today than could comparable ones with respect to atomic energy be met by the physicist fifteen years ago. I can, however, indicate a few of the reasons for asserting that conventional assumptions about the human side of enterprise are inadequate. And I can suggest—tentatively—some of the propositions that will comprise a more adequate theory of the management of people. The magnitude of the task that confronts us will then, I think, be apparent.

II.

Perhaps the best way to indicate why the conventional approach of management is inadequate is to consider the subject of motivation. In discussing this subject I will draw heavily on the work of my colleague, Abraham Maslow of Brandeis University. His is the most fruitful approach I know. Naturally, what I have to say will be overgeneralized and will ignore important qualifications. In the time at our disposal, this is inevitable.

Physiological and Safety Needs

Man is a wanting animal—as soon as one of his needs is satisfied, another appears in its place. This process is unending. It continues from birth to death.

Man's needs are organized in a series of levels—a hierarchy of importance. At the lowest level, but preeminent in importance when they are thwarted, are his physiological needs. Man lives by bread alone, when there is no bread. Unless the circumstances are unusual, his needs for love, for status, for recognition are inoperative when his stomach has been empty for a while. But when he eats regularly and adequately, hunger ceases to be an important need. The sated man has hunger only in the sense that a full bottle has emptiness. The same is true of the other physiological needs of man—for rest, exercise, shelter, protection from the elements.

A satisfied need is not a motivator of behavior! This is a fact of profound significance. It is a fact which is regularly ignored in the conventional approach to the management of people. I shall return to it later. For the moment, one example will make my point. Consider your own need for air. Except as you are deprived of it, it has no appreciable motivating effect upon your behavior.

When the physiological needs are reasonably satisfied, needs at the next higher level begin to dominate man's behavior—to motivate him. These are called safety needs. They are needs for protection against danger, threat, deprivation. Some people mistakenly refer to these as needs for security. However, unless man is in a dependent relationship where he fears arbitrary deprivation, he does not demand security. The need is for the "fairest possible break." When he is confident of this, he is more than willing to take risks. But when he feels threatened or dependent, his greatest need is for guarantees, for protection, for security.

The fact needs little emphasis that since every industrial employee is in a dependent relationship, safety needs may assume considerable importance. Arbitrary management actions, behavior which arouses uncertainty with respect to continued employment or which reflects favoritism or discrimination, unpredictable administration of policy—these can be powerful motivators of the safety needs in the employment relationship *at every level* from worker to vice president.

Social Needs

When man's physiological needs are satisfied and he is no longer fearful about his physical welfare, his social needs become important motivators of his behavior—for belonging, for association, for acceptance by his fellows, for giving and receiving friendship and love.

Management knows today of the existence of these needs, but it often assumes quite wrongly that they represent a threat to the organization. Many studies have demonstrated that the tightly knit, cohesive work group may, under proper conditions, be far more effective than an equal number of separate individuals in achieving organizational goals.

Yet management, fearing group hostility to its own objectives, often goes to considerable lengths to control and direct human efforts in ways that are inimical to the natural "groupiness" of human beings. When man's social needs—and perhaps his safety needs, too—are thus thwarted, he behaves in ways which tend to defeat organizational objectives. He becomes resistant, antagonistic, uncooperative. But this behavior is a consequence, not a cause.

Ego Needs

Above the social needs—in the sense that they do not become motivators until lower needs are reasonably satisfied—are the needs of greatest significance to management and to man himself. They are the egoistic needs, and they are of two kinds:

1. Those needs that relate to one's self-esteem—needs for self-confidence, for independence, for achievement, for competence, for knowledge.
2. Those needs that relate to one's reputation—needs for status, for recognition, for appreciation, for the deserved respect of one's fellows.

Unlike the lower needs, these are rarely satisfied; man seeks indefinitely for more satisfaction of these needs once they have become important to him. But they do not appear in any significant way until physiological, safety, and social needs are all reasonably satisfied.

The typical industrial organization offers few opportunities for the satisfaction of these egoistic needs to people at lower levels in the hierarchy. The conventional methods of organizing work, particularly in mass production industries, give little heed to these aspects of human motivation. If the practices of scientific management were deliberately calculated to thwart these needs—which, of course, they are not—they could hardly accomplish this purpose better than they do.

Self-Fulfillment Needs

Finally—a capstone, as it were, on the hierarchy of man's needs—there are what we may call the needs for self-fulfillment. These are the needs for realizing one's own potentialities, for continued self-development, for being creative in the broadest sense of that term.

It is clear that the conditions of modern life give only limited opportunity for these relatively weak needs to obtain expression. The deprivation most people experience with respect to other lower-level needs diverts their energies into the struggle to satisfy *those* needs, and the needs for self-fulfillment remain dormant.

III.

Now, briefly, a few general comments about motivation:

We recognize readily enough that a man suffering from a severe dietary deficiency is sick. The deprivation of physiological needs has behavioral consequences. The same is true—although less well recognized—of deprivation of higher-level needs. The man whose needs for safety, association, independence, or status are thwarted is sick just as surely as is he who has rickets. And his sickness will have behavioral consequences. We will be mistaken if we attribute his resultant passivity, his hostility, his refusal to accept responsibility to his inherent "human nature." These forms of behavior are *symptoms* of illness—of deprivation of his social and egoistic needs.

The man whose lower-level needs are satisfied is not motivated to satisfy those needs any longer. For practical purposes they exist no longer. (Remember my point about your need for air.) Management often asks, "Why aren't people more productive? We pay good wages, provide good working conditions, have excellent fringe benefits and steady employment. Yet people do not seem to be willing to put forth more than minimum effort."

The fact that management has provided for these physiological and safety needs has shifted the motivational emphasis to the social and perhaps to the egoistic needs. Unless there are opportunities *at work* to satisfy these higher-level needs, people will be deprived; and their behavior will reflect this deprivation. Under such conditions, if management continues to focus its attention on physiological needs, its efforts are bound to be ineffective.

People *will* make insistent demands for more money under these conditions. It becomes more important than ever to buy the material goods and services which can provide limited satisfaction of the thwarted needs. Although money has only limited value in satisfying many higher-level needs, it can become the focus of interest if it is the *only* means available.

The Carrot and Stick Approach

The carrot and stick theory of motivation (like Newtonian physical theory) works reasonably well under certain circumstances. The *means* for satisfying man's physiological and (within limits) his safety needs can be provided or withheld by management. Employment itself is such a means, and so are wages, working conditions, and benefits. By these means the individual can be controlled so long as he is struggling for subsistence. Man lives for bread alone when there is no bread.

But the carrot and stick theory does not work at all once man has reached an adequate subsistence level and is motivated primarily by higher needs. Management cannot provide a man with self-respect, or with the respect of his fellows, or with the satisfaction of needs for self-fulfillment. It can create conditions such that he is encouraged and enabled to seek such satisfactions *for himself*, or it can thwart him by failing to create those conditions.

But this creation of conditions is not "control." It is not a good device for directing behavior. And so management finds itself in an odd position. The high standard of living created by our modern technological know-how provides quite adequately for the satisfaction of physiological and safety needs. The only significant exception is where management practices have not created confidence in a "fair break"—and thus where safety needs are thwarted. But by making possible the satisfaction of low-level needs, management has deprived itself of the ability to use as motivators the devices on which conventional theory has taught it to rely—rewards, promises, incentives, or threats and other coercive devices.

Neither Hard nor Soft

The philosophy of management by direction and control—*regardless of whether it is hard or soft*—is inadequate to motivate because the human needs on which this approach relies are today unimportant motivators of behavior. Direction and control are essentially useless in motivating people whose important needs are social and egoistic. Both the hard and the soft approach fail today because they are simply irrelevant to the situation.

People, deprived of opportunities to satisfy at work the needs which are now important to them, behave exactly as we might predict—with indolence, passivity, resistance to change, lack of responsibility, willingness to follow the demagogue, unreasonable demands for economic benefits. It would seem that we are caught in a web of our own weaving.

In summary, then, of these comments about motivation:

Management by direction and control—whether implemented with the hard, the soft, or the firm but fair approach—fails under today's conditions to provide effective motivation of human effort toward organizational objectives. It fails because direction and control are useless methods of motivating people whose physiological and safety needs are reasonably satisfied and whose social, egoistic, and self-fulfillment needs are predominant.

IV.

For these and many other reasons, we require a different theory of the task of managing people based on more adequate assumptions about human nature and human motivation. I am going to be so bold as to suggest the broad dimensions of such a theory. Call it "Theory Y," if you will.

1. Management is responsible for organizing the elements of productive enterprise—money, materials, equipment, people—in the interest of economic ends.

2. People are *not* by nature passive or resistant to organizational needs. They have become so as a result of experience in organizations.

3. The motivation, the potential for development, the capacity for assuming responsibility, the readiness to direct behavior toward organizational goals are all present in people. Management does not put them there. It is a responsibility of management to make it possible for people to recognize and develop these human characteristics for themselves.

4. The essential task of management is to arrange organizational conditions and methods of operation so that people can achieve their own goals *best* by directing *their own* efforts toward organizational objectives.

This is a process primarily of creating opportunities, releasing potential, removing obstacles, encouraging growth, providing guidance. It is what Peter Drucker has called "management by objectives" in contrast to "management by control."

And I hasten to add that it does *not* involve the abdication of management, the absence of leadership, the lowering of standards, or the other characteristics usually associated with the "soft" approach under Theory X. Much on the contrary. It is no more possible to create an organization today which will be a fully effective application of this theory than it was to build an atomic power plant in 1945. There are many formidable obstacles to overcome.

Some Difficulties

The conditions imposed by conventional organization theory and by the approach of scientific management for the past half century have tied men to limited jobs which do not utilize their capabilities, have discouraged the acceptance of responsibility, have encouraged passivity, have eliminated meaning from work. Man's habits, attitudes, expectations—his whole conception of membership in an industrial organization—have been conditioned by his experience under these circumstances. Change in the direction of Theory Y will be slow, and it will require extensive modification of the attitudes of management and workers alike.

People today are accustomed to being directed, manipulated, controlled in industrial organizations and to finding satisfaction for their social, egoistic, and self-fulfillment needs away from the job. This is true of much of management as well as of workers. Genuine "industrial citizenship"—to borrow again a term from Drucker—is a remote and unrealistic idea, the meaning of which has not even been considered by most members of industrial organizations.

Another way of saying this is that Theory X places exclusive reliance upon external control of human behavior, while Theory Y relies heavily on self-control and self-direction. It is worth noting that this difference is the difference between treating people as children and treating them as mature adults. After generations of the former, we cannot expect to shift to the latter overnight.

V.

Before we are overwhelmed by the obstacles, let us remember that the application of theory is always slow. Progress is usually achieved in small steps.

Consider with me a few innovative ideas which are entirely consistent with Theory Y and which are today being applied with some success:

Decentralization and Delegation

These are ways of freeing people from the too-close control of conventional organization, giving them a degree of freedom to direct their own activities, to assume responsibility, and, importantly, to satisfy their egoistic needs. In this connection, the flat organization of Sears, Roebuck and Company provides an interesting example. It forces "management by objectives" since it enlarges the number of people reporting to a manager until he cannot direct and control them in the conventional manner.

Job Enlargement

This concept, pioneered by I.B.M. and Detroit Edison, is quite consistent with Theory Y. It encourages the acceptance of responsibility at the bottom of the organization; it provides opportunities for satisfying social and egoistic needs. In fact, the reorganization of work at the factory level offers one of the more challenging opportunities for innovation consistent with Theory Y. The studies by A. T. M. Wilson and his associates of British coal mining and Indian textile manufacture have added appreciably to our understanding of work organization. Moreover, the economic and psychological results achieved by this work have been substantial.

Participation and Consultative Management

Under proper conditions these results provide encouragement to people to direct their creative energies toward organizational objectives, give them some voice in decisions that affect them, provide significant opportunities for the satisfaction of social and egoistic needs. I need only mention the Scanlon Plan as the outstanding embodiment of these ideas in practice.

The not infrequent failure of such ideas as these to work as well as expected is often attributable to the fact that a management has "bought the idea" but applied it within the framework of Theory X and its assumptions.

Delegation is not an effective way of exercising management by control. Participation becomes a farce when it is applied as a sales gimmick or a device for kidding people into thinking they are important. Only the management that has confidence in human capacities and is itself directed toward organizational objectives rather than toward the preservation of personal power can grasp the implications of this emerging theory. Such management will find and apply successfully other innovative ideas as we move slowly toward the full implementation of a theory like Y.

Performance Appraisal

Before I stop, let me mention one other practical application of Theory Y which—while still highly tentative—may well have important consequences. This has to do with performance appraisal within the ranks of management. Even a cursory examination of conventional programs of performance appraisal will reveal how completely consistent they are with Theory X. In fact, most such programs tend to treat the individual as though he were a product under inspection on the assembly line.

Take the typical plan: substitute "product" for "subordinate being appraised," substitute "inspector" for "superior making the appraisal," substitute "rework" for "training or development," and, except for the attributes being judged, the human appraisal process will be virtually indistinguishable from the product inspection process.

A few companies—among them General Mills, Ansul Chemical, and General Electric—have been experimenting with approaches which involve the individual in setting "targets" or objectives *for himself* and in a *self*-evaluation of performance semi-annually or annually. Of course, the superior plays an important leadership role in this process—one, in fact, which demands substantially more competence than the conventional approach. The role is, however, considerably more congenial to many managers than the role of "judge" or "inspector" which is forced upon them by conventional performance. Above all, the individual is encouraged to take a greater responsibility for planning and appraising his own contribution to organizational objectives; and the accompanying effects on egoistic and self-fulfillment needs are substantial. This approach to performance appraisal represents one more innovative idea being explored by a few managements who are moving toward the implementation of Theory Y.

VI.

And now I am back where I began. I share the belief that we could realize substantial improvements in the effectiveness of industrial organizations during the next decade or two. Moreover, I believe the social sciences can contribute much to such developments. We are only beginning to grasp the implications of the growing body of knowledge in these fields. But if this conviction is to become a reality instead of a pious hope, we will need to view the process much as we view the process of releasing the energy of the atom for constructive human ends—as a slow, costly, sometimes discouraging approach toward a goal which would seem to many to be quite unrealistic.

The ingenuity and the perseverance of industrial management in the pursuit of economic ends have changed many scientific and technological dreams into commonplace realities. It is now becoming clear that the application of these same talents to the human side of enterprise will not only enhance substantially these materialistic achievements but will bring us one step closer to "the good society." Shall we get on with the job?

STORM OVER MANAGEMENT DOCTRINES

Corporate organization planners—a growing body—are in the middle as critics assail "authoritarian" rule from top, and businessmen stick even closer to classic principles.

To give an award to a recognized authority for his latest book, then "pound him over the head" until he admits he would change some sections of it if he were to write it again, may seem an odd procedure. But it's indicative of the present state of confusion about organization theory and of the controversy that's raging around the work of the organization planners around the world.

The combined honor and headpounding is what happened to Douglas McGregor of MIT when he received the annual publications award of the Organization Development Council—largest and oldest of the three bodies devoted exclusively to the interests of the organization planners—at its last monthly meeting.

The award to the one-time MIT psychologist and present professor of industrial management was for his book, *The Human Side of Enterprise*.

THREE-WAY DEBATE. The book's title is a clue to the arguments that are being tossed back and forth. McGregor represents a general movement of criticism and protest against the kind of managerial organization that has always dominated U.S. industry, as it has most economic organization throughout history. He is a forthright critic of what is called "authoritarian" management, and argues that conventional organization leaves untapped and even frustrates many of the capacities that human beings possess.

"Storm over Management Doctrines," *BusinessWeek*, Jan. 6, 1962, pp. 72–74.

The proponents of the classic management principles questioned by McGregor are far from silent under onslaught. They have run up their flag again in a survey released last month by the National Industrial Conference Board and prepared by Harold Stieglitz, assistant director of its Div. of Personnel Administration.

In the middle, and on the spot, are the organization planners—one of the newer and more important groups of staff experts who surround company chief experts who surround company chief executives at corporate headquarters. Their specialty, almost unknown 30 years ago when Standard Oil Co. of California first set up a department of that name [BW Aug. 6 '49, p30], is growing as companies grow and corporate organization becomes more complex.

But however much any of them might be drawn to the more revolutionary theories of management, in their jobs they are a cog in the traditional management machinery, and many of them have come up through the practical working of the machine. So their reaction to McGregor and the management uplift movement is somewhat mixed. As members of the Organization Development Council, they take refuge in refusing to be quoted.

ANTI-AUTHORITARIAN. From McGregor and his fellow critics—called variously behaviorists, participationists, human relationists, and half dozen other terms—the organization planners hear an anti-authoritarian chorus. McGregor refuses to accept the assumptions that he says underlie both textbook descriptions of management and most company practices. According to him, orthodox management theory assumes:

- Average people have an inherent dislike of work and will avoid it if they can.
- So most people must be controlled and directed to work hard enough to achieve company objectives.
- Anyway, the average person isn't very ambitious for responsibility, and really wants to be guided.

McGregor rejects this "mediocrity of the masses" theory and, with it, reliance on authority as the central principle of organization.

MUTUALITY. What McGregor wants is greater collaboration or interdependence between management and employees through the development of mutual target setting. His basic assumptions reveal his thinking:

- Work is as natural as play or rest. Men will exercise self-direction and self-control in working toward ends they are committed to. Their commitment depends most on satisfaction of their own egos.
- Lack of ambition and avoidance of responsibility are not inherent. Above-average imagination, ingenuity, and creativity in solving organizational problems are widely distributed. But modern industrial life only partially utilizes the intellectual potentialities of the average man. Traditional control and direction by management frustrate all sorts of undeveloped capacities.

EMPLOYEE-CENTERED. McGregor is joined in this general viewpoint by many others, almost all professors and academic researchers with a background of social science. Chris Argyris, associate professor in Yale's Dept. of Industrial Administration, is sure that individuals could grow, be more satisfied, enjoy better mental health, except for the demands of organization as management now knows and uses it. He urges more employee-centered leadership, enlargement of individual jobs, more reality-oriented managers.

Much of the same argument, but based on voluminous research data collected by the staff of the University of Michigan's Institute for Social Research, was made recently by professor of psychology and sociology Rensis Likert [BW Aug. 19 '61, p34].

LITTLE HEADWAY. Whether or not this line of thought strikes a responsive chord among individual planners, few of their companies are "messing around with it," in the words of a senior member of the Organization Development Council.

The Stieglitz survey for the NICB shows what is actually going on organizationally in U.S. business. It details the organization plans of 61 companies, including some represented in ODC. Among them are American Radiator and Standard Sanitary Corp., Radio Corp. of America, Sylvania Electric Products, Inc., and U.S. Rubber Co.

TREND OF CHANGE. According to the NICB report, the organization of the typical U.S. corporation is indeed changing—but not from having adopted any new-fangled theory.

The changes add up, too, to more than simply a trend to greater decentralization, which many continue to praise as evidence that authority is being distributed more generously and on lower levels. In fact, the trend of change provides little to hearten the reformers:

- Companies have been dropping functional organization for divisionalization, usually on a product basis, as they diversify and face new technological and marketing problems. Old subsidiaries and new acquisitions often lose some of their former autonomy in the process.
- The corporate staff has begun to play a changed and more elaborate role, emerging as a major force at company headquarters—a process sometimes called recentralization.
- Some companies have introduced a new executive level at the top—general executives responsible for two or more divisions (more common for product divisions than for corporate staff divisions).
- To help the chief executive cope with expanding responsibilities, his office has been enlarged and elaborated—through personal staff assistants, or upgrading other top executives to share his function in an executive council or "office of the president."

STICKING TO PRINCIPLES. The conclusion from the Stieglitz survey is that the classic management principles—the object of the attacks of McGregor and other critics—still guide U.S. management in refining and revamping its organization.

Stieglitz stresses 11 basic principles as "those most frequently mentioned or emphasized by both analysts and companies." They include such familiar statements as these: The objective of the enterprise and its component elements should be clearly defined and stated in writing. The organization should be kept simple and flexible. There should be clear lines of authority running from top to bottom, and accountability from bottom to top. Everyone in the organization should report to only one supervisor.

PLANNER'S JOB. The Stieglitz report also spots the job of the growing clan of organization planners. It is to study, analyze and recommend. Final decisions on company structure and the staff that make up the management organization remain the prerogative of top management.

Because the organization expert's job is rarely to invent a new organization from scratch, he might better be called a reorganization planner. But he's perpetually involved in a review of the current organization—from the point of view of classic management, Stieglitz makes clear. Once top management has determined company objectives and stated its policies, the organization planner's job is to:

- Inventory existing personnel to find out who does what, who reports to whom, who has authority, and how much.
- Draw up an ideal organization chart as a long-term project.
- Determine how to shape the existing organization closer to it—normally step-by-step through short term "phase plans."

SCHIZOPHRENIC. With the behaviorists and humanitarians to the left, orthodox doctrine to the right, and top management perhaps just down the hall, it would be natural if organization planners developed at least a slight case of schizophrenia.

Members of ODC insist they have not opted for the newest panaceas on "the human side of organization." One admits he'd like to believe "a majority of us are over on the non-authoritarian side."

But another explains "it's just the more academic ones who are hottest for this behavioral science thing."

To avoid the danger of chronic schizophrenia, it's not surprising that the organization experts have banded together in discussion groups. ODC organized as early as 1951, formalized itself five years later. In 1954 NICB organized a Council on Organization Planning, now numbering 21. Two years later, the West Coast Organization Planning Round Table, a group of about 20, started in San Francisco.

Whatever management philosophy the members follow, it's clear that ODC, for one, doesn't sell organization short: for 30 members, it has four officers, plus a board of seven, plus three vice-presidents, plus a couple of committee chairmen.

MIT FACULTY RESOLUTION

The following resolution was formally presented to the assembled M.I.T. faculty on October 21, 1964.

The Faculty records with deep regret the death of Douglas McGregor on October 13, 1964. At the same time, it records with deep pride the contributions he made to M.I.T., to higher education throughout the United States, to the advancement of his chosen profession, to industry both here and abroad, and, above all, to the development of a great many individuals.

It is easy to relate the simple facts of his life. He was born in Detroit in 1906. He received his Bachelor's degree from Wayne University in 1932, his Master's degree from Harvard in 1933, and his Doctorate from Harvard in 1935. He came to M.I.T. in 1937, as one of the founders of the Industrial Relations Section. In 1948, when he was Professor of Psychology and Executive Director of the Industrial Relations Section, he accepted the position of President of Antioch College. After six years in this post, he returned to M.I.T. as Professor of Industrial Management, and in 1962 became the first incumbent of the Sloan Fellows Professorship. Along the way, he served in many diverse capacities, among others as Director of Industrial Relations for the Dewey and Almy Chemical Company, as Trustee of Antioch College, as a Director of the Social Science Research Council, as a Director of the National Training Laboratories, as a Director of the Psychological Corporation, as Chairman of our own Discipline Committee, and as a consultant to government and industry.

It is less easy to describe in brief compass the many facets of the man that Douglas McGregor was. He was a man of wide interests, from music to gardening, from company reorganization to sharing of jokes, from education in India to the life of his family. To none of these interests was he content to play the role of mere spectator; always he was an active participant.

In the very best sense of the term, Douglas McGregor was a crusader. He believed in the work he was doing, and he believed that others could benefit by what he had to offer. He took himself seriously; otherwise he could not have accomplished what he did. But he never took himself too seriously, and therein lay much of the basis of his effectiveness. Because he understood himself and his own foiblies, he was able to appreciate and sympathize with the foibles of others. His sense of humor was robust, but never manifested itself in ridicule.

His professional contributions were of the highest order. As one of his colleagues said: "A large segment of his professional field operated in an environment which he created. Much of the work that goes on now couldn't have happened if he had never been."

Through his writings, particularly *The Human Side of Enterprise*, and through personal contacts, he was known throughout the world. Although he traveled widely, it was impossible for him to meet all or even most of the demands to serve as teacher, speaker, consultant, or counselor. To his office came a constant stream of people from all parts of the globe. For all of them, it was a rewarding experience.

Douglas McGregor led a full life. Not in the least of the measures of its fullness was the enrichment he gave to the lives of countless others.

Benson R. Snyder

Charles A. Myers

Donald G. Marquis

Howard W. Johnson

Warren G. Bennis

Douglass V. Brown, Chairman

October 21, 1964

BEYOND McGREGOR'S THEORY Y: HUMAN CAPITAL AND KNOWLEDGE-BASED WORK IN THE TWENTY-FIRST-CENTURY ORGANIZATION

*Thomas Kochan, Wanda Orlikowski, and Joel Cutcher-Gershenfeld**

Prepared for the Sloan School 50th Anniversary Session on October 11, 2002

This conference presentation was subsequently published as: Thomas Kochan, Wanda Orlikowski, and Joel Cutcher-Gershenfeld, "Beyond McGregor's Theory Y: Human Capital and Knowledge-Based Work in the 21st-Century Organization," in *Management: Inventing and Delivering Its Future*, Thomas Kochan and Richard Schmalensee, eds., Cambridge, MA: MIT Press (2003).

* Thomas Kochan is the George M. Bunker Professor of Management in MIT's Sloan School of Management; Wanda Orlikowski is Professor of Information Technologies and Organization Studies at MIT's Sloan School of Management and holds the Eaton-Peabody Chair of Communication Sciences at MIT; Joel Cutcher-Gershenfeld is a Senior Research Scientist in MIT'S Sloan School of Management and the Executive Director of the Engineering Systems Learning Center in MIT's Engineering Systems Division (Joel is also a Sloan Alum, Ph.D., 1988). Invaluable assistance in this research was provided by Natasha Iskander, Jen Fabas, Lynn Dovey, Carolyn Corazo, and many other participants in the Sloan seminar 15.343 on "Transforming Work, Organizations, and Society." Support for this paper was provided through MIT's Sloan School of Management and the Cambridge-MIT Initiative (CMI).

INTRODUCTION

Nearly 50 years ago, at the Sloan School's Fifth Anniversary Convocation, Douglas McGregor launched a debate over how to manage *The Human Side of the Enterprise.*[1] By comparing what he called Theory X and Theory Y perspectives, he challenged the management profession to reexamine its assumptions about the motivations employees bring to their jobs. The question was: Could employees be trusted and empowered to do good work, or did they have to be closely directed, monitored, and controlled to act in the interests of the firm? While McGregor's Theory Y sparked important innovations in human resource practices, it did not challenge other fundamental assumptions underpinning the twentieth-century organizational model. If, as is widely recognized, human capital and knowledge are the most important sources of value for the twenty-first-century organization, then fundamental assumptions about the relationship between work and organizations will also need to be challenged.

The approach that dominated organizational theory, teaching, and practice for most of the twentieth century looked at organizations from the top down, starting with a view of the CEO as the "leader" who shapes the organization's strategy, structure, culture, and performance potential. The nature of work and the role of the workforce enter the analysis much later, after considerations of technology and organization design have been considered. However, if the key source of value in the twenty-first-century organization is to be derived from the workforce itself, an inversion of the dominant approach will be needed. The new perspective will start not at the top of the organization, but at the front lines, with people and the work itself—which is where value is created. Such an inversion will lead to a transformation in the management and organization of work, workers, and knowledge. This transformation was signalled by McGregor, but we must go further.

We believe accomplishing this inversion is among the most important challenges facing organization and management theory, research, teaching, and practice today. In fact, these challenges have been at the forefront of the research of a number of Sloan School research groups (see Figure 1). Furthermore, several Sloan faculty recently stated these challenges in the provocative form of a "Manifesto for the Twenty-First-Century Organization."[2] And, over the past semester, we have explored these challenges with a range of industry experts, Sloan School students, and alumni in our course on "Managing Transformations in Work, Organizations, and Society."

FIGURE 1. ***Selected Sloan Faculty Research Reexamining Assumptions about People, Work, and Organizations***

Piore and Sabel on "The Second Industrial Divide" (1984)
Kochan, Katz, and McKersie on "The Transformation of American Industrial Relations" (1986)
Schein on "Culture and Leadership" (1988)
Senge on "Learning Organizations and Systems Thinking" (1990)
Bailyn on "Integrating Work and Family" (1992)
Orlikowski on "Use of Technology in Organizations" (1992)
Ancona, Kochan, Scully, Van Mannen, and Westney on "Organizational Processes" (1994)
Walton, Cutcher-Gershenfeld, and McKersie on "Strategic Negotiations" (1994)
Orlikowski and Yates on "Collaborative Technologies" (1994)
Cutcher-Gershenfeld et al. on "Knowledge-Driven Work" (1998)
Osterman, Kochan, Locke, and Piore on "Working in America: A Blueprint for the New Labor Market" (2001)
Carroll on "Organizational Learning in the Midst of Crisis" (2001)
Sterman and Repenning on "Nobody Ever Gets Credit for Fixing Problems That Never Happened" (2001)
Murman et al. on "Lean Enterprise Value" (2002)
Malone and Scott Morton on "Inventing Organizations of the 21st Century" (forthcoming)

In this paper, we build on these efforts to first contrast the twentieth- and twenty-first-century organizational models and then to examine how organizations are attempting to move toward a human capital and knowledge-based model of organizing (see Figure 2 for our methods and process). Finally, we explore the implications of this

FIGURE 2. ***Methods and Process in Developing this Paper***

This paper has its roots in an MIT course entitled "Transforming Work, Organizations, and Society," which was first offered in the spring of 2001 and again offered in the spring of 2002. The course, which was developed under the leadership of Tom Kochan in partnership with Joel Cutcher-Gershenfeld, Wanda Orlikowski, and others, focused on all of the themes covered in this paper. From the outset, the course involved participation from Sloan and other graduate students on campus, as well as System Design and Management (SDM) students on rotation back in their home organizations. It also included lifelong learning participants from partner corporations such as the U.S. Air Force, Pratt & Whitney, Ford, Hewlett-Packard, Lucent, NASA, Otis Elevators, Polaroid, Qualcomm, Saturn, Teradyne, Visteon, and Xerox. It involved both in-class discussion, remote video participation, and on-line discussions.

In honor of Sloan's fiftieth anniversary, we offered Sloan alums the opportunity to participate directly in the sessions as well as the chance to follow the discussions and make contributions through the Internet. Over 100 Sloan alums signed up at the Web site and contributed comments or vignettes on the topics covered in the course. Students in the class drew on their own experience and interviewed some of the alums to generate additional vignettes on all of these topics. They also organized all of this data into integrative final papers that corresponded to the themes for the course. The analysis in this paper draws on independent research conducted by all three authors as well as the many vignettes, comments, and papers generated. Current Sloan student experience and the experience of Sloan alums are woven throughout the text (with the names of specific individuals and organizations deleted for confidentiality).

alternative organizational model for the future of management education.

CONTRASTING ASSUMPTIONS: TWENTIETH- AND TWENTY-FIRST-CENTURY ORGANIZATIONAL MODELS

As evident in Figure 3, the organizational model that dominated the past century embodied assumptions (about people, work, technology, leadership, and goals) that contrast with the model that may come to dominate the next century.

FIGURE 3. *Contrasting Assumptions in Twentieth- and Twenty-First-Century Organizations*

Assumption About:	Assumptions Characterizing Twentieth-Century Organizations	Assumptions That May Characterize Twenty-First-Century Organizations
People	Theory X: People are a cost that must be monitored and controlled	Theory Y: People are an asset that should be valued and developed
Work	Segmented, industrially based, and individual tasks	Collaborative, knowledge-based projects
Technology	Design technology to control work and minimize human error	Integrate technology with social systems to enable knowledge-based work
Leadership	Senior managers and technical experts	Distributed leadership at all levels
Goals	Unitary focus on returns to shareholders	Multidimensional focus on value for multiple stakeholders

Like McGregor, we are counterposing two alternative models, each of which involves competing assumptions. Reality, of course, may involve a spectrum of choices between these extremes, but it is helpful to understand the way alternative choices will pull organizations in one direction or the other. In the balance of this section, we will examine the implications of each of these assumptions.

People: Labor Costs or Human Assets?

Conventional economic and organization theory views labor as a cost to be controlled. Moreover, since labor cannot be separated from its human motivation and free will, incentives are needed to ensure employees will commit their full energies and skills to the goals of the organization. Labor also brings its own interests and sources of power to the organization. Therefore, efforts on the part of employees to use their collective power by forming unions or other organizations to represent their own interests need to be discouraged or defeated.

A human capital, knowledge-based perspective understands workers as human assets who create the value of the organization. By joining and staying in the organization, employees invest and put at risk some of their human capital. By taking advantage of opportunities for continued learning and development, their human capital is deepened and expanded. Since employees have interests and obligations outside of work—to their professions, families, communities, and themselves—they cannot and do not wish to commit their full energies to the organization. Therefore, efforts are needed to integrate work and personal aspects of life. Employees also bring a variety of expectations to their jobs, including an interest in having meaningful influence and voice in matters that are important to them. At the same time, employers can reasonably expect employees and their representative organizations to contribute to the continued viability and effectiveness of the enterprise. Therefore, efforts are needed to engage employees individually and collectively in ways that simultaneously address organizational and individual interests and expectations.

Work: Industrial or Knowledge-Based Systems?

The early years of the twentieth century witnessed the gradual movement from agrarian and craft to an industrial model of work organization. The latter part of the century has witnessed efforts to continue the transformation from the industrial to a knowledge-based system of work organization. That transformation process continues today.

The industrial model created sharp legal and status distinctions between managers who conceived and directed how work was done and nonmanagers who executed their tasks as directed. Productivity was maximized by organizing tasks into well-defined jobs and functions. Efficiency gains were achieved through increased specialization and formalization of reporting relationships, promotion paths, and compensation rules.

The transformation in work systems underway today involves efforts to shift from industrial to knowledge-based work systems that blur the lines between managerial and nonmanagerial work. These systems assume that in a knowledge-based economy, high levels of performance can only be achieved by organizing work in ways that allow workers to utilize and deepen their knowledge and skills, while working collaboratively on multiple, temporary projects to accomplish flexible and innovative operations. As a result, there is an emphasis on horizontal interrelationships among diverse groups (both internal and external) and the coordinated use of teams, cross-functional task forces, and cross-organizational alliances and networks.

Technology: A Mechanistic or Integrative Perspective?

Technology is conventionally viewed as a physical asset—a piece of machinery or an information system—that is initially developed and designed by technical experts and then implemented for use by the workforce. This view emphasizes the mechanistic dimensions of technology, while disregarding or attempting to eliminate the human side. For example, a major function of technology in this view is to reduce reliance on human inputs—both the quantity of labor and the variance (error) that can result from human judgment, fatigue, lack of motivation, or direct challenges or conflicts with management decisions or actions. Even today, the dominant assumption in much of the machine tool industry, for example, involves designing people out of the process—even at the expense of flexibility and innovation.

A human capital, knowledge-based view of technology is best captured by the saying that it is "workers who give wisdom to the machines."[3] Technology is understood to be simultaneously physical and social, and its capabilities are only effective when utilized in practice by workers operating in a variety of social/organizational contexts. This relational view of technology recognizes that technological outcomes are highly contingent and emergent—depending on how the technical capabilities interact with human choices, political actions, cultural norms, and learning opportunities over time. In this view, benefits from technologies can only be realized when the technical and social dimensions are integrated through the design, implementation, and ongoing adaptation of the technologies employed in an organization.

Leadership: Exclusive Role of the CEO or a Distributed Capability?

Leadership is conventionally viewed as being vested primarily in the role of the CEO and other top executives. The CEO is to provide vision and broad strategic direction to the rest of the organization and in doing so shape the culture and values of the enterprise. The search process for CEOs therefore focuses on identifying individuals in top positions in apparently successful organizations who appear to have these personal attributes. Wall Street analysts, the business press, and business school case studies often attribute organizational success (or failure) to the quality of the CEO's leadership, thereby perpetuating this image of what leadership is and where it resides in organizations.

A human capital, knowledge-based view of the enterprise envisions leadership as a distributed capability that involves multiple people and groups at all levels of the organization. To be sure, the CEO and other executives are critical players in leading a process which generates a clear and compelling shared vision for the organization. However, such action by senior executives is not sufficient unless and until it engages the aspirations and energies of all organizational participants. Leadership is thus more than a set of individual traits or abilities; it is a set of capabilities that extends throughout the organization and over time. In this view, a CEO would be seen to be effective if she/he creates the conditions that enable people at all levels in the organization to exercise leadership in their everyday activities. Performance in the twenty-first-century organization is a function of the quality of leadership capabilities in action throughout the organization.

Goals: Value for Shareholders or Multiple Stakeholders?

This brings us to a fundamental question: What purpose(s) do organizations serve? With the rise to prominence of the modern corporation, the answer that dominated American organizations and management education throughout most of the twentieth century was that business organizations exist to maximize shareholder value. This reflects a recognition of the role played by owners, who provide and put at risk the critical resource—significant pools of financial capital—needed to build large corporations. As a result, the governance structure and processes are seen to be the exclusive domain of the financial owners and their direct agents, the CEO and other top executives.

Knowledge-based organizations depend on employees to invest and put at risk their human capital in joining and remaining with the firm. This places human capital in an analogous position in the twenty-first-century organization to that of financial capital in the twentieth-century corporation. Thus, employees could claim a legitimate role in shaping the objectives of the organization to be consistent with their interests and values. Other stakeholders can make similar claims. Suppliers, for example, are increasingly responsible for critical aspects of product design, inventory management, and other tasks that require long-term partnership agreements. Communities have legitimate claims to the social and environmental impacts generated by the products and processes of organizations. Governments today are more interested in long-term public-private partnerships (government as "enabler" rather than "enforcer"). Even regulatory agencies are exploring more interactive relationships with the regulated community. Thus, processes of stakeholder—not just shareholder—governance assume strategic significance in the twenty-first-century organization. Viewed one way, these many embedded stakeholder relationships represent complex constraints on organizational flexibility and innovation. Viewed another way, these same stakeholder relationships constitute an extended enterprise capable of delivering value to the organization and to these many stakeholders in unprecedented ways.[4]

Today, organizations are connected to these many stakeholders in complex networks including strategic alliances, public-private partnerships, and other collaborative initiatives. In all cases, there are both common interests that bring these parties together and conflicting interests that threaten the viability of the cooperative venture. In many cases, individual organizations may come and go, but others will take their place in these emerging institutional arrangements. Therefore, organizations are called upon to take a longer view—ensuring today's actions do not make it more difficult for future generations of citizens and communities to realize their aspirations and objectives. Management and management education need to take a longer-term, sustainability perspective and a broader, networked view of organizations. More emphasis is needed on developing professional standards, ethics, and norms that hold individuals and organizations accountable for their effects on multiple stakeholders, both today and in the future.

TAKING STOCK OF CURRENT ORGANIZATIONAL PRACTICE

The above distinctions between twentieth- and twenty-first-century organizational models are somewhat oversimplified. Few organizations could survive by completely ignoring some of the assumptions underlying either model. And, as noted, many organizations have been pursuing aspects of a human-centered, knowledge-based approach for some time. So the reality today is that organizations have implemented different sets of assumptions drawn from both the twentieth- and twenty-first-century organizational models depicted above. Below, we draw on the data collected from our industry participants, students, and alumni to take stock of current organizational practices as experienced by the people in these organizations. These are among the people who will collectively shape the organizations of the twenty-first century. In this section, we summarize their experiences and assessments of current practice, their visions for where they want their organizations to be in the future, and their ideas for what it will take to get there.

People: The Workforce of the Twenty-First Century

One word best captures the contemporary workforce: *diversity*. A second key word applies to the workforce of the future: *scarcity*.

DIVERSITY AND ITS IMPLICATIONS. Tomorrow's workforce, even more than today's, will depart dramatically from the twentieth-century image of the average (some would say "idealized") worker as a male breadwinner or organization man with a wife at home attending to family and community affairs. Today, workers are more diverse in gender, race, ethnicity, age, nationality, and culture, just to mention the more obvious and visible features. The households that workers come from are equally diverse, with less than 20 percent fitting the old image. The majority either have both spouses/partners in the paid labor force or are headed by an individual who is a working, single parent. Work and family decisions are highly interdependent.

Leading firms are recognizing the importance of both the need to attend to demographic diversity and work and family issues, as the following boxed text illustrates. Our research and the views of our students and alumni suggest that most firms have internalized the legal and social responsibilities introduced by the civil rights movement and laws enacted in the 1960s and 1970s. For example, there is considerable training aimed at "valuing diversity." Today's workforce generally also shares these values, especially younger workers who have grown up in more diverse cultural and racial settings. Many of our students and alumni therefore are more frustrated than supported by this type of training. They are ready for something more substantive.

A More Diverse Pool of Future Leaders

"Over the past 20 years the demographics of our company's professional staff have been changed dramatically. Female engineers today represent a large percentage of the population and a large percentage of its high-potential future leaders. These are employees we desperately want to hold onto for the long run."

Contribution to Sloan Student/Alum Dialogue in Course on "Transforming Work, Organizations, and Society" (Spring 2002).

The current challenge in managing diversity is to go beyond efforts to change attitudes to focus on building the skills needed to facilitate work in diverse teams and to learn from the variety of backgrounds and knowledge people bring to their jobs. This is how the diversity in our contemporary workforce can be used to add value to both workers and their organizations. The following boxed text provides a vivid example of this opportunity, drawing on the efforts of Japanese managers teaching their U.S. counterparts how to relate and sell to their Japanese customers.

> ***Learning Across Cultures***
>
> **"As the number of Japanese sales staff was reduced, the local staff built good connections with Japanese OEMs and delivered the same quality services without the assistance of Japanese expatriates. To do this, the local sales staff needed to learn skills and know-how to build the relationships with Japanese OEMs ... This change did not happen naturally."**

Contribution to Sloan Student/Alum Dialogue in Course on "Transforming Work, Organizations, and Society" (Spring 2002).

People are also highly diverse in the expectations they bring to their work and organizations. To be sure, as survey data and labor market behavior continue to demonstrate, good wages and benefits remain a high priority for all workers. But these, by and large, are taken as a given—a necessary condition for individuals to consider a prospective job offer. Beyond these essentials, as a recent survey supplied by Towers Perrin indicated (see Figure 4), jobs have to be tailored to the priorities of different groups. Young workers place highest priority on possibilities for learning and developing their skills; mid-career and mid-life workers value the opportunity to integrate work and family life; and older workers assign highest priority to long-term employment and income security. Most workers, young and old alike, appear to have learned the lesson of the past decades' breakdown in the prospect of long-term jobs. Over 40 percent of those employed actively look at alternative job opportunities on a regular basis, and few see it as their responsibility to stay with a given employer for any particular length of time.[5]

Clearly, the actions of organizations in the last decade have shaped the expectations of the current workforce. Few are ready to commit their loyalty and put their trust in any single firm to provide lifetime

FIGURE 4. ***What Attracts Employees by Age***

Top Attractors	U.S. Overall	Age 18–29	Age 30–44	Age 45–54	Age 55+
Competitive base pay/salary	®	®	®	®	®
Competitive health-care benefits package	®	®	®	®	®
Opportunities for advancement	1	1	2		3
Work-life balance	2	2	1	2	
Competitive retirement benefits package	3			1	1
Pay raises linked to individual performance	3		3	3	2
Learning and development opportunities		3			

Source: Towers Perrin, Talent Report 2001: New Realities in Today's Workforce, New York: Towers Perrin, 2002.
Key: ® Core rewards that rank at the top for all groups
1–3 Top differentiators in rank order

jobs and careers. This, does not, however, mean that they all want to be "free agents." As these data and others show, employees still expect firms to manage in ways that offer learning and career development opportunities. Also, with age comes the heightened priority of and expectation for long-term security. Fairness in employment decisions—layoffs, compensation, and promotion opportunities—are just as much an expectation today as in the past.

Work-family integration serves as today's frontier workforce issue. Of all the issues we examined, it generated the most interest among our alumni, students, and industry participants. They documented a wide range of "family-friendly" policies and procedures offered in their organizations today, including flexible hours, part-time options, assistance with domestic services, and backup day care. They also indicated that these policies and procedures often remained underutilized and, consequently, were ineffective. This is not for lack of thought on these matters. As one individual observed, being a "married couple with dual careers requires a constant evaluation of [our] roles as parents and professionals."

Two factors stand out as constraints, limiting the use and effectiveness of work-family policies. In many professions and organizations, the use of part-time options is still interpreted as signaling less commitment to the organization and to one's professional career. This was brought home vividly by our expert panel from the legal profession. Beth Boland, a partner in the Boston law firm of Mintz Levin, Cohn, Ferris, Glovsky, and Popeo, P.C., reported that although over 90 percent of leading law firms in Boston now provide a part-time option for associates and partners, less than 5 percent of those eligible actually take advantage of the option. Moreover, more than one-third of lawyers believe doing so would hurt their careers.

Similar low rates of uptake on work-family policies are reported in other studies and by our students and alumni in their organizations, for comparable reasons. The importance of face time and full-time commitment appears to still permeate the culture of many organizations and professions, dominating the image of the ideal worker or high-potential employee in the eyes of senior executives and even peers. As one student commented, "Unfortunately, there still does occur this notion of 'face time' that seems to equate the number of times your face is seen to that of a higher performer." The

Gap between Policy and Practice

"All of the work-life programs, however, are in reality used by only a small proportion of employees. The reasons for this are:

1. **Rarely do male employees ever use them. Female employees therefore don't use them because they don't want to be seen as different than other employees.**
2. **With today's culture of starting work earlier than required and working later than required, many employees are reluctant to leave the office before their colleagues.**
3. **As others in the class pointed out, face time is very important. Out of sight is out of mind."**

Contribution to Sloan Student/Alum Dialogue in Course on "Transforming Work, Organizations, and Society" (Spring 2002).

above boxed text from another student further elaborates on this issue and the overall gap between policy and practice.

The second constraint lies in the need to focus on changing the work itself, collectively among peers and supervisors. Our colleague Lotte Bailyn[6] has documented this in her work and suggests the need to design work collaboratively around a dual agenda: achieving high performance *and* allowing individuals to integrate their work schedules with personal and family obligations. This connects to Douglas McGregor's conception of integration. In the legal community, for example, Beth Boland pointed out that the legal work itself is well suited to part-time arrangements, because most lawyers divide their time among many clients. As a result, reduced-time arrangements just mean a reduced number of clients, not a reduction of effort in support of any one client. This sort of thinking is at the core of the approach that Lotte Bailyn has advocated.

The difficulty and yet the potential for addressing the stresses associated with the long hours professionals put into their work was brought home vividly through a vignette offered in the following boxed text by the spouse of a physician-resident.

> ***Reflections from the Spouse of a Medical Resident***
>
> **"In addition, in spite of the fact that she was putting in all this effort, the head of the program, coming from a time when surgeons were men, with wives at home taking care of everything, could not understand how this lifestyle was not maintainable for her. There were no support programs or other alternatives available. Surgeons were supposed to do their job, not complain, and stick it out."**

Contribution to Sloan Student/Alum Dialogue in Course on "Transforming Work, Organizations, and Society" (Spring 2002).

The biggest uncertainty and most interesting source of debate involves whether the next generation, the so-called Gen Y cohort, will bring and maintain different values and expectations than those of their parents. After all, they will have observed the breakdown in the social contract experienced by their parents and experienced the increased number of hours their parents have been devoting to the paid workforce. There is some anecdotal evidence to suggest that this generation is deeply committed to building individual skills and capabilities, but highly distrustful of organizations and other workplace institutions. There are even some indications of an unwillingness to work long hours of overtime at the expense of personal and family matters. If these are indeed defining characteristics of this cohort—shaped by their experiences growing up during the eras of rightsizing, downsizing, reengineering, and outsourcing—then there will be significant human capital challenges for organizations and industries in the future. These challenges appear to be particularly acute in such fields as autos, aerospace, and NASA, all of which are facing a demographic shock with as many as one-third of the employees eligible to retire in the next five years.

THE COMING LABOR FORCE SCARCITY? Predicting future labor supply/demand balances is tricky because multiple variables—including the rate of economic growth, productivity, immigration, working hours, retirement trends, and global sourcing of work—all interact to affect this balance. Nevertheless, straightforward projections by the Bureau of Labor Statistics, using moderate estimates of these variables, suggested that by 2010, labor supply in the United States could fall approximately five to ten million workers short of demand.[7]

The challenge is clear: workers will be a scarce resource, and those with the most knowledge and skills will be among the most scarce, as the following boxed text illustrates. The organization that seeks to compete on the basis of human capital and knowledge will need to learn how to attract and retain these valued workers. Thus, if anything, the individual and collective power of the workforce will continue to increase.

The vision for the future that emerged from our discussions and interviews is one that addresses the frontier challenges—managing diversity and addressing the different expectations of the workforce—by letting the people solve these problems themselves. This is a refrain

Stress and Shortage for Technical Professionals

"Having entered the workforce in '49 has allowed a unique perspective. Several factors contributed to the present condition. In the late '60s and early '70s corporations became increasingly concerned with mergers, acquisitions, global considerations, and the issues associated with high technology. As a result, pay scales for 'in-demand' positions such as patent law and technology specialties increased to attract talent. However, as salaries increased, there was also an expectation of 60- to 70-hour workweeks. Also, as pay increased, many companies could not afford to continue adding staff, so they began loading people down to accomplish the work. This carries through to today, where people in technical shortage categories are still expected to perform to their pay level. Also, where supply is an issue for these positions, it is easier to get one person than two, so the one hired may end up being asked to do more than the work of one."

Contribution to Sloan Student/Alum Dialogue in Course on "Transforming Work, Organizations, and Society" (Spring 2002).

that will echo through the visions expressed not just for this challenge, but for all those discussed in this paper. Young lawyers aspire to succeed in their profession just as much as their counterparts of an earlier generation. But they also want to attend to their family and personal lives and to rearrange work processes and caseloads to better meet their dual agendas. They recognize they cannot do this unless others in their profession and in leading companies work together to change the culture and norms of their profession. The same movement is underway among residents in the medical profession. They are ready to transform the way they do their work, and, in the process, gradually change the culture of their professions and organizations. Will those in power in organizations support or frustrate these efforts? The answer to this question will influence the way this transformation process plays out in the years ahead.

Knowledge-Based Work

The last quarter century has witnessed the gradual diffusion of what are called knowledge-based work systems among front-line manufacturing and service workers. The general consensus derived from a broad range of studies and the experience of our industry participants is that these produce higher levels of organizational performance and higher levels of learning and employee satisfaction than the industrial models of work organization they are replacing.[8] Yet, the best-known examples of knowledge-based work systems are generally in what are termed "greenfield" facilities (literally new facilities built in open, green fields). Most organizations fall into the "brownfield" category—existing operations with many of the legacy twentieth-century assumptions firmly in place.

Implementing the new work systems in these existing operations requires extended and continued effort. Leaders from one Pratt & Whitney facility participated in our class and cataloged their fluctuating efforts to implement team-based work systems and sustained labor-management cooperation. Successes were periodically set back by turnover of plant managers or union leaders, and by decisions to outsource work or lay off employees, which undermined the trust needed to build and retain employee support for these workplace changes and innovations. This is not an isolated example. The best estimates from our research and others are that about one-third of U.S. establishments have implemented some features of knowledge-based work systems in their operations.[9] Very few have achieved what might be termed a transformation. Whether these efforts will be maintained and whether further diffusion will occur depends on the actions of a variety of stakeholders—managers, workers, labor union representatives, Wall Street analysts, and government policy makers. The key issue is whether these stakeholders will recognize the value that knowledge-based work systems offer the workforce and the economy, and choose to work together to sustain the momentum already underway, or whether short-term decisions by these groups will limit or even undermine transformation efforts.

Alongside the implementing of new work systems is another key labor market development: the increased use of various types of contract, consultant, and project work arrangements. From the demand side of the labor market, these arrangements offer employers access to specialized knowledge from outside sources, flexibility, reduced headcount and associated labor cost reductions, and the opportunity to focus on core competencies. From the supply side, these arrangements can also offer opportunities to learn across jobs and organizational assignments, while also providing more options for integrating work with different stages of personal and/or family life, for example, combining work with further education, child- or elder-care duties, or as a bridge into retirement. The downside of these arrangements lies in the reduction of benefits, employment security, status, and influence, and in more variable earnings for contractors. The costs to the organization include increased coordination requirements, potential safety or security risks, and the potential loss of organizational knowledge or capability—all downsides that become more visible after the outsourcing decision.

Clearly, if managed well, there are potential benefits to both organizations and individuals from sensible use of contracting arrangements. Our students and alumni see both the benefits and the pitfalls of these work arrangements playing out in their organizations (see boxed text for one student's experiences with contracting). Their hopes and aspirations for the future are that they and their organizational peers will learn to use these flexible arrangements sensibly, to draw on the knowledge and skills of independent contractors/consultants or those in transition stages of their life cycle, and to not use this option as a short-term way to simply reduce headcount or compensation costs.

Mixed Results with Contracting

For many tasks and positions, a contracting arrangement does indeed provide a benefit to the government. After all, there is probably little difference with regard to maintenance workers, technicians, and other unskilled or low-skill support personnel as to whether they are government or private-sector employees. Tasks for these employees also tend to be better defined, and supervisory functions are limited to general personnel-related issues. My observation, however, is that when the jobs that are contracted out become more complex, requiring higher-level skills and increased experience, then the system breaks down and ceases to function properly. This leads to more waste, less productivity, and more frustration on the part of both the civil servants and the private-sector employees. I believe that this is due to several interrelated causes:

- **First, the structure of the contract is usually such that there is no incentive for the private contractor to hire the best-qualified candidate. Instead, the least-costly candidate that meets the minimum criteria as specified in the job description is the person that is hired. This is because if the contractor hired a more costly candidate, then he might exceed his proposed budget, which would count against him when profit is calculated or when the contract is up for renewal.**

Mixed Results with Contracting (Continued)

- Second, a weaker candidate that is available immediately is preferable over a stronger candidate who may be available in one or two months. The reason for this is that every month that the position goes unfilled will usually count against the contractor's performance or profit. So the private contractor has every reason to fill every position as fast as possible. Whether the candidate is the best or not does not really matter to the bottom line.
- Third, in positions requiring more experience or skills, supervisor, reporting, and chain-of-command-related issues become more common and more complex.
- Fourth, one of the reasons that is often used to justify the on-site contractor structure is that it allows government programs to be more flexible in adjusting personnel levels, since the theory is that private contractors can lay off people more easily than the government. However, while this is true for many low-wage, low-skill positions, my observation is that most of these on-site contracts have significant job-protection guarantees built in. In one case, three-month notices are required before a layoff can occur. These policies, while socially laudable, diminish the value of the on-site contractor arrangement, making the need for such arrangements, especially with regard to higher-skilled jobs, questionable.

Contribution to Sloan Student/Alum Dialogue in Course on "Transforming Work, Organizations, and Society" (Spring 2002).

Integrating Technical and Social Dimensions of Technology

In the last quarter of the twentieth century, U.S. manufacturing industries learned about the need to understand technology as an integrated system of technical and social dimensions. That is, they learned that a return on their investments in hardware could only be realized if these investments were linked to complementary investments in education, work redesign, and cultural change. The U.S. auto industry learned this the hard way, by losing market share to Japanese competitors in the 1980s—competitors who were quicker to build this sociotechnical principle into their production systems, employment practices, and work operations.

Our research has documented that the greatest returns to both manufacturing and information technologies come when the technical dimensions of technology are appropriately integrated with the organizational and human dimensions. Two Sloan students, John Krafcik[10] and John Paul MacDuffie,[11] demonstrated that world-class productivity and quality performance were achieved in auto plants that integrated deployments of technology with the development of flexible, knowledge-based work systems, deep investments in training and development, and high levels of employee participation in problem solving and decision making. Plants that adopted this integrated approach outperformed plants that invested more in technology without corresponding investments in human resources and work system innovations and plants that continued to operate with more traditional industrial models of production and work organization. Later, the same results were replicated not only in other manufacturing industries, but with information technologies as well.[12]

The relationship between the technical and social dimensions of technology has been further elaborated by Wanda Orlikowski's research on the uses of information technologies in the workplace.[13] Her studies investigated the implementation of new information technologies in U.S., European, and Japanese firms. With a few exceptions, she found that these firms had failed to realize the benefits anticipated by their technological investments—not because of some failure in strategy, technology, or deployment, but because these firms had failed to manage the most critical determinant of technological effectiveness in organizations: how people actually use the technologies to get their work done. These findings suggest the importance of shifting management attention from being primarily focused on managing technologies as physical assets to being focused on managing the human and organizational *use of technologies*. Managing the use of technology requires recognizing the critical interdependence between technical capabilities and the human capital (knowledge, skills, motivations) and work systems (norms, incentives, practices) that realize the value of those technical capabilities in practice. It also recognizes that use of technology will change over time—as requirements evolve, market conditions change, learning occurs—and thus resources need to be dedicated to enable workers to adapt and augment their technologies and their use routines, as appropriate, over time.

These same lessons are now being learned in the area known as "knowledge management." As the following text box indicates, there are many dilemmas associated with the narrow concept of "capturing" knowledge. Note that this example links issues of knowledge management with issues of labor turnover.

One of the pioneers in the area of knowledge management, Larry Prusak from IBM's Institute for Knowledge-Based Organizations, built on this point in his presentation to our class, as illustrated in the boxed text on the next page.

The Dilemma of What Knowledge to Capture

The constant turnover of personnel in our organization has made even assuring short-term knowledge continuity very problematic.... First we tried to capture the basics, without focusing so much on the step-by-step instructions. This proved to be unsuccessful.... There is an extreme reluctance on the part of the users (scientists) to assume anything that was not explicitly written down.... In response to these comments ... we would write down every step, providing checkpoints, approximate times of completion, etc. The result was that the procedures grew from a single 30-page manual to over a 500-page book.... This approach was as unsuccessful as the first one.... Some people are asking for more detail, others are asking for less. No matter what we do, someone will be disappointed.

Contribution to Sloan Student/Alum Dialogue in Course on "Transforming Work, Organizations, and Society" (Spring 2002).

> ### *Information Technology and Knowledge Creation*
>
> It has been argued "technology's most valuable role in knowledge management is extending the reach and enhancing the speed of knowledge transfer." Information technology is indeed very useful in capturing, storing, and distributing structured and codified knowledge, therefore enabling other individuals in the organization to have access to it. However, IT plays a much more limited role in knowledge creation, which is very much a social process involving the exchange of hard-to-codify knowledge and personal experiences. Also, IT, by itself, cannot create a knowledge-based environment that promotes knowledge use and sharing. For any technology to be optimized, it must be augmented by strategy, process, culture, and behavior that support knowledge sharing and knowledge-based work.

Contribution by Larry Prusak to Sloan Course on "Transforming Work, Organizations, and Society" (Spring 2002).

Building Leadership Capabilities

Most business school cases are written and discussed from the vantage point of the CEO or others positioned at the top of their functional areas or departments. This sends the signal that it is the brilliance or individual leadership of those at the top who solve critical organizational problems which accounts for the success or failure of organizations. The leadership model implicit (and sometimes explicit) in these cases is one of the charismatic, visionary, and powerful strategist alongside a top-down model of innovation and change. Some have argued that in the last decade, corporate boards of directors have been seduced by the business press (a seduction possibly reinforced by business schools) to search for a charismatic CEO to be the "leader" who will provide the new vision and direction to transform organizational performance.[14]

At Sloan, we are in a process (led by Deborah Ancona) of developing an alternative view of leadership better suited to modern organizational realities.[15] We see leadership as a distributed capacity, exercised individually and collectively at multiple levels of the organization. This capacity is constituted by four interdependent capabilities: visioning, sensemaking, relating, and inventing. As organizations decentralize and flatten hierarchies, engage in greater cross-functional teamwork, and participate in multiple, dynamic, networklike interactions, we believe that the capabilities of this distributed model of leadership become even more relevant and effective in practice. Moreover, as organizations form more cross-boundary strategic alliances and become part of larger networks, leadership capabilities must be shared across these boundaries. In this way, leadership and change are highly interdependent processes.

While the Sloan distributed leadership model continues to stress the importance of developing individual capabilities, it recognizes that leadership is a collective phenomenon that requires engaging the energies, interests, and aspirations of the many people that constitute the organization—those involved in doing the everyday work of the enterprise. In this respect, distributed leadership cuts across all of the topics covered in this paper. As the following text box illustrates, for example, diversity training can and should bridge into broader leadership capabilities.

Linking Diversity Training and Leadership Skills

"Diversity training is mainly to help employees better understand other employees who are different from them. Additional training would be valuable if it worked more on the group process and leadership necessary to translate diversity into positive organizational results."

Contribution to Sloan Student/Alum Dialogue in Course on "Transforming Work, Organizations, and Society" (Spring 2002).

Redefining Organizational Goals

One inevitable consequence of adopting a human capital, knowledge-based organizational model is that the voices of employees will become more influential in shaping the values, goals, and priorities of the twenty-first-century organizations. Judging from the level of interest exhibited by our Sloan Fellows students, high on the list of priorities of employees today are concerns for social and environmental sustainability. These leaders want to work in and lead organizations in ways that ensure their children and future generations have the same opportunities as they do. This is the vision they express in their thesis projects and comments. Thus, sustainability may be the frontier example of how the underlying objectives of organizations may change in human-centered organizations.[16]

A number of organizations have made highly visible commitments to managing from a sustainability perspective.[17] This movement is farther advanced in Europe, in part because the European Community will shortly require companies to report outcomes related to what they view as their "triple bottom line," i.e., people, profits, and planet. Shell and British Petroleum are among the leaders in emphasizing sustainability, as documented in a thesis by two recent Sloan Fellows, Clare Mendelsohn and Sunil Pangarkar.[18]

Social and Environmental Sustainability: The Athabasca Oil Sands Project

The objective of the Athabasca Oil Sands Project (a joint venture effort led by Shell Canada) is to mine the estimated 100-year supply of oil. While this oil field had been discovered as early as 1956, two prior attempts to mine the oil had failed on technical and environmental grounds. A big concern was the large environmental footprint associated with the mine and the 300 miles of pipeline. It was only on the third attempt, begun in 1996, that a breakthrough was reached, and oil was success-

Social and Environmental Sustainability: The Athabasca Oil Sands Project (Continued)

fully produced. This third attempt was uniquely steered by social and environmental sensitivities and community need for involvement. Shell Canada's success came from being able to demonstrate to all the critical stakeholders that the project could provide economic, social, and environmental benefits. Through a participatory, collective approach—including and engaging local communities, experts, and NGOs—Shell Canada was able to realize numerous advantages for the community of Athabasca:

- 1,000 permanent jobs were established within the local community, with as many as 12,000 employed during the construction peak.
- The community benefits from substantial tax revenues.
- The project helped to build and augment the skills of the local people.
- Process water was recycled, thereby reducing demand on local rivers.
- A domestic supply of gas was developed, resulting in less dependency on oil imports.
- No chemicals were utilized in the oil separation process, and mine lands will eventually be restored to a natural condition.
- A groundbreaking climate change program was developed to address international concerns and to identify ways to reduce CO_2 emissions.
- An independent panel of experts continues to identify other means for carbon offsets as well as renewable energy alternatives.

Contribution to Sloan Student/Alum Dialogue in Course on "Transforming Work, Organizations, and Society" (Spring 2002).

In the United States, we examined the Ford Motor Company's highly visible effort to refurbish its River Rouge manufacturing complex following principles of sustainability. The result has been a bold rethinking of the relationship between a factory, its products, and the environment. Ford's CEO, William Clay Ford, has been an outspoken advocate of the River Rouge initiative, and the corporation has even added "environment" to its traditional set of standard metrics on safety, quality, delivery, cost, and morale. Still, the concept of sustainability has not yet become deeply embedded in the values and beliefs of the company's managers or in the corporation's manufacturing processes and product development processes. A small staff and a handful of strong line leaders support Ford's sustainability initiatives, but it remains to be seen if the vision will continue beyond the current CEO. That is, is the commitment to sustainability itself sustainable?

Another area where managing multiple stakeholders is critical is that of strategic partnerships, including labor-management partnerships, public-private partnerships, customer-supplier partnerships, and even strategic alliances among competitors. In class, we observed that these strategic partnerships are characterized by constant tensions—such as the tension between the personal relationships between individuals in the respective organizations and the formal roles that these individuals have—which can lead them to withhold information, act unilaterally, and otherwise undermine the relationships they have built. Similarly, there is a constant tension between the pressure to deliver short-term results and the long-term process of constructing and sustaining a partnership. These and other tensions reveal that strategic partnerships are fundamentally unstable organizational forms, dependent on a constantly adapting agenda which continues to deliver value to all parties.

We examined one unique labor-management partnership on this issue: the Kaiser-Permanente health plan partnership, which involves eight unions representing 55,000 workers in 26 bargaining units across 18 states. We heard evidence of the way that these partnership efforts have helped to grow the business by valuing employee knowledge, as well as by constructing path-breaking joint initiatives on work-family matters, the reduction of medical errors, systems for conflict resolution, and even methods of compensation. At the same time, we also learned of the constant difficulties of incorporating innovative lessons into ongoing organizational operations, as well as the difficulty of addressing key stakeholders who are not part of the partnership, whether they are the doctors who have a separate organizational structure within Kaiser-Permanente or the other unions and bargaining units that have chosen not to be part of the partnership.

Beyond the issues of strategic partnerships, we also explored examples of innovation in local, state, and federal government. Here the issues involved not only mechanisms to value employee knowledge and capability, but also transformation around redefined outcomes, greater collaboration, and new roles for the "clients" being served by the agencies. In her thesis on social sustainability, Sloan Fellow Lynne Dovey[19] found that broader social systems change requires a new role for governments (whether local or national): a role where they engage in power sharing and joint accountability with organizations and communities, enable valued outcomes rather than only enforce regulations, create incentives for collaboration with multiple stakeholders, participate in longer-term, relational contracting, and practice distributed leadership.

Implications for Management Education

As business schools rose to prominence over the twentieth century, organization theory and education focused more and more on management within the individual firm. Organizational control, autonomy, flexibility, and managing uncertainty became key issues. Priority was given to strategies for attracting and allocating financial capital, managing these and other firm assets in ways that return value to shareholders, and protecting the firm from the influence of agents, groups, and organizations that lie outside the firm's boundaries. Organizations were conceived as "going concerns" that survive indefinitely, so potential future liabilities or costs were discounted and incorporated into current decision making.

As we rethink assumptions about the nature and value of work and organizations, key adjustments to business school curricula are needed. Just as we inverted the analysis of work and organizations to reflect where value is created, so too do we need to revamp teaching to provide future managers and leaders with the perspectives, knowledge, and tools that enable organizations to realize the potential value from the workforce and their knowledge. Each dimension highlighted in this paper—workforce demographics, knowledge-based work, integration of social and technical systems, distributed leadership, and expanded organizational goals—will need to be integrated in the curricula and supported with practical tools and experiences.

We need, for example, to prepare business leaders to address high-priority, sensitive workforce issues such as diversity and fair treatment, as well as career development and work-life integration. The management skills and tools needed here are straightforward: engaging, listening to, negotiating with, and facilitating different forms of individual and collective employee voice. Whereas twentieth-century workforce management focused on control, the twenty-first-century workforce is directly engaged in the management process. Skills in negotiation, problem solving, conflict resolution, and coordination of horizontal, cross-boundary interactions need to become the standard tools of the trade.

Similarly, knowing how to implement and sustain mechanisms for knowledge creation and application is essential in the knowledge-based organization. This requires an understanding of the needed knowledge, skills, and abilities at every phase of what is sometimes termed a value stream in an organization. Most efforts to manage value streams effectively are focused on mapping the flow of products or services from conception to ultimate customers—looking for constraints and improvement opportunities. Our analysis would call for training next-generation managers to be able to do a parallel mapping of knowledge and capabilities—looking for constraints and opportunities along the dimensions of knowledge and human capital.

In the domain of technology, we would call for deeper and more explicit attention to the interdependence of social and technical aspects of business operations. The MBA degree grew to prominence in the twentieth century as a specialized profession, separate from the disciplinary training of other university departments. This reinforced the view that issues of training, development, teams, and even leadership should be treated separately from efforts to design, implement, and innovate with various types of new technology. Managing the twenty-first-century organization will require integrating state-of-the-art knowledge and skills that cut across traditional disciplinary boundaries. The implication here is clear: management schools need to be better integrated with their physical and social science and engineering counterparts, and vice-versa.

As we educate next-generation business leaders, we must better understand and appreciate the leadership development that has occurred over the past decade. Even if the so-called Internet bubble has burst, what still remains is a cohort of young, talented people who have developed valuable insights and capabilities in this concentrated e-business crucible. Already there is anecdotal evidence to suggest that this cohort is less interested in traditional business cases centered on large, multidivisional corporations and more interested in learning that incorporates what they now know, as well as the kinds of organizational settings to which they aspire. Leadership, as Robert Thomas and Warren Bennis emphasize,[20] is often best learned through experiences of failure. The lesson here is obvious: we simply have to work with our students to help them and us to reflect on and learn from the rich experiences they bring into our classrooms.

The basic assumption of a shareholder- and customer-driven, profit-maximizing organization is woven throughout business school education. Much less common is attention to the multiple stakeholders associated with any business operation and the objectives or metrics relevant to these other stakeholders—whether they be the workforce, communities, regulatory agencies, strategic partners, or suppliers. Our challenge is to build on and go beyond such initiatives as "the balanced scorecard,"[21] "stakeholder value,"[22] reciprocal contracts, and related mechanisms for attending to outcomes for multiple stakeholders. We have found the best way to do this is by bringing representatives of these different stakeholders into our classes—to hear directly about their perspectives, interests, and the value they can add to organizations and to build cases and simulations that put students in these different stakeholder roles and hold them accountable for addressing these multiple criteria.

CONCLUSION

We draw three broad conclusions about the diversity of practice in organizations today, the process of transformation, and the leverage associated with broader assumptions on work and organizations. First, the differences between the two organizational models outlined at the outset of this paper are reflected in organizational practices today, where organizations are seen to be positioned at various points along the continuum characterizing these two organizational models. Many organizations are currently trying to transform themselves as they recognize the importance of human capital and knowledge to their future effectiveness.

Second, there is no guarantee that such a transformation process will continue or succeed. It is not guided by some invisible hand or market imperative. Indeed, we have encountered many "disconnects" between rhetoric and reality. Organizational change is a highly political, contested process involving individuals and groups with different, often conflicting interests, beliefs, and power. Therefore, whether the various transformations currently underway will result in organizations more suited to the demands of the twenty-first century will depend on management's willingness to challenge fundamental assumptions about organizations and the quality of the negotiated change processes they engage in with various stakeholders.

Third, we have outlined a broader set of assumptions about work and organizations that represents a powerful set of levers for transformation. Yet to put this larger set of assumptions "on the table" for discussion and change will require opening a dialogue with the various stakeholders who share an interest in and commitment to building effective twenty-first-century organizations. The implication here is simple but blunt: the future of management (and management education) is too important to leave to managers alone! Employees from the front lines through middle management and the executive ranks, professional associations and unions, families and communities, partner organizations, as well as nongovernmental organizations and government policy makers, are all part of the network of leaders who need to be engaged and involved in shaping the organizations of the twenty-first century.

McGregor asked us to rethink our assumptions about people. Now our task is to examine an even broader set of assumptions around the very nature of work and organizations. The choices we make will determine whether the rhetoric around the twenty-first-century organizations will become a reality.

ENDNOTES

1. Presentation at the Sloan School's fifth anniversary on "The Human Side of Enterprise" by Douglas McGregor, later expanded into a book: Douglas McGregor, *The Human Side of Enterprise*, New York: McGraw-Hill, 1960.
2. MIT 21st-Century Manifesto Working Group, Sloan School of Management, "What Do We Really Want? A Manifesto for the Organizations of the 21st Century," November 1999.
3. Shimada, Haruo, and John Paul McDuffie, "Industrial Relations and Humanware," Sloan School of Management Working Paper, 1987.
4. Murman, Earll, Tom Allen, Kirkor Bozdogan, Joel Cutcher-Gershenfeld, Hugh McManus, Debbie Nightingale, Eric Rebentisch,

Tom Shields, Fred Stahl, Myles Walton, Joyce Warmkessel, Stanley Weiss, and Sheila Widnall, *Lean Enterprise Value: Insights from MIT's Lean Aerospace Initiative*, New York: Palgrave/Macmillan, 2002.

5. Towers Perrin, *Talent Report 2001: New Realities in Today's Workforce*, New York: Towers Perrin, 2002.

6. Bailyn, Lotte, *Breaking the Mold*, New York: Maxwell MacMillan, 1993.

7. Fullerton, Howard, Jr., and Mitra Toossi, "Employment Outlook: 2000–2010—Labor Force Projections to 2010: Steady Growth and Changing Composition," *Monthly Labor Review*, November 2001, pp. 21–38.

8. Ichniowski, Casey, Thomas Kochan, David Levine, Craig Olson, and George Strauss, "What Works at Work?" *Industrial Relations*, vol. 35, issue 3, 1996, pp. 299–333.

9. Osterman, Paul, "Work Organization in an Era of Restructuring: Trends in Diffusion and Impacts on Employee Welfare," *Industrial and Labor Relations Review*, vol. 53, 2000, pp. 179–196.

10. Kraftcik, John, "Triumph of Lean Production," *Sloan Management Review*, vol. 30, 1988, pp. 41–52.

11. MacDuffie, John Paul, and John Krafcik, "Integrating Technology and Human Resources for High-Performance Manufacturing: Evidence from the International Auto Industry," in Thomas A. Kochan and Michael Useem (eds.), *Transforming Organizations*, New York: Oxford University Press, 1992, pp. 209–227; MacDuffie, John Paul, "Human Resource Bundles and Manufacturing Performance: Organizational Logic and Flexible Production Systems in the World Auto Industry," *Industrial and Labor Relations Review*, vol. 48, 1995, pp. 197–221.

12. Bresnahan; Timothy F., Erik Brynjolfsson, and Lorin M. Hitt, "Information Technology, Workplace Innovation, and the Demand for Skilled Labor: Firm Level Evidence," in Margaret M. Blair and Thomas A. Kochan (eds.), *The New Relationship*, Washington, D.C., The Brookings Institution, 1999.

13. Orlikowski, Wanda J., "Learning from Notes: Organizational Issues in Groupware Implementation," *Information Society Journal*, vol. 9, 1993, pp. 237–250.

14. Prusak, Laurence, and Salvatore Parise, "Information Systems as a Conduit for the Transfer of Knowledge," paper produced by the IBM Institute for Knowledge Management, Cambridge, Mass., 2002.

15. Khurana, Rakesh, *Searching for a Corporate Savior: The Irrational Quest for Charismatic CEOs*, Princeton, N.J.: Princeton University Press, 2002.

16. Ancona, Deborah G., Thomas W. Malone, Wanda J. Orlikowski, and Peter Senge, "Distributed Leadership," Sloan School of Management Workshops, Cambridge, Mass., 2001/2002.

17. Senge, Peter, and Gören Carstedt, "Innovating Our Way to the Next Industrial Revolution," *Sloan Management Review*, January–February 2001.

18. Mendelsohn, Clare, and Anirudha Pangarkar, "Case Studies of How BP and Shell Are Approaching Sustainable Development," Master's Thesis, Sloan School of Management, Cambridge, Mass., May 2002.

19. Dovey, Lynne, "Achieving Better Social Outcomes in New Zealand through Collaboration: Perspectives from the United States," Master's Thesis, Sloan School of Management, Cambridge, Mass., May 2002.

20. Bennis, Warren, and Robert J. Thomas, *Geeks and Geezers*, Boston: Harvard Business School Press, 2002.

21. Kaplan, Robert, *Strategy Focused Organizations: How Balanced Scorecard Companies Thrive in the New Business Environment*, Boston: Harvard Business School Press, 2001.

22. Murman Earl, Tom Allen, Kirkor Bozdogan, Joel Cutcher-Gershenfeld, Hugh McManus, Debbie Nightingale, Eric Rebentisch, Tom Shields, Fred Stahl, Myles Walton, Joyce Warmkessel, Stanley Weiss, and Sheila Widnall, *Lean Enterprise Value: Insights from MIT's Lean Aerospace Initiative*, New York: Palgrave/Macmillan, 2002.

INDEX

Page numbers followed by "*n*" indicate material in footnotes.

ABOUT THE AUTHOR

Douglas McGregor is one of the most influential management thinkers of all time. Born in Detroit in 1906, he received his bachelor's degree from Wayne University in 1932, his master's degree from Harvard in 1933, and his doctorate from Harvard in 1935. McGregor joined the MIT faculty in 1937 as one of the founders of what was then the Industrial Relations Section (now the Institute for Work and Employment Research). In 1948, when he was professor of psychology and executive director of the Industrial Relations Section, he accepted the position of president of Antioch College, which has undergraduate and graduate programs in management, conflict resolution, educational administration, and other topics, and which has recently (in 2000) renamed the campus in his honor as Antioch McGregor University. After six years of service as Antioch's president, he returned to MIT as professor of Industrial Management, and in 1962 became the first incumbent of the Sloan Fellows Professorship. At various points in his career, he served as director of Industrial Relations for the Dewey and Almy Chemical Company, as trustee of Antioch College, as a director of the Social Science Research Council, as a director of the National Training Laboratories, as a director of the Psychological Corporation, and as a consultant to government and industry. Douglas McGregor died in 1964, having transformed our understanding of the human side of enterprise, but leaving so much yet to be done in service of his vision.

ABOUT THE EDITOR

Joel Cutcher-Gershenfeld is a senior research scientist in MIT's Sloan School of Management, with affiliations in MIT's Engineering Systems Division and the Program on Negotiation at Harvard Law School. His scholarship spans new work systems, labor-management relations, complex engineered systems, negotiations, and dispute resolution systems. Joel is coauthor of *Valuable Disconnects in Organizational Learning Systems* (Oxford University Press, 2005), *Lean Enterprise Value* (Palgrave, 2002), *Knowledge-Driven Work* (Oxford University Press, 1998), *Strategic Negotiations* (Harvard Business School Press, 1994), additional coauthored and coedited books, and over 70 articles and book chapters. Joel has extensive experience leading large-scale change initiatives. He has worked with a wide range of public and private sector employers and unions in Australia, Bermuda, Canada, Denmark, England, Italy, Japan, Mexico, New Zealand, Panama, Poland, Spain, South Africa, and the United States. In the McGregorian tradition, both his scholarship and field practice center on surfacing and addressing underlying values and assumptions about people at work, in organizations, and in society. Joel holds a Ph.D. in Industrial Relations from MIT (where he had a Scanlon Fellowship, a part of the legacy of Douglas McGregor) and a B.S. in Industrial and Labor Relations from Cornell University. As part of the Sloan School's 50th Anniversary, Joel coauthored a specially commissioned essay connecting McGregor's Theory Y approach to the challenges of the twenty-first century.